Making Culture

Making Culture provides an in-depth discussion of Australia's relationship between the building of national cultural identity – or 'nationing' – and the country's cultural production and consumption. With the 1994 national cultural policy *Creative Nation* as a starting point for many of the essays included in this collection, the book investigates transformations within Australia's various cultural fields, exploring the implications of nationing and the gradual movement away from it. Underlying these analyses are the key questions and contradictions confronting any modern nation-state that seeks to develop and defend a national culture while embracing the transnational and the global.

Including topics such as publishing, sport, music, tourism, art, Indigeneity, television, heritage and the influence of digital technology and output, *Making Culture* is an essential volume for students and scholars within Australian and Cultural Studies.

David Rowe FAHA, FASSA is an Emeritus Professor of Cultural Research in the Institute for Culture and Society, Western Sydney University. Internationally recognized for his extensive and influential publications on sport, media and popular culture, his most recent books are *Global Media Sport: Flows, Forms and Futures* (2011), *Sport Beyond Television: The Internet, Digital Media, and the Rise of Networked Media Sport* (2012) and *Digital Media Sport: Technology, Power and Culture in the Network Society* (2012) (both with Brett Hutchins), and (with Jay Scherer) *Sport, Public Broadcasting, and Cultural Citizenship: Signal Lost?* (2014).

Graeme Turner is an Emeritus Professor of Cultural Studies in the Institute for Advanced Studies in the Humanities at the University of Queensland. He has published 24 books in film, media, communications and cultural studies, and his work has been translated into ten languages. One of the founding figures in media and cultural studies in Australia and internationally, his primary research interests over the last decade have been focused on television and new media in the post-broadcast and digital era. His most recent books include *Re-Inventing the Media* (2016), *Television Histories in Asia: Issues and Contexts* (co-edited with Jinna Tay) (2015), a revised edition of *Understanding Celebrity* (2014) and *Locating Television: Zones of Consumption* (co-authored with Anna Cristina Pertierra) (2013).

Emma Waterton is an Associate Professor in the Geographies of Heritage at Western Sydney University. She was a Research Councils UK (RCUK) Academic Fellow at Keele University from 2006–2010 and a DECRA Fellow at WSU from 2012–2016. Her research explores the interface between heritage, identity, memory and affect in both Australian and international contexts. She has published 19 books, including the monographs *Politics, Policy and the Discourses of Heritage in Britain* (2010, Palgrave Macmillan), *Heritage, Communities and Archaeology* (co-authored with Laurajane Smith; 2009, Duckworth) and *The Semiotics of Heritage Tourism* (co-authored with Steve Watson; 2014, Channel View Publications).

Making Culture
Commercialisation, transnationalism, and the state of 'nationing' in contemporary Australia

Edited by David Rowe, Graeme Turner and Emma Waterton

LONDON AND NEW YORK

First published 2018
by Routledge
2 Park Square, Milton Park, Abingdon, Oxon OX14 4RN

and by Routledge
711 Third Avenue, New York, NY 10017

Routledge is an imprint of the Taylor & Francis Group, an informa business

© 2018 selection and editorial matter, David Rowe, Graeme Turner and Emma Waterton; individual chapters, the contributors

The right of David Rowe, Graeme Turner and Emma Waterton to be identified as the authors of the editorial material, and of the authors for their individual chapters, has been asserted in accordance with sections 77 and 78 of the Copyright, Designs and Patents Act 1988.

All rights reserved. No part of this book may be reprinted or reproduced or utilised in any form or by any electronic, mechanical, or other means, now known or hereafter invented, including photocopying and recording, or in any information storage or retrieval system, without permission in writing from the publishers.

Trademark notice: Product or corporate names may be trademarks or registered trademarks, and are used only for identification and explanation without intent to infringe.

British Library Cataloguing-in-Publication Data
A catalogue record for this book is available from the British Library

Library of Congress Cataloging-in-Publication Data
A catalog record has been requested for this book

ISBN: 978-1-138-09412-3 (hbk)
ISBN: 978-1-315-10620-5 (ebk)

Typeset in Times
by Apex CoVantage, LLC

Contents

Figure vii
Tables viii
Notes on contributors ix
Acknowledgements xii

Introduction: making culture 1
DAVID ROWE, GRAEME TURNER AND EMMA WATERTON

PART 1
The cultural fields 13

1 **The book trade and the arts ecology: transnationalism and digitization in the Australian literary field** 15
DAVID CARTER AND MICHELLE KELLY

2 **Beyond nation, beyond art? The 'rules of art' in contemporary Australia** 28
TONY BENNETT

3 **The Australian art field: fairs and markets** 40
DEBORAH STEVENSON

4 **The 'music nation': popular music and Australian cultural policy** 51
SHANE HOMAN

5 **Television: commercialization, the decline of 'nationing' and the status of the media field** 64
GRAEME TURNER

6   A history of heritage policy in Australia: from hope
    to philanthropy   75
    EMMA WATERTON

7   The sport field in Australia: the market, the state,
    the nation and the world beyond in Pierre Bourdieu's
    favourite game   87
    DAVID ROWE

PART 2
Across cultural fields   101

8   'Crossing the technical rubicon': marketizing culture
    and fields of the digital   103
    BRETT HUTCHINS

9   Touring nation: the changing meanings of cultural
    tourism   116
    CHRIS GIBSON

10 Indigeneity, cosmopolitanism and the nation:
    the project of NITV   129
    BEN DIBLEY AND GRAEME TURNER

11 Making multiculture: Australia and the ambivalent
    politics of diversity   140
    IEN ANG AND GREG NOBLE

    Afterword: undoing the bonds of nation/
    rediscovering dead souls   154
    TOBY MILLER

    Index   167

Figure

11.1 Dimensions of diversity according to the Australia Council's
Cultural Engagement Framework 144

Tables

7.1	Rugby union in the Australian anti-siphoning regime	92
7.2	Involvement in rugby union by sex	94
7.3	Total annual household income from all sources and involvement in rugby union	95
7.4	Nominated social class and watching rugby union live through the media	96

Notes on contributors

Ien Ang is a Distinguished Professor of Cultural Studies at the Institute for Culture and Society, Western Sydney University. Her work focuses on broad issues of cultural diversity and cultural exchange in a globalized world. Her books include *Watching Dallas* (1985), *On Not Speaking Chinese: Living Between Asia and the West* (2001), *The SBS Story* (2008) and *Chinatown Unbound: Trans-Asian Urbanism in the Age of China* (forthcoming in 2019).

Tony Bennett is a Research Professor in Social and Cultural Theory in the Institute for Culture and Society at Western Sydney University. His books include *Formalism and Marxism* (1979), *Bond and Beyond: The Political Career of a Popular Hero* (1987, with Janet Woollacott), *Outside Literature* (1991), *The Birth of the Museum* (1995), *Culture: A Reformer's Science* (1998), *Pasts Beyond Memory: Evolution, Museums, Colonialism* (2004), *Making Culture, Changing Society* (2013) and *Museums, Power, Knowledge* (2018). He is lead co-author of *Accounting for Tastes: Australian Everyday Cultures* (1999), *Culture, Class, Distinction* (2009) and *Collecting, Organising, Governing: Anthropology, Museums and Liberal Government* (2017).

David Carter is a Professor of Australian Literature and Cultural History at the University of Queensland and a Fellow of the Australian Academy of the Humanities. His books include *Always Almost Modern: Australian Print Cultures and Modernity* and *Making Books: Contemporary Australian Publishing*. He is a contributor to the *Cambridge History of Australia*, the *Cambridge History of Australian Literature* and the *Routledge International Handbook of the Sociology of Art and Culture*. His new book, *Australian Books and Authors in the American Marketplace*, will be published in early 2018.

Ben Dibley is a Research Fellow at the Institute for Culture and Society at Western Sydney University, Australia. He has research interests in social and cultural theory, particularly around questions concerning cultural institutions, colonialism, and the environment. His essays have appeared in *Australian Humanities Review, Cultural Studies Review, History and Anthropology, International Journal of Cultural Studies, Museum and Society, New Formations* and *Transformations*. He is the co-author of *Collecting, Ordering, Governing: Anthropology and Liberal Government* (Duke University Press, 2017).

Chris Gibson is a Professor of Human Geography and Director of the interdisciplinary Global Challenges Program at the University of Wollongong, Australia. His research spans interests in cultural economy, music, tourism and, more recently, cultural policy-making around the links between creative industries and manufacturing. He is a Fellow of the Academy of Social Sciences in Australia and currently Editor-in-Chief of *Australian Geographer*.

Shane Homan is an Associate Professor and Research Coordinator of the School of Media, Film and Journalism at Monash University, Melbourne. He is the lead Chief Investigator in the Australian Research Council project *Interrogating the Music City: cultural economy and popular music in Melbourne*. His most recent book, with Professor Martin Cloonan and Dr Jen Cattermole, is *Popular Music and the State: Policy Notes* (Routledge, 2016).

Brett Hutchins is a Professor of Media and Communications Studies in the School of Media, Film & Journalism at Monash University. His research focuses on the social, economic and political implications of technological transformation and, in particular, the movement from analogue-print to mobile-digital media systems and markets. He is presently writing a monograph on mobile media and sport for Oxford University Press (http://artsonline.monash.edu.au/mobilemediasport/), and his recent articles appear in *Media, Culture & Society*, *Digital Journalism* and *International Communication Gazette*.

Michelle Kelly is the Senior Research Officer and Project Manager of 'Australian Cultural Fields: National and Transnational Dynamics', a Discovery Project funded by the Australian Research Council (DP140101970). Her research interests include reading practices, public libraries, Aboriginal and Torres Strait Islander literature and contemporary fiction. She is co-editor of 'Transforming cultures? From Creative Nation to Creative Australia', a special section of *Media International Australia* (2016), and *The Politics and Aesthetics of Refusal* (2007). She has published in *Australian Literary Studies*, *Rhizomes* and several edited collections. She is based at the Institute for Culture and Society, Western Sydney University, Australia.

Toby Miller is a Distinguished Professor of the Graduate Division at University of California, Riverside; the Sir Walter Murdoch Professor of Cultural Policy Studies at Murdoch University; Profesor Invitado at the Escuela de Comunicación Social, Universidad del Norte; Professor of Journalism, Media and Cultural Studies at Cardiff University/Prifysgol Caerdydd; and Professor in the Institute for Media and Creative Industries at Loughborough University London. The author and editor of over 40 books, his work has been translated into Spanish, Chinese, Portuguese, Japanese, Turkish, German, Italian, Farsi and Swedish. His most recent volumes are *Greenwashing Culture* (2018), *Greenwashing Sport* (2018), *The Routledge Companion to Global Cultural Policy* (edited with Victoria Durrer and Dave O'Brien, 2018), *Global Media Studies* (with Marwan M. Kraidy, 2016), *The Sage Companion to Television Studies* (edited with Manuel Alvarado, Milly Buonanno, and Herman Gray, 2015) and *The Routledge Companion to Global Popular Culture* (edited, 2015).

Greg Noble is a Professor at the Institute for Culture and Society at Western Sydney University. He has been involved in research in multiculturalism for 30 years, with a special interest in the relations between youth, ethnicity and gender; migration and cosmopolitanism; cultural pedagogies and habitus; multicultural education and cultural complexity. He is the editor or co-author of several books, including *Cultural Pedagogies and Human Conduct* (2015), *Disposed to Learn* (2013), *On Being Lebanese in Australia* (2010) and *Bin Laden in the Suburbs* (2004).

Deborah Stevenson is a Professor of Sociology and Urban Cultural Research in the Institute for Culture and Society at Western Sydney University. Her research interests are focused on cities and urban life, arts and cultural policy, and place and tourism, and her many publications include the books *Cities of Culture: A Global Perspective*; *The City*; *Tourist Cultures: Identity, Place and the Traveller*; *Cities and Urban Cultures*; and *Art and Organisation: Making Australian Cultural Policy*. She is also the co-editor of *The Ashgate Research Companion to Planning and Culture*.

Acknowledgements

This volume is an outcome of an Australian Research Council-funded Discovery Project 'Australian Cultural Fields: National and Transnational Dynamics', led by Tony Bennett. In addition to *Making Culture*'s editors – Rowe, Turner and Waterton – the researchers contributing to the project and to the development of this book include Ien Ang, David Carter, Ben Dibley, Michelle Kelly, Fred Myers, Greg Noble, Anna Cristina Pertierra, Tim Rowse and Deborah Stevenson. David Rowe would like to acknowledge the support of the Institute for Culture and Society at Western Sydney University, and Emma Waterton would like to acknowledge the support of the School of Social Sciences and Psychology at Western Sydney University.

Introduction
Making culture

David Rowe, Graeme Turner and Emma Waterton

This collection of essays is an outcome of a multi-disciplinary research project[1] devoted to investigating the transformation of Australian cultural fields over the last two decades. While the larger project has mapped the changing dynamics within and across each field in order to provide a historicized account of the shifts, both general and detailed, in culture and policy over the period from 1994 to the present, this book has a more specialized focus. It is interested in one key shift in particular: an uneven but nonetheless incremental withdrawal from the policy approach that we refer to as 'nationing', the objective of developing a national culture through the deployment of policy. Such an objective had been an explicit component of Australia's (and many other nation-states') cultural and development policies for many years; the contributions to this book would suggest that this is no longer so clearly the case. They provide evidence of the part played in that policy realignment by a pervasive tendency towards the commercialization of national culture and by the increasing influence of globalism and/or transnationalism. *Making Culture* approaches these issues through case studies of selected cultural fields (the literary, sport, visual art, music, television and heritage) and analyses of certain influences active across those fields (Indigeneity, transnationalism, multiculturalism and the rise of the digital), as well as drawing from time to time on original survey data examining Australian consumers' choices and preferences in cultural consumption. None of these influences, tendencies or political shifts is unique to Australia, of course, even though they have their own distinctive dynamics within that society, and these are our major concerns here. Indeed, they constitute a widespread complex of issues, contradictions and competing imperatives that must be dealt with by many, if not most, nation-states at the moment, as fundamental considerations in the design and management of national projects of economic modernization and cultural development.

The historical starting point for many of the case studies in this collection is the Paul Keating Labor government's release of Australia's first national cultural policy, *Creative Nation*, in October 1994 (Commonwealth of Australia 1994). With the publication of *Creative Nation*, an interest in the production of an Australian national culture was formally placed right at the centre of Australian cultural policy. In turn, cultural policy was overwhelmingly framed around a particular conception of the national interest – supporting home-grown national cultural activity and, in some cases, protecting it from competition from outside Australia. The 'ultimate aim' of *Creative Nation*, as outlined in the policy's introduction, was to 'increase the comfort and enjoyment of Australian life', heightening Australian experience by 'shoring up our heritage in new or expanded national institutions', while adding to 'our security and well-being' (1994, p. 7). As such, the document claimed, the Commonwealth's cultural policy statement would pursue 'similar ends to any social policy' (1994, p. 7). There was a sign of competing formulations, though, in the very next paragraph, where culture was carved out in equally clear economic terms:

> This cultural policy is also an economic policy. Culture creates wealth. Broadly defined, our cultural industries generate 13 billion dollars a year. Culture employs. Around 336,000 Australians are employed in culture-related industries. Culture adds value, it makes an essential contribution to innovation, marketing and design. It is a badge of our industry. The level of our creativity substantially determines our ability to adapt to new economic imperatives. It is a valuable export in itself and an essential accompaniment to the export of other commodities. It attracts tourists and students. It is essential to our economic success.
>
> (1994, p. 7; see also Stevenson 2000)

Over the more than two decades since the release of this document, such an emphasis has become more prominent as the purpose of cultural policy has gradually been articulated to, or perhaps subsumed within, its economic significance. An approach which regarded cultural policy as a means of planning the project of nationing has given way to a position that views the state of the national culture as an object of industry policy. Making culture, within a context of increased globalization and commercialization, seems increasingly likely to become a by-product of economic policy rather than an end in itself.

The contributions to this book focus in various ways, and within various contexts, on the tensions generated between two broad overlapping and often competing influences – the public and political aspirations towards the maintenance of a distinctive national culture and cultural identity on the one hand, and the market-oriented imperatives towards greater economic integration with the increasing transnational flows of capital, people and cultural texts on the other. The essays which follow consider the varying responses to these influences across a range of cultural fields, highlighting what amount to major changes in policy focus and in the dynamics of cultural production in Australia over the period studied.

The state of 'nationing'

We need to explain our coining of the term 'nationing' and why it seems a useful way of focusing on the core issues dealt with in this book. The value of this term is that it enables us to cover what is now a range of purposes for the production and representation of the nation; there is currently no other inclusive term that can adequately cover the proliferating uses of the discourses and strategies now in play. We have long been accustomed to talking about strategies of nation formation, the political investment in the promotion of national culture aimed at constructing Benedict Anderson's (1983) widely used concept of 'imagined communities'. The purpose of projects of nation formation has included the establishment of an inclusive national identity and a sense of belonging as a means of cohering diverse ethnic, racial, political and cultural elements into a functioning, modern and largely, but not exclusively, democratic nation-state. This aim has been particularly important in nation-states dealing with longstanding ethnic, religious or racial tensions, where it has been hoped that the construction of a consensual national identity would help transcend such differences. At times, the process may be described a little more actively as nation-building – itself a term that as often refers to material development projects as to the development of a national consciousness – but in both cases, the formation of the nation was an end in itself. The construction of a national identity was thought to underpin the social viability of the nation-state while also figuring as a fundamental component of the modern sense of belonging. In Australia, that project was articulated to a cultural nationalism which was highly influential in cultural policy over many years, as well as supporting a long history of economic protectionism aimed at securing employment for Australian citizens. At the level of the social, Australia shares with many other settler-colonial societies the challenges of constructing a shared identity for a population that was created, after the dispossession of their Indigenous peoples, by successive waves of immigration from other, more historically and culturally defined nations.

Since the 1980s, the influence of globalization has been significant as the network of economic interdependencies that it encouraged tended to weaken positions of economic nationalism, as well as spilling over into debates surrounding the continuing relevance of cultural nationalism. A greater transnational orientation in trade policy had local political and social effects that needed to be managed and, in many ways, the strategies used to effect such management ran against the grain of earlier traditions of nation formation. In place of 'the nation', Australian policy makers began to talk of 'the national economy' as the core context of policy formation. Following what was a common view internationally at the time, some argued that the nation-state would be superseded under the influence of globalization (Beck 2007), and this view was in part responsible for the widespread enthusiasm for deregulatory policies in many areas of cultural and economic activity. It is true that this argument has now been largely discredited, and the 'trickle-down economics' that tended to accompany it has turned out to have very different effects to those proposed (Flew et al. 2016). In response to this challenge to globalizing discourse, as well as to a number of other factors that we won't discuss here, there are indications of a partial return to more regulatory and culturally nationalist politics in many locations – the US, France and the UK among them. However, and notwithstanding that tendency, the discourses which now circulate in relation to the relative importance of culture and the economy, and the policy objectives which lie behind them, have shifted in significant ways that seem to constitute a withdrawal of political interest from some of the earlier objectives of nation formation.

A key aspect of the next phase of projects of nationing can be exemplified by the Tony Blair New Labour government's investment in re-branding and re-vitalising Britain's art and culture, culminating in the promotion of the UK as 'Cool Britannia' and 'a young country' in the 1990s. Capitalizing on the burgeoning art scene in London and the rebirth of mainstream British music through bands such as Oasis and Blur, Blair's New Labour sought to place 'youthful' creative industries, as commodities, at the heart of the government's PR campaign (Urban 2004). Here, the construction of national identity was packaged and delivered as a marketing operation. Its aim was not to find an inclusive mode of constructing a shared identity for its citizens, but rather to commodify a substantially revised national identity. True, Cool Britannia drew upon some of the home-grown stars from the UK's contemporary popular culture – David Beckham and the Spice Girls, for instance – but it was also clearly an invention: a simulated national identity drawing its referents from the fashion and media culture of London and aimed at global retail and tourism markets.

Since then, we have seen what has come to be called 'nation-branding' turn into a relatively routine avenue for countries seeking to establish an image in order to engage with transnational markets. Nadia Kaneva (2012) has described the outbreak of nation-branding that followed the break-up of the former Yugoslavia as new nations were established through international political settlements. With their newly constituted populations riven by long-standing ethnic, religious and racial conflicts, many of these countries had little sense of a shared or agreed cultural identity upon which to build. Kaneva describes the use of nation-branding in such circumstances as a 'quick fix' for the 'identity malaise' of just about every Central and Eastern European nation-state from 1989 onwards. This development turned the more familiar process of nation formation on its head: instead of building a cultural identity more or less 'from below', to be formalized and deployed in the representation of the state, nation-branding sought to promote assent to the representations generated to promote a brand that was constructed and imposed 'from above', creating what Milhelj (2011) has called 'media nations'. The components used within this kind of nationing program – publicity promotions and advertisements invoking longstanding cultural identities, iconic physical locations and shared histories – were, of course, in most cases confected markers of national identities sold to communities as a means of s(t)imulating a sense of belonging.

Once we enter such a domain, nationing loses the connection to its earlier purpose of nation formation. Rather, it is a marketing strategy, a mode of political and, as we shall see, commercial, performance. As such, it is highly adaptable and can be deployed to quite diverse ends. In India, for instance, media products are being used as the frontline in a project of rebranding which seeks to capitalize on their current international commercial success in order to modernize India's international image and increase the purchase of its 'soft power' (Athique 2012). Over the past few decades in Britain, heritage has been reimagined in planning frameworks and regeneration policies as an economic catalyst for reviving broken places and dysfunctional communities – for fixing a 'Broken Britain' – by a government that sees heritage as providing new forms of capital accumulation and competitive advantage (Watson and González-Rodríguez 2015). Then there is the development that Zala Volcic and Mark Andrejevic (2016) have labelled 'commercial nationalism'. In some transitional states where the media and other commercial interests seem to have more power than the state, political discourses of nationing have been deployed to achieve unequivocally commercial ends. Volcic and Andrejevic cite examples from Serbia and Slovenia, among others, where commercial reality television formats have used divisive ethnic, religious and racial stereotypes in ways that are deliberately provocative and inflammatory. The core objective, however, is not to influence political debate and certainly not to assist in the construction of a political consensus on national identity. Indeed, the likely political effects seem not to interest media producers for whom such consequences are simply collateral damage. These producers have exploited socio-cultural tensions because it has proven a highly successful strategy for winning audience ratings. While the producers may be unconcerned by the political by-products of their commercial exploitation of competing nationalisms, these consequences are the primary focus of Volcic and Andrejevic's work.

Although the discourses of nationing are ever more widely and variously deployed, they have begun to lose their connection to their earlier purposes, and to the project of successfully building an imagined community. Those purposes have given way to the nation-state's prioritizing of particular kinds of economic development and the making of culture has assumed secondary importance. In Australia, we can trace this trajectory through a history that takes us from the launch of *Creative Nation* in 1994 to the present. Over this time, the cultural nationalist model of nationing has been reconfigured and its discourses and principles, on the whole, devalued. This shift in position is discernible in a wave of deregulation and disinvestment across a range from the late 1990s onwards (film, broadcasting, literature, conservation and heritage, community arts and related activities, for some examples), particularly under the leadership of John Howard's Liberal-National Party government, as well as in the arrangement of ministerial portfolios. Unlike, for example, in the UK, with its prominent Department for Culture, Media and Sport (DCMS – with Digital added in July 2017), culture in Australia no longer has its own dedicated portfolio. While the federal government's ministerial structure has changed frequently, culture now tends to be located in those portfolios most directly responsible for national economic and industrial development. In such locations, the dominance of economic concerns serves as a buffer against cultural nationalist policy settings. Indeed, cultural policy in Australia has now become a subset of economic and industry policy, eliciting calls in some quarters for remedial strategies such as the development of a policy framework for a 'cultural economy' (O'Connor 2016).

In an example of this shift, Emma Waterton (Chapter 6) in this collection notes how Australian heritage policy has been articulated in recent years, where the reliance on voluntary community initiatives is now underpinned by a rhetoric that requires heritage venues to earn their place, justify investment and provide a return in terms of economic regeneration. Shane Homan (Chapter 4) notes that, while the federal government has largely, if perhaps only temporarily, abandoned its investment in the popular music industry, state governments have taken a greater interest in it. Significantly, this latter development is not concerned with any nationing or generally cultural imperative, but is rather in response to state government interest in the commercial potential of creative industries and in the establishment of certain kinds of creative precinct for the purposes of urban renewal. In a further variation of the contingent settlements required to deal with the competing imperatives that we have been outlining, David Rowe's analysis (Chapter 7) of the professionalization of rugby union describes a complex interface between potentially contradictory systems of support: from government funding arrangements for the national team to the enlistment of large corporate sponsors, including nationally-based companies, such as Qantas, as well as major transnational corporations, such as Samsung and HSBC. As is clear right across the sports field, both within and outside Australia, even such an apparently straightforward representative of the nation as a national sporting team is now enmeshed in a complex web of government investment, local corporate sponsorship, international sports commerce and global media deals.

Finally, here, it is important to acknowledge explicitly the wisdom of resisting too simple a narrative of decline in our account of the fate of the project of nationing. Two of the cross-field chapters in *Making Culture* examine issues which demonstrate continuing interest in the principles behind the more traditional projects of nation formation, while also revealing how difficult and potentially contestable such initiatives can be in practice. Ben Dibley and Graeme Turner's account of the National Indigenous Television Network (commonly referred to as NITV) (Chapter 10) demonstrates how institutional imperatives, as well as commercial considerations even within the context of a publicly funded broadcasting organization, can frustrate and complicate what are self-evidently worthwhile initiatives. The task of mounting an Indigenous network that is programmed with entirely Indigenous material, and which speaks both to the Indigenous and wider Australian communities, is revealed to face considerable challenges – some of them, structural and institutional. In their chapter on Australia's longstanding but increasingly embattled policy of multiculturalism, moreover, Ien Ang and Greg Noble (Chapter 11) express their concerns at the policy's capacity to deal effectively with the 'diversity of diversity' that some Australian communities are now facing. This issue is further complicated by the contradiction between elements of current Australian multicultural policy in both emphasizing common heritage, shared identity and values while also foregrounding the increasing diversification in the cultural practices of Australians. In both these contributions (Chapters 10 and 11), we see the persistence of a policy formation aimed at the public good that is nonetheless confronted by a range of difficulties and ambiguities that threatens to frustrate these good intentions.

Globalization and transnationalism

As a number of the chapters demonstrate, the forces of globalization have had complex and varied effects on the cultural fields that this volume examines. We know that it has not been uncommon for its proponents to exaggerate the scale and provenance of the processes of globalization, and many of the earlier totalizing narratives have required significant revision (Sparks 2016). Such reconsideration is especially necessary once we focus on the circumstances within specific cultural fields and in particular nation-states (Voltmer 2013). Research on the media industries, for instance, far from documenting the further entrenchment of 'Global Hollywood' (after Miller et al. 2001), has shown how local media production hubs have emerged elsewhere – in Asia, Latin America and Africa, for example – in response to new conditions of production and distribution, and feeding the development of strong regional and linguistic markets. Michael Curtin (2003) has described locations such as Hong Kong as the new 'media capitals', challenging globalist assumptions about the continuing global dominance of Anglo-American media conglomerates. As Curtin demonstrates, the corporate concentration of global media has gone hand-in-hand with the fragmentation and diversification of media content markets and, paradoxically, a confirmed commercial preference for local content in many such markets. Outside the Anglo-American media centres, there is now a significant localization of production underway, developing new content and formats, indigenizing global television genres, and marketing content to local and regional geo-linguistic markets (Moran 2009). Graeme Turner's contribution (Chapter 5) on the contemporary influence of global media within Australian television points to the shifts in the local production industry which have reoriented interest in the local production of quality drama while, on the other hand, negatively affecting the continuing profitability of not only the broadcast networks, but also the major pay-TV operator. Scherer and Rowe (2014) have noted, in the key area of free-to-air and subscription television sport, the widely variable ways in which local, national, public and commercial interests are accommodated across the globe. As such evidence demonstrates, the narrative of globalization is not nearly as straightforward as originally believed, nor are its characteristics as 'global' as was once assumed by those initial analysts who focused mostly on the more developed sectors of the global North.

Consequently, for our purposes with this volume, we have chosen to work with the more modest concept of transnationalism. It would be hard to deny the contemporary necessity, for any nation-state seeking economic growth, of engaging with transnational markets. Among developing nations and those transitioning from non-democratic or non-market systems, participation in the global marketplace has become a fundamental component of the process of developing a modern economy. While transnationalism does chime with the standard rhetoric of globalization – which could represent such a tendency as proof of the declining relevance of the nation-state, for instance – there is also evidence in such countries of a clear connection between the internationalization and modernization of the local economy and a process of nation-building (Tay and Turner 2015). As noted earlier in reference to India and to the nations emerging out of the former Yugoslavia, this change can also involve policy investment in campaigns of nation-branding as the outward-facing dimension of such a process. This point further highlights the contradictory relationship noted above: a partnership between the internationalist embrace of a global economy and a nationalist program of modernization and cultural development.

In Australia, in some of the fields that we have surveyed, the tactics employed to address that contradiction are manifest. There can be little doubt that strengthening tendencies towards transnationalism are implicated in the moderation of the nationing imperatives underpinning the policy settings used to shape Australian cultural fields such as art, music, literature, media and, to a lesser extent, heritage and sport. Indeed, in some instances such tendencies are a direct and deliberate consequence of broader policy settings within which engagement with the global or the transnational has an explicitly higher priority than is applied to an earlier model of cultural nationalism, and in which once again we can see the consequences of a shift in government interest from cultural to industry policy. The Australian literary field was once regarded as something of a cultural flagship, particularly from the 1960s through to the 1980s. More recent changes in government policy settings in relation to Australia's participation in the international book trade, as well as the increasing internationalization of Australian publishing and bookselling industries and a declining investment in arts funding across the board, have taken us well away from what David Carter and Michelle Kelly (Chapter 1) describe as Australia's 'literary nationalism'. Tony Bennett's (Chapter 2) analysis of the art field deals with the transition from the 'resolutely national' focus of *Creative Nation*'s discussion of the visual arts to that of the contemporary art field which is more outward looking – the engagement with Asian markets is of particular note here – as well as being more substantially integrated into an international art market that is itself now less dominated by the traditional centres of London, Paris or New York. That market is thus more diverse and inclusive, and Bennett discusses the complex implications that arise for Indigenous artists, and for what he describes as the normal 'rules of art'. Deborah Stevenson's contribution (Chapter 3) also provides evidence of the growing internationalization of the Australian art field through her discussion of the art fair/art market as a highly scale-able, commercially diverse and strategically adaptable means of linking host cities, rather than host nations, with transnational art markets.

Foremost among the cross-field factors implicated in the influence of the global or the transnational has been the significant changes in technologies of production, distribution and consumption enabled by the rise of the digital. Bennett points to the effects of these processes on formal experimentation and innovation within the art field, as well as to the implications of digital technologies for the cultural status of the contemporary art object (Chapter 2). Carter and Kelly (Chapter 1) also point to the impact of digital technologies on the literary field, while Turner (Chapter 5) argues that the introduction of the online streaming service Netflix to the Australian television sector has turned out to be a 'game-changer' – not only in terms of what it offers to consumers as content, but also in the problems that it introduces for existing national regulatory arrangements. In his contribution, focused entirely on the cultural and regulatory implications of the digital, Brett Hutchins (Chapter 8) argues that the influence of digital technologies across cultural fields is setting a 'confounding' set of challenges for national governments and policy makers as they attempt to balance issues of public good and public utility against the commercial requirements of an 'agile' and 'innovative' digital economy. For Australia, as it aims at transitioning from a raw material and manufacturing economy into a services economy, these issues are now of major strategic importance.

Commercialization

The most common analytical element in this collection is the acknowledgment of the influence of commercialization or marketization upon the cultural fields that it addresses, and upon their changing status within national policy frameworks. If there ever was a time when government investment in building national culture was seen as an unproblematically appropriate activity, it would be safe to say that such a time has now passed. In a broad policy context in which governments of many political persuasions have come to regard the market as a mechanism preferable to government as a means of allocating resources, distributing opportunity and regulating industries, it is hardly surprising that this principle is being applied even to activities which might be regarded as primarily cultural rather than commercial. As noted earlier, making culture for its own sake is far less in favour now than it was even in 1994, when the preamble to *Creative Nation* could confidently declare that, 'the Government accepts its responsibility for creating an environment in which culture may flourish' (Commonwealth of Australia 1994, p. 2). At that time, it was probably still the case that investment in the production of culture was regarded as, on balance, an appropriate and necessary activity for government, even if that position was coming under significant challenge from more neoliberal policy proposals. Now, it is almost routine for cultural policy to be framed around the notion that cultural activities should be able to demonstrate their value in the marketplace and should seek commercial viability rather than rely on continued government subvention. Its successor, *Creative Australia: National Cultural Policy* (Commonwealth of Australia 2013, p. 7), while retaining elements of *Creative Nation's* commitment to the role of government, was emphatic that '[t]he cultural sector has always been central to the social life of Australians, but it is now an increasingly important part of the economic mainstream'.

The consequences of this shift in approach have varied significantly across Australia's cultural fields, as each has had their own contingent relation to the forces of marketization. In their discussion of the Australian literary field, Carter and Kelly (Chapter 1) note the significance of the reframing of the literary field as 'the book industry', while nonetheless asking whether or not 'commercialization' is the most accurate or comprehensive way of describing what has occurred in this sector. In the art field, the commercialization of the visual arts evident in the proliferation of the art markets and art fairs described by Stevenson (Chapter 3) may actually have the positive effect of breaking down the exclusivity and elite status of the art object. Bennett (Chapter 2) also points to the knock-on effects of reduced public funding for the arts and the increased marketization of the field, while also noting an increased openness to new art practices as drivers of change.

Turner (Chapter 5) argues that the media in general, but particularly the news media, are far more unequivocally focused on their commercial interests than ever before, and thus far less committed to their traditional national role as the primary sources of information for citizens. Homan's (Chapter 4) discussion of the popular music industry frames recent investigation of the creative industries model as almost entirely driven by the search for a means of commodifying not only the products of these industries, but also their putative capacity to provide for urban planners a core of activity and innovation within urban settings. In his contribution to cross-field analysis, Chris Gibson's account (Chapter 9) of the changing meanings of cultural tourism in Australia devotes its attention not only to the changing batteries of representation in the promotion of Australian tourism – notably, the recent shift towards representing Australia as an urban and cosmopolitan culture – but also to how tourism has reoriented itself around the commercial opportunities available through commodifying, rather than making, Australian culture.

Taken as a whole, then, the essays in this collection suggest that the commercialization of the production of national culture, in various ways and to varying degrees, constitutes an important factor in the configuration of the relations between state and economic power. Therefore, the commercialization of the signification of nation is one of the key influences on the progress of change in Australian culture over the decades since the release of *Creative Nation*. It is a change that is also visible elsewhere in the world, of course, and we are not arguing that this development is unique to Australia, although the specifics of its elaboration may well be so. Furthermore, it is not only the cultural industries which are being marketized; we can see this strategy determining policy regarding, for instance, higher education funding and health care – cases where the choices involved in managing government investment in a public good or public utility are being outsourced to the market environment. For politicians, there has been the consequent benefit of putting difficult decisions at arms' length, while gradually assuming the status of a natural or inevitable process (evident when they talk of a certain level of funding for such activities as being 'unsustainable', rather than as a creation of political will or the lack thereof). As noted earlier in our discussion of nation-branding, it would not be too much of an exaggeration to say that much of the contemporary processes of nationing have been handed over to the market as well. Indeed, some of it resembles what has been described, often in relation to sport and media, as 'corporate nationalism' (Silk et al. 2005). The chapters that follow examine what has happened within Australia as it has shifted its location of the management of the production of culture; where once it sat within a context of nation formation and cultural production, it now sits, arguably, within a marketized context of economic development and consolidation.

The organization of this book

The chapters in this book are organized into two principal parts. Part 1 is composed of individual case studies of the internal dynamics of the selected cultural fields – literature, art, music, sport, heritage and the media. The potential scale of such an undertaking in relation to sport and the media has required us to restrict our analysis of these fields to what we regard as particularly relevant and resonant sites. Given their expansiveness and cultural, institutional, and industrial complexity, in comparison, say, to the literary field, we have selected a particular element from each of these fields as the focus of our case study: respectively, the sport of rugby union and the medium of television. In relation to the music field, we have focused on popular music as the form within which cultural nationalist policy initiatives have been most vigorously applied over the last two decades or so, and in which the changing objectives of contemporary cultural policy are most clearly traced.

Part 2 examines what we think of as 'cross-field' capacities, where a particular domain or technology exercises such a pervasive influence upon other fields as to play a significant, perhaps even determining, role in their definition and development. The spread of digital technologies, and their implications for the reconfiguration of the production, distribution and consumption of culture, is dealt with in this section of the book. Similarly, tourism, with its influence over the marketing of heritage, for instance, but also regarding the manner in which it generates and recycles a repertoire of images that define the nation both for its citizens and visitors, is also the subject of a chapter in this section. This part of the book also examines two cultural influences which are not confined to one particular cultural field, but which have been the focus of discussion, debate and activism aimed at establishing or reinforcing their significance within the culture as a whole. The increasingly ambiguous and contested location of multiculturalism in Australian culture generally, as well as the manner in which an Indigenous presence might be appropriately affirmed within such a powerful cultural field as the media, are both discussed in chapters in Part 2. Finally, Toby Miller (Chapter 12) provides a reflection on this book's contributions in an Afterword, locating the debates canvassed in *Making Culture* within the broader international context. The book closes, then, just as it began, with a focus on the ways in which commercial, governmental, communal, national, transnational and (potentially) global forces coalesce in fashioning how culture is made, and on the profound symbolic and material consequences of their constantly shifting interplay.

Note

1 The Australian Cultural Fields: National and Transnational Dynamics project was supported by the Australian Government through the Australian Research Council (DP140101970). The project was awarded to Tony Bennett (Project Director, Western Sydney University), to Chief Investigators Greg Noble, David Rowe, Tim Rowse, Deborah Stevenson and Emma Waterton (Western Sydney University), David Carter and Graeme Turner (University of Queensland), and to Partner Investigators Modesto Gayo (Universidad Diego Portales) and Fred Myers (New York University). Michelle Kelly (Western Sydney University) was appointed as Project Manager/Senior Research Officer. The project has additionally benefited from inputs from Ien Ang, Ben Dibley, Liam Magee, Anna Pertierra and Megan Watkins (Western Sydney University).

References

Anderson, B., 1983. *Imagined communities: Reflections on the origin and spread of nationalism*. London: Verso.

Athique, A. M., 2012. *Indian media*. London: Polity Press.

Beck, U., 2007. The cosmopolitan condition: Why methodological nationalism fails. *Theory, Culture and Society*, 24(7–8), 295–310.

Commonwealth of Australia, 1994. *Creative nation: Commonwealth cultural policy* (revised ed.). Canberra: Department of Communications and the Arts.

Commonwealth of Australia, 2013. *Creative Australia: National cultural policy*. Canberra: Australian Government. Available from: http://apo.org.au/system/files/33126/apo-nid33126-39286.pdf [Accessed 22 June 2017].

Curtin, M., 2003. Media capital: Towards the study of spatial flows. *International Journal of Cultural Studies*, 6(2), 201–228.

Flew, T., Iosifidis, P. and Steemers, J., eds., 2016. *Global media and national policies: The return of the state*. London: Palgrave Macmillan.

Kaneva, N., 2012. *Branding for post-communist nations: Marketizing national identities in the 'new' Europe*. New York: Routledge.

Milhelj, S., 2011. *Media nations: Communicating belonging and exclusion in the modern world*. London: Palgrave Macmillan.

Miller, T., Govil, N., McMurria, J. and Maxwell, R., 2001. *Global Hollywood*. London: BFI.

Moran, A., 2009. *Television formats worldwide: Localizing global programs*. Bristol: Intellect.

O'Connor, J., 2016. *After the creative industries: Why we need a cultural economy*. Strawberry Hills: Currency House Platform Papers No. 47.

Scherer, J. and Rowe, D., 2014. Sport, public service media, and cultural citizenship. *In*: J. Scherer and D. Rowe, eds. *Sport, public broadcasting, and cultural citizenship: Signal lost?* New York: Routledge, 1–29.

Silk, M. L., Andrews, D. L. and Cole, C. L., 2005. *Sport and corporate nationalisms*. Oxford: Berg.

Sparks, C., 2016. Global integration, state policy and the media. *In*: T. Flew, P. Iosifidis and J. Steemers, eds. *Global media and national policies: The return of the state*. London: Palgrave Macmillan, 49–74.

Stevenson, D., 2000. *Art and organisation: Making Australian cultural policy*. St Lucia: University of Queensland Press.

Tay, J. and Turner, G., eds., 2015. *Television histories in Asia: Issues and contexts*. London: Routledge.

Urban, K., 2004. Towards a theory of cruel Britannia: Coolness, cruelty and the 'nineties'. *New Theatre Quarterly*, 80, 354–372.

Volcic, Z. and Andrejevic, A., eds., 2016. *Commercial nationalism: Selling the nation and nationalizing the sell*. Basingstoke: Palgrave Macmillan.

Voltmer, K., 2013. *The media in transitional democracies*. London: Polity Press.

Watson, S. and González-Rodríguez, M. R., 2015. Heritage economies: The past meets the future in the mall. *In*: E. Waterton and S. Watson, eds. *The Palgrave handbook of contemporary heritage research*. Basingstoke: Palgrave Macmillan, 458–477.

Part 1
The cultural fields

1 The book trade and the arts ecology

Transnationalism and digitization in the Australian literary field

David Carter and Michelle Kelly

Introduction

The effects of globalization and the digital revolution on the Australian literary field have undeniably been significant, if unequal, across the different spheres of production, distribution and reception. According to one industry commentator, Australian trade publishing has recently faced a 'perfect storm' (O'Shaughnessy 2016, p. 89), and in the words of the most recent large-scale report:

> It has been a difficult period for the industry and the contributory factors to its structural transformation are well known. They include the development of technology that has enabled digital publishing, distribution and retailing; secure e-commerce systems; the entry of disruptive players including Amazon, Google and Apple; the introduction of hand-held reading platforms and devices; changes in the bricks and mortar retailing sector; and the rise of online and social media as important channels for promoting books.
>
> (Zwar 2016, p. 1)

Yet the publishing industry and the broader field of books and reading also show a surprising level of stability or continuity. This chapter will argue that these recent agents of change need to be understood in the context of the long history of transnationalism in Australian publishing and bookselling and their equally longstanding commercialism. While the impacts of online bookselling and e-readers have been relatively sudden and transformative, they have largely been absorbed within existing industry structures; and while digital technologies have given publishers and booksellers new access to book consumers, as well as providing new opportunities for consumers to access books, it is difficult to see any sudden 'increasing commercialization' in the field.

Similarly, in the policy domain, we see both change and recurrence. While there has been a relative decline of 'nationing' discourses in providing the key rationales for government intervention in the literary field since the 1980s, the foregrounding of economic rather than cultural imperatives extends back at least as far as the national cultural policy *Creative Nation* in 1994. And if *Creative Nation* was largely silent about the national literature, this silence was in part because the notion of subsidizing literature's producers, both publishers and individual writers, was already well established in Australia Council programs. While government and associated reports have focused on the book publishing industry, discursive appeals to forms of 'national story-telling' and cultural value have never disappeared. If the cultural grounds for *subsidy* have been weakened within the cultural industries paradigm, literature has been the subject of a new kind of validation as one domain among others of creativity and entertainment, a legitimate object of *investment*.

The sections below analyse the Australian literary field since the early 1990s, drawing parallel chronologies of developments in policy, publishing, digital technologies, bookselling, and the role of literary agents and writers festivals. The domestic literary field is framed by its location within a transnational publishing industry and book market. While the big players in international publishing and bookselling are as global and globalizing as any large-scale media organization – we need only mention Amazon or the Bertelsmann-Pearson-owned Penguin Random House – the Anglophone publishing industry and book market are more accurately represented through the notion of transnationalism rather than globalization. 'Transnationalism' better captures the way that domestic markets and national policy settings, not least those governing copyright, shape the flow of books and authors across national borders and the local operations of 'global' players.

Policy

The Australia Council's 1996–97 annual report began as follows: 'Australia is a culturally rich nation and artists are central to our sense of national identity and the way we are perceived by the world' (Commonwealth of Australia 1997, p. 7). By contrast, in 2015–16, the first full reporting year following the implementation of the Council's new Strategic Plan, the predominant discourse is that of investment: the Council's purpose is 'to champion and invest in Australian arts' (Australia Council 2016, p. 13). While the Chair could still refer to 'our unique collective identity' (p. 5), defined most prominently by Indigenous and immigrant cultures, the report is organized less around ideas of a national culture than 'investment in the arts to support and build a vibrant arts ecology' (p. 13). These statements occurred in the context of the Council's reformed structure in which grants for writers, publishers, literary magazines or other literary projects are part of the general mix of 'grants program and initiative funding' rather than within a specific literary portfolio primarily driven by and responsive to the sector itself. Literature still does well in this part of the Council's programs, attracting 12.3 per cent of grant dollars in 2015–16, just behind the visual arts and music but just ahead of theatre (p. 24). However, literature is not granted the same status as the major arts companies or institutions: at 2.7 per cent of *total* Council funding (its lowest percentage over the previous five years), it lags far behind symphony orchestras, theatre, opera, dance and the visual arts.

Literature and the book industry have long been viewed through the lenses of both economic and cultural policy, from the establishment of the Commonwealth

Literary Fund (CLF) in 1908 to the regular Tariff Board enquiries considering duties on imported books and magazines. Literature was the earliest target of national cultural policy through the CLF, especially from 1939–40, when it began supporting universities offering lectures in Australian literature (Butterss 2015). Its status was confirmed with the Literature Board, a key part of the Australia Council from its foundation in 1972 until a major restructure in 2013. Over the intervening decades, the policy situation for literature was relatively stable, if periodically controversial, based primarily on grants for individual writers and publishers, with more than half of the Board's budget dedicated to funding individual writers (Stevens 2004, p. 11). The Board also developed international programs supporting overseas tours and residencies for Australian writers, funding offshore magazines to publish Australian writing, engaging overseas publicists to promote Australian work in foreign markets and assisting exhibitions of Australian books overseas (Stevens 2004, pp. 18–26).

Creative Nation (Commonwealth of Australia 1994) did nothing to disturb or enhance this situation. It records the history of subsidy, and by noting increases in sales and book exports, it implies a connection between Commonwealth support and the industry's expansion, but no overt claims about literature's role in the national culture are made. Literature is mentioned as a source of content and 'entrepreneurial skills' for the development of multimedia platforms, but otherwise it is not given any privileged role in terms of national culture or artistic excellence. It is assumed, rather, within a creative industries model and 'back-grounded' through broader notions of creative expression, heritage and multimedia potential. As Stuart Glover (2005, p. 103) argued, *Creative Nation* was poised 'between market deregulation and cultural protectionism', its 'economic imperatives ... balanced against a commitment to nation-building'.

The Labor Party's next iteration of national cultural policy, *Creative Australia* (Commonwealth of Australia 2013), said even less about literature. It defined 'writing and publishing' as one of the domains covered by the report, but says little about them. With the change of government in September 2013, *Creative Australia* was shelved. In any case, as cultural economist David Throsby shows, new initiatives were concentrated in 'state of the industry' reports rather than cultural policy (Throsby 2017, pp. 3–12).

All told, of the almost 20 reports pertaining to publishing, authorship or reading that we have identified from 1994 onwards, five analyse the publishing industry and five others survey reading. The word 'book' appears in the titles of nine of these reports; 'literature' or 'literary' appears in three only, all of which were connected to the Australia Council.

But although economic discourses have become prominent in cultural policy documents, it would be misleading to pose a simple opposition between concerns with the industry or marketplace and appeals to Australian culture. Industry reports have made an impressive case for the cultural significance of the book industry; cultural policy, in turn, acknowledges the economic significance of the industry; and books and writing continue to be supported through Australia Council programs. Literature's role in 'nation branding' has long been present in

Council objectives; however, it would appear that its role in such activities is perceived to be a modest one, hence, in part, literature's small slice of the Council's overall budget.

The then Labor government had resisted the Productivity Commission's 2009 recommendation that existing parallel importation restrictions on books be lifted; but in acknowledging the challenges the book trade faced it established the Book Industry Strategy Group (BISG) to review the industry.[1] The BISG, in turn, recommended the establishment of a Book Industry Collaborative Council (BICC). Despite reporting to the Department of Industry, the BICC's extensive report, submitted in June 2013, a month after *Creative Australia*, 'recognized that the book industry's claim on the attention of government lay primarily in its cultural role' (Throsby 2017, p. 8). A separate section on 'The Book Industry and Australian Culture' linked books to new media, highlighting cultural, civic and economic values equally:

> Books stimulate debate and informed discussion of public issues in Australia and beyond, and are a primary vehicle for the production and dissemination of Australian content across all genres ... Australian stories are the bedrock of our culture. Australian books reflect who we are as a nation, where we've been and where we are going.
>
> (BICC 2013, p. 47)

Indeed, this industry report is more overt about national cultural claims than either *Creative Nation* or *Creative Australia*. It also deliberately opens out to include graphic novels, popular fiction and emerging digital genres such as e-poetry. It does not use the term 'literature', but gives books, story-telling and literary creativity a broad role in Australian culture, in the civic sphere, in new media contexts and in producing intellectual property and economic benefits.

Outside the new strategy for the Australia Council, there has been little policy activity in recent years. The history of what might have been the final major development of the period, the Book Council of Australia (BCA), is indicative of policy indecision. Announced in September 2015, the proposed new body soon found itself in disorder, not least because it was to be funded controversially by AU$6 million pulled from the Australia Council. By December, plans for the BCA had been shelved. Nonetheless, its terms of reference, like the BICC report, embraced a mixed 'ecology' of national, civic, industry and commercial imperatives with a dash of nation-branding: 'Australian literature is vital to our cultural and intellectual life. Australian writers are ambassadors for our stories and experiences, reflecting the diverse and exceptional creativity of the nation' (Ministry for the Arts 2015).

In these new formulations of literature's place within an arts ecology, it's possible to see the basis for a robust cultural policy and an innovative sense of books and writing in a new media landscape. What is much harder to see in the short-to-medium term is any political investment in new policy developments at the national level. The function of the Parliamentary Friends of Australian Books and

Writers, launched in September 2017, remains to be seen. It aims to create a forum for Members of Parliament and Senators 'to meet and interact' with publishing industry representatives (Parliament of Australia 2017).

Industry

Australian publishing was certainly affected by the successive waves of business mergers, acquisitions and closures that occurred across the 1980s and 1990s in Anglophone trade publishing (Lee 2007; Thompson 2012). But in the decades since 1994, perhaps the main story for Australian publishing is the relative stability of ownership structures and of relations between large multinational and small-to-medium local publishers. The mergers and takeovers in the US and UK industries were driven by genuinely global enterprises: Bertelsmann (Random House), Pearson (Penguin), Hachette, HarperCollins, Holtzbrinck (Macmillan), plus Simon & Schuster in the USA. But with two major exceptions – the 2013 merger of Random House and Penguin and HarperCollins's 2015 purchase of Harlequin – the situation in Australia has been relatively quiet since the late 1980s when HarperCollins acquired Angus & Robertson and Penguin absorbed Lloyd O'Neill and McPhee Gribble (Lee 2007, p. 23). Penguin Random House, Hachette, Pan Macmillan, HarperCollins/Harlequin and Simon & Schuster (to a lesser extent) are all major players, not least as publishers of Australian books for Australian audiences (Carter 2016, pp. 7–8). But the size of the domestic market means they function more like 'medium-sized' publishers, alongside local independents such as Allen & Unwin (by far the largest), Text, University of Queensland Press, Black Inc. and Fremantle Press. Although collectively, the big players dominate the market, the number of takeovers and acquisitions has been limited.

In the decades leading up to the 1990s, one of the major changes for Australian publishing, not least for international publishers operating in Australia, was the 1976 collapse of the Traditional Markets Agreement through which British and US publishers had divided the English-speaking world into two markets, in effect locking Australian books and authors into the British sphere. From that time, Australian firms became active players in the international rights market as Australia became truly an independent copyright territory. Indeed, these 'transnational' moves often had a cultural nationalist dimension, as with the efforts of both Penguin Australia, under Brian Johns's leadership, and the University of Queensland Press to sell Australian books into the USA (Poland and Indyk 2010; Jordan 2010). While Australian authors and publishers (including the Australian branches of multinational firms) are still often at a disadvantage in terms of scale and bargaining power, the international trade in rights has become part of 'business as usual' for local small-medium sized firms. It is no longer rare even for first novels to find overseas buyers (for example, the sale of UK rights in Kate Mildenhall's debut novel, *SkyLarking*, published locally by Black Inc: Stegink 2016, pp. 8–9).

In terms of ownership structures, we cannot say that the local industry has been rapidly or profoundly transformed by globalization or transnationalism in recent years. As a mid-sized industry and market, publishing and the book trade have long been 'transnational' and defined by their relation to the larger Anglophone industries. Multinationals have been dominant since the 1980s, and earlier in the guise of British firms. Over the same period, the lifespan of local independents has been extended and their contribution to adult fiction publishing has increased; since 2000, there has been a slight decline in the proportion of Australian fiction titles produced by the multinationals (Carter 2016, p. 8). Of course, there have also been casualties: we have tracked 13 small-to-medium publishers, from Hale & Iremonger in 2002 to Pier 9 in 2012, that have folded, been acquired or shifted operations away from literary publishing. But many more have stayed afloat and new publishers have been launched. Those surviving to the present include Scribe, Boolarong, Magabala and Text, among others (we count over 20). Digital technologies have lowered the bar to entry into publishing even further, in an industry where it has long been possible for very small publishing operations to come into being. Despite the new affordances, however, marketing and 'discoverability' remain major issues for the smaller players.

Digital publishing

If there has been relative stability on the production side, the picture does need to be recalibrated with a closer focus on the rise of digital publishing, especially in genre fiction. The multinationals have boosted production and sales by being better positioned to invest in digital releases. The number of fiction titles published annually in Australia jumped dramatically from 2011 and 2016, with ebooks and self-publishing via online platforms contributing a major part of the increase. Ebooks have proven to be especially popular for adult fiction, and in particular for popular genres such as crime, science fiction and romance: Australian ebook sales for romance have risen from 10.2 per cent in 2009 to 58.9 per cent in 2014 (Driscoll et al. 2016, p. 71). Mainstream fiction titles such as Graeme Simsion's *The Rosie Project* might now have a 50/50 print to ebook sales ratio (Barrett 2015), while it has been estimated that 17–20 per cent of most large trade publishers' turnover comes from digital sales (Zwar 2016, p. 7). At the same time, the initial rapid growth in ebook production and sales after 2009 has slowed or stalled: in 2013 ebooks and other digital formats accounted for 29 per cent of all titles published but by 2015 this figure had fallen to 22 per cent (Jefferies 2016, p. 6). Further, some key 'digital only' imprints launched by the multinationals around 2012 have had limited life-spans. Pan Macmillan's Momentum was 'scaled down and folded back into the publisher' in early 2016 (Jefferies 2016, p. 4), while Penguin Australia's Destiny Romance imprint began dwindling around the same time.

Nonetheless, genre fiction publishing has driven innovation in publishing models and in modes of publishers connecting directly with readers. Like television, publishing has been transformed by multi-platforming, such that the link between a particular genre and a specific technology has been broken (Davis 2013, p. 4). But rather than being rendered obsolete, the result for books, even in print, is that they no longer appear as 'old technology'. At the time of writing, the degree of disruption that the new technologies will produce remains uncertain, but it does seem that digital publishing has been absorbed within modified but not radically transformed business models. Even where ebooks account for 10 or even 20 per cent of a firm's revenues, 'the core functions of contemporary book publishing remain remarkably similar to those it possessed throughout the twentieth century' (Stinson and Mannion 2016, p. vii). While ebooks have offset declining print sales for some firms – despite meaning 'more units but less revenues' (Donoughue 2013, p. 17) – print has remained core business. In general terms, Emmett Stinson's summary from 2013 still holds: 'ebooks have not really provided either a new business model or a particularly significant income stream for most Australian publishers, but have instead complicated and problematized existing models' (Stinson 2013, p. ix). The most recent industry survey presents a largely positive story of innovation in the publishing industry, even if many of the new developments were forced rather than foreseen (Zwar 2016).

In many ways the most striking effect of digital publishing technologies has been the rise of *self-publishing* options and *online publishing* platforms such as Amazon. While the vast majority of self-published titles remain unknown and unsold, self-publishing is now much more a question of choice or strategy than simply a last resort. There are enough success stories (following the *Fifty Shades of Grey* phenomenon) to change perceptions in the trade and the marketplace: stories of self-published books becoming bestsellers, self-published authors transitioning to mainstream publishers and established authors choosing to self-publish. Self- or micro-published titles are generally not recorded in the industry surveys that report declining ebook sales; by contrast, Amazon, which stocks many of these titles, reports increases in both sales and revenues (Earls 2017). If ebook growth has stabilized or stalled for larger mainstream publishers, the online world of 'self, indie or Amazon-published authors' (Earls 2017) is still multiplying.

It's some time now since we've heard predictions of the 'death of the book'. Digital publishing appears to have underwritten growth in the number of titles produced in both ebook *and* print forms and the volume of sales has been maintained. We might say that these new developments have flooded the basement of book publishing and forced some renovations inside and out, but there has as yet been no foundational structural transformation. The bigger change agents locally have occurred in retailing, not least through the impact of online booksellers and e-readers and in the new relationships between publishers, booksellers and consumers these changes have produced.

Bookselling

The major changes in Australian bookselling and consumer behaviour since the early 1990s have been through the rise of online booksellers, the uptake of e-readers, especially Amazon's Kindle, and the 2011 demise of the REDgroup, owners of the Australian Borders and Angus & Robertson bookstore chains. Amazon is the key player, not simply as a global online bookseller but, above all, through its Kindle, a tipping point in the uptake of digital reading and bookselling technologies in that it combines e-reading and book purchasing/distribution capacities in a single device. But in the short term, the most dramatic impact was the collapse of the REDgroup, due it appears to bad management rather than the impact of online retailing or ebooks per se (Lim 2011). The market shrank by around 20 per cent, the proportion the chains had held, and became polarized between the 'discount department stores' (DDSs) and independent bookstores. It continued to fall from its 2010 peak (AU$1290m) before a turnaround in 2014–15 (Zwar 2016, p. 3).[2] This reduction occurred just when online and ebook sales were increasing. The DDSs have attained enormous power in the fiction market, potentially influencing publishers' investments towards fewer, 'bigger' titles, and, together with ebooks, increasing consumers' expectations of lower-priced books. Some have also seen the widespread uptake of Nielsen Bookscan from 2001 as a gamechanger, providing publishers with point-of-sale information and so increasing focus on commercial imperatives (Driscoll 2016). Big W is now believed to be 'the single biggest retailer of books in Australia' (Zwar 2016, p. 6). Latest estimates give the book chains 38 per cent, DDSs 28 per cent and independents 27 per cent of the market (Zwar 2016, p. 5).

The impact of 'digital globalization' in this domain is such that in recent years, according to one estimate, AU$250 million in Australian books sales annually 'has been lost to offshore retailers such as Amazon, Amazon's Book Depository and through ebook sales from other providers', and the short-term prediction is for around 20 per cent of trade sales to be through online retailers (Zwar 2016, pp. 3, 8). In effect, online retailing has enabled individual consumers to compete with local booksellers, bypassing Australia's parallel importation restrictions by 'importing' cheaper books into Australia via their internet browser or Kindle (Ensor 2015). Indeed, a longer-term effect could be the erosion of the established business model for many Australian publishers, where the production of local works is cross-subsidized with income derived from buy-ins of overseas-originated titles, as individual consumers can now directly source these books. Digital technologies have also enabled or forced publishers to invent a raft of new strategies for dealing directly with book-buyers and readers: selling directly to consumers instead of through bookstores, providing notes for reading groups online or in print, building communities of readers online, using social media, distributing pre-publication copies to YouTube reviewers and book bloggers and harvesting consumer data to shape future publishing and marketing plans (Zwar 2016, p. 12; c.f. Davis 2016, pp. 53–55, for a critical perspective).

Despite the growth in online retailing and consumer grooming, industry commentators point to the ways in which many independent bookstores have survived, even thrived, in the new environment. The Australian Booksellers Association estimated a 5 per cent growth in bookstores in 2016 (Earls 2016), while the survey conducted by the Australian Cultural Fields project (Carter and Kelly 2017) indicates the local bookstore is the most popular site for obtaining books (65 per cent of those surveyed said they had bought books in local books shops over the previous year), ahead of online retailers (38 per cent) and ebook purchases (27 per cent). Independent bookstores, like the book itself, have found new roles and an expanded space for themselves in the reconfigured field of reading and book culture.

Literary agents and festivals

The industry directory *Australian Writer's Marketplace* puts the number of Australian literary agents and agencies at 14 in the late 1990s, 24 in 2006 and 23 in 2015–16. The size of the sector thus fluctuates, but within a narrowly defined band, which is predictable for a service industry that is small in international terms and, until recently, minimally professionalized. It was still possible in the late 1990s to see 'agenting' as an amateur enterprise where anyone 'can hang out a shingle as a literary agent' (Wynhausen and Perkins 1997; Lurie 2002, p. 10). The new century has seen rapid professionalization, with the formation of the Australian Literary Agents Association in 2003, a consolidation rather than dramatic expansion or segmentation of the field.

Thompson has identified a dramatic and inexorable rise of the literary agent in the US and the UK (2012, pp. 59–100), a situation not replicated in Australia. The recent Macquarie University Book Authors survey found that only 18.8 per cent of respondents had an agent (Throsby et al. 2015, p. 31). The difference is explained on the one hand by the smaller advances paid in Australia and on the other by the smaller pool of Australian writers seeking overseas rights sales. Agents seem, nonetheless, to play a major role in *fiction* publishing, especially for print books.

One of the most dramatic developments in the Australian literary field since the early 1990s has been the rise of literary or writers festivals. Many of the capital cities had writers festivals by 1997 including Adelaide, Brisbane, Melbourne and Perth, and Sydney in its first year. The Northern Territory/Darwin followed in 1998 and Tasmania/Hobart in 2001 (as part of Ten Days on the Island). The establishment of festivals for young and/or emerging writers clustered around 2004–05, with Melbourne's Emerging Writers Festival and New Voices, but these were preceded by Newcastle's original National Young Writers Festival in 1998, run as part of This is Not Art since 2000. From the beginning of our timeframe in 1994, marked by the establishment of the Mildura Writers Festival, there has also been a steady flow of new regional literary festivals – and a torrent from 2008 or thereabouts. Alongside the major metropolitan festivals, we see an increasing specialization or segmentation of the festival domain, with the emergence of festivals dedicated to specific groups, genres or registers: Jewish, women and Greek-Australian writers, nature writers, crime writing, experimental writing, literary non-fiction and short stories.[3]

The larger festivals typically celebrate both the literary 'in its own terms' and offer a 'festival' of commercialization. Commentators have described publisher involvement and the festivals' own promotional objectives as being among 'the most prominent marketing strategies for literature' (Stewart 2009, p. 27). Following Giorgi, we also note the tendency of festivals to morph 'from amateur to professional organizations' (2011, pp. 41–42). We see the rapid expansion of literary festivals that seek to extend commercial opportunities *and* cultural access, especially in regional areas, an expansion broadly in line with international trends. Agencies, by contrast, have followed their own domestic trajectory, but both sectors show increasing professionalization.

Conclusion

Operating within a global or transnational economy has long been the reality for Australian publishing and bookselling, and any model proposing a sudden shift from a literary field defined primarily in national or domestic terms to one profoundly redefined by globalization or increasing commercialization would be misleading. Multinational publishing firms have been dominant in Australian publishing and central to the promotion of the national literature since at least the 1970s. Imported titles have always been dominant in the marketplace. If anything, the ecology of small-to-medium publishers has become more diverse and sustained, a development that has underwritten the growth of literary festivals and prizes.

There is much that has persisted in the field since the early 1990s, in spite of unpredictable changes in government policy, the rise of ebooks and e-readers, the collapse of the REDgroup and the increased bargaining power of the DDSs. There has been spectacular growth in ebook production and sales in certain areas, and digital technologies have affected every sector of the industry, above all through the rise of self-publishing, online bookselling and reader engagement through digital platforms. Indeed, these developments still have the power to be more profoundly disruptive in the literary field than anything we have seen to date. But the printed book, the brick-and-mortar bookstore and the market for Australian books have shown remarkable resilience.

There have certainly been marked changes in the discourse of cultural policy in relation to Australian literature and the book publishing industry, with a shift in the balance of power from the former to the latter. The industry received new kinds of policy attention (if with no lasting institutional impacts), while literature's slice of the federal funding pie diminished. The sector still struggles to be heard, to be recognized as a major cultural industry, despite the noise that literary prizes, say, can create. But here too, we argue, the changes are neither sudden nor dramatic. If literature as a distinctive art form, privileged in claims for national identity, has undergone a certain dissolution, invocations of literature's national significance have persisted in both old and new configurations.

Literature has been woven into broader discourses of creativity, digital innovation, civic value and international promotion, while the notion of the book trade operating within and alongside an arts ecology, we argue, offers a more robust model than older representations of the national culture for capturing the kinds of developments explained above. The Australian literary field will continue to be defined by its mixed character as a medium-sized industry, market and culture within a larger transnational space and by the dynamics of disruption within institutional resilience. Part of this resilience is without doubt the symbolic and economic salience of the concept of the 'book' itself. Should the book's centrality be challenged, the potential for foundational transformation in the field would increase dramatically.

Notes

1 Parallel Importation Restrictions were first introduced by Labor in 1991 to 'provide protection for authors and publishers holding rights in Australian-published books, against the importation and sale of the books from overseas suppliers' (Throsby 2017, p. 3). A book published in Australia must be released within 30 days of its publication elsewhere, and resupply must be guaranteed within 90 days. Since 2012, the industry has voluntarily adopted a 14/14 rather than a 30/90-day rule. Most recently, in November 2015, the Turnbull government announced its support for the removal of parallel importation restrictions, but no policy changes have been announced at the time of writing.
2 Total turnover in the Australian print book market fell 18 per cent in value in 2011 and bottomed out in 2013 at AU$917m before rising to $938m in 2014 and $979m in 2015 (Jefferies 2016; Earls 2017).
3 Literary prizes have also grown over the period, with new regional and state honours and genre-based awards as well as inaugural major prize programs like the Prime Minister's Literary Awards and the Stella Awards, following a similar trajectory to festivals in terms of proliferation and diversification (Driscoll 2016).

References

Australia Council, 2016. *Annual report 2015–16* [online]. Surry Hills, NSW: Australia Council for the Arts. Available from: www.australiacouncil.gov.au/workspace/uploads/files/_aca_annual_report_2015-16-58058c6e60676.pdf/ [Accessed 3 September 2017].
Barrett, J., 2015. Unlikely saviours as bookshops win battle to stay in business. *Australian Financial Review* [online], 21 March. Available from: www.afr.com/lifestyle/arts-and-entertainment/books/unlikely-saviours-as-bookshops-win-battle-to-stay-in-business-20150317-1m17yq [Accessed 3 September 2017].
Book Industry Collaborative Council (BICC), 2013. *Final report 2013* [online], Canberra: Australian Government. Available from: www.publishers.asn.au/documents/item/157 [Accessed 3 September 2017].
Butterss, P., 2015. Australian literary studies in the 1940s: The Commonwealth Literary Fund lectures. *Australian Literary Studies*, 30(4), 115–127.
Carter, D., 2016. The literary field and contemporary trade-book publishing in Australia: Literary and genre fiction. *Media International Australia*, 158(1), 48–57.
Carter, D. and Kelly, M., 2017. Australian stories: Books and reading in the nation. *In*: A. Mannion, M. Weber and K. Day, eds. *Publishing means business: Australian perspectives*. Clayton, Vic.: Monash University Publishing, 147–181.
Commonwealth of Australia, 1994. *Creative nation: Commonwealth cultural policy* (revised ed.). Canberra: Department of Communications and the Arts.
Commonwealth of Australia, 1997. *Australia Council annual report 1996–97*. Redfern, NSW: Australia Council.
Commonwealth of Australia, 2013. *Creative Australia: National cultural policy*. Available from: http://apo.org.au/node/33126 [Accessed 3 September 2017].
Davis, M., 2013. Publishing in the end times. *In*: E. Stinson, ed. *By the book? Contemporary publishing in Australia*. Clayton, Vic.: Monash University Publishing, 3–14.

Davis, M., 2016. The changing literary ecology. *In*: E. Stinson and A. Mannion, eds. *The return of print? Contemporary Australian publishing*. Clayton, Vic.: Monash University Publishing, 47–66.

Donoughue, P., 2013. At war with the future: The publishing industry and the digital revolution. *In*: E. Stinson, ed. *By the book? Contemporary publishing in Australia*. Clayton, Vic.: Monash University Publishing, 15–21.

Driscoll, B., 2016. *Contemporary Australian literary culture*. Oxford Research Encyclopedia, Literature. Available from: www.literature.oxfordre.com [Accessed 12 November 2017].

Driscoll, B., Fletcher, L. and Wilkins, K., 2016. Women, akubras and ereaders: Romance fiction and Australian publishing. *In*: E. Stinson and A. Mannion, eds. *The return of print? Contemporary Australian publishing*. Clayton, Vic.: Monash University Publishing, 67–88.

Earls, N., 2016. All hail the bookshop: Survivor against the odds. *The Conversation* [online], 11 August. Available from: http://theconversation.com/all-hail-thebookshop-survivor-against-the-odds-63758 [Accessed 3 September 2017].

Earls, N., 2017. Has the print book trumped digital? Beware of glib conclusions. *The Conversation* [online], 9 May. Available from: http://theconversation.com/has-the-print-book-trumped-digital-beware-of-glib-conclusions-77174 [Accessed 3 September 2017].

Ensor, J., 2015. Read it and weep: The book trade needs more than parallel import restrictions. *The Conversation* [online], 2 December. Available from: http://theconversation.com/read-it-and-weep-thebook-trade-needs-more-than-parallel-import-restrictions-51585 [Accessed 3 September 2017].

Giorgi, L., 2011. Between tradition, vision and imagination: The public sphere of literature festivals. *In*: L. Giorgi, M. Sassatelli and G. Delanty, eds. *Festivals and the cultural public sphere*. London: Routledge, 29–44.

Glover, S., 2005. *Literature and cultural policy studies*. Thesis (PhD). University of Queensland.

Jefferies, B., 2016. The market down under. *In*: *Think Australian 2016* [online]. Melbourne: Thorpe-Bowker, 4–7. Available from: www.booksandpublishing.com.au/ThinkAustralian/ThinkAustralian2016.pdf [Accessed 3 September 2017].

Jordan, D., 2010. American dreams and the University of Queensland Press. *In*: R. Dixon and N. Birns, eds. *Reading across the Pacific: Australia-United States intellectual histories*. Sydney University Press, 323–338.

Lee, J., 2007. Exploiting the imprint. *In*: D. Carter and A. Galligan, eds. *Making books: Contemporary Australian publishing*. St Lucia, Qld.: University of Queensland Press, 17–33.

Lim, K., 2011. What really went wrong for Border and Angus & Robertson. *The Conversation* [online], 24 March. Available from: http://theconversation.com/what-really-went-wrong-for-borders-and-angus-and-robertson-341 [Accessed 3 September 2017].

Lurie, C., 2002. Agents united. *Australian Author*, November, 8–15.

Ministry for the Arts, 2015. *Terms of reference: Book Council of Australia* [online]. Attorney-General's Department. Available from: http://arts.gov.au/sites/default/files/literature/Book-Council-Terms-of-Reference.pdf [Accessed 30 November 2015].

O'Shaughnessy, T., 2016. Deckchairs and life rafts: Australian trade publishing's perfect storm. *In*: E. Stinson and A. Mannion, eds. *The return of print? Contemporary Australian publishing*. Clayton, Vic.: Monash University Publishing, 89–114.

Parliament of Australia, 2017. *Parliamentary Friendship Groups (non-country)* [online]. Available from: www.aph.gov.au/About_Parliament/Parliamentary_Friendship [Accessed 8 November 2017].

Poland, L. and Indyk, I., 2010. Rejected by America? Some tensions in Australian-American literary relations. *In*: R. Dixon and N. Birns, eds. *Reading across the Pacific: Australia-United States intellectual histories*. Sydney University Press, 309–322.

Stegink, V., 2016. Selling strong. *In*: *Think Australian 2016* [online]. Melbourne: Thorpe-Bowker, 8–11. Available from: www.booksandpublishing.com.au/ThinkAustralian/ThinkAustralian2016.pdf [Accessed 3 September 2017].

Stevens, I., 2004. *A short history of the Literature Board, 1986–2000*. Sydney: Australia Council for the Arts.

Stewart, C., 2009. *The culture of contemporary writers' festivals*. Thesis (PhD). Queensland University of Technology.

Stinson, E., 2013. Introduction. *In*: E. Stinson, ed. *By the book? Contemporary publishing in Australia*. Clayton, Vic.: Monash University Publishing, vii–xii.

Stinson, E. and Mannion, A., 2016. Post-digital publishing: An introduction. *In*: E. Stinson and A. Mannion, eds. *The return of print? Contemporary Australian publishing*. Clayton, Vic.: Monash University Publishing, vii–xii.

Thompson, J. B., 2012. *Merchants of culture: The publishing business in the twenty-first century* (2nd ed.). New York: Plume.

Throsby, D., 2017. Commerce or culture? Australian book industry policy in the twenty-first century. *In*: A. Mannion, M. Weber and K. Day, eds. *Publishing means business: Australian perspectives*. Clayton, Vic.: Monash University Publishing, 1–21.

Throsby, D., Zwar, J. and Longden, T., 2015. *Book authors and their changing circumstances: Survey method and results* [online]. Available from: www.businessandeconomics.mq.edu.au/our_departments/Economics/econ_research/reach_network/book_project/authors/BookAuthors_WorkingPaper_2015.pdf [Accessed 3 September 2017].

Wynhausen, E. and Perkins, M., 1997. Agents – who needs them? *The Australian*, 28 June, Factiva.

Zwar, J., 2016. *Disruption and innovation in the Australian book industry: Case studies of trade and educational publishers*. Macquarie Economic Research Papers. Research Paper 1/2016. Sydney: Department of Economics, Macquarie University.

2 Beyond nation, beyond art? The 'rules of art' in contemporary Australia

Tony Bennett

Introduction

The claim that 'the visual arts have helped more than any other to forge our national identity' (Department of Communications and the Arts 1994, p. 33) sets the tone for the emphasis that the *Creative Nation* policy statement placed on art as a technology of nationing. This had several dimensions. The *Visions of Australia* program, established the previous year, was singled out for extending art's reach to the furthest-flung corners of the nation through its travelling exhibitions. Equal stress was placed on the need to reposition Australian art within a broadened conception of international art, encompassing Asia as well as Europe and the US. This formed a part of the self-confident nationhood to which *Creative Nation* aspired in aiming to go beyond the languages of both the 'cultural cringe' and the 'cultural strut': the belief, respectively, that either nothing of cultural value could be produced in Australia or that only Australian culture had true merit. The National Gallery of Australia (NGA) was accorded particular significance in this regard. Initially opened in 1982, it had, in 1994, 're-opened its Australian galleries to provide a comprehensive survey of Australian Art', while also being committed to 'the collection and display of cultures of non-European societies, particularly those of indigenous Australia and South-East Asia', thereby strengthening 'the pluralistic nature of Australia's culture' (p. 34). The attention accorded Aboriginal art here – recognized as 'a strong and increasingly visible aspect of the visual arts sector' (p. 33) – echoed the emphasis that *Creative Nation* placed on the 'culture and identity of Aboriginal and Torres Strait Islander people' as heirs to the 'magnificent heritage of the oldest civilization on earth' in providing 'an essential element of *Australian* identity, a vital expression of who we *all* are' (p. 6, emphasis in original).

Simon Knell (2016) offers a different assessment, interpreting the NGA's collection and exhibition of Aboriginal art since the 1980s as profoundly re-imagining the relations between art and nation. Not because the NGA has produced a new art historical narrative of nationhood but, to the contrary, because it has called into question the categories of both art and nation: the former in its collection of Indigenous art practices whose ancestral narratives are at odds with Western conceptions of art and art history, and the latter in its presentation of Australia as a land and people whose histories exceed the 'problematic fantasy' of 'the nation' (Knell 2016, p. 14).

Although, for reasons that I shall come to, I think Knell's assessment is somewhat overstated, it nonetheless provides a useful way into my concerns. For it is precisely because Indigenous art practices often bend or bypass the normal 'rules of art' that they can serve to highlight the respects in which those rules have been suspended or qualified by recent developments in the Australian art field.

The 'rules of art' I have in mind here are those which, in Pierre Bourdieu's classic formulation, refer to the production of art in accordance with the principles of judgement that were autonomous to the French art field during the period (the late nineteenth century) of its hard-won (relative) independence from the economic and political fields. In his 1996 postscript to *The Rules of Art*, however, Bourdieu stressed the '*threats to autonomy*' resulting from 'the increasingly greater interpenetration between the world of art and the world of money' (Bourdieu 1996, p. 344). The resulting erosion of the division between 'the narrow field of producers for producers' – in which artists are in control of the instruments of artistic production, circulation, evaluation and consecration – and the field of mass production could only by warded off, he argued, by a 'corporatism of the universal' (p. 348) in which artists and intellectuals would combine to create a 'veritable *Internationale of intellectuals* committed to defending the autonomy of the universes of cultural production' (p. 344). While this hasn't happened – no more in Australia than elsewhere – I shall argue that Indigenous art practices have provided alternatives to, and complex alignments with, the ways in which the rules of art have been inflected by the trajectories that have characterized the recent development of the Australian art field.[1] This calls for a brief sketch of the main economic, policy and institutional drivers of these trajectories.

Art field trajectories: policies, institutions, markets and publics

The key policy shifts have consisted in the increasing influence of neoliberal policy agendas. Annette Van den Bosch (2005) traces the influence of these agendas back beyond *Creative Nation* to the McLeay Report *Power, Patronage and the Muse* (House of Representatives Standing Committee on Expenditure, 1986) The developments that this report set in tow, she argues, led to: (i) an increased commercial gallery sector, with the role of owner-collector and commercial galleries as purchasers of art increasing relative to the public gallery sector; (ii) new ways of producing artistic reputations which reduced the significance of pro-art world values (usually dependent on peer evaluation) relative to market values; (iii) funding pressures on public galleries leading to an increased reliance on temporary exhibitions, usually involving a shift of government funding and institutional support away from Australian to international artists; and (iv) the increased involvement of private corporations and wealthy benefactors in the sponsorship of galleries, exhibitions and special events. The *Creative Australia* policy statement of the Gillard Labor government proposed limited checks to these tendencies (Australian Government 2013). However, the election of the Tony Abbott Coalition government in 2013 saw, instead, a reversion to the neoliberal principles that had shaped arts policies under the 1996–2007 Howard Coalition governments. This shift was most dramatically evident in the cuts to arts funding, the downsizing of the Australia Council, and the partial defunding of artist's organizations implemented by George Brandis as Minister for the Arts in the 2013–2015 Coalition government.

While Bourdieu's ideal of autonomous art values adjudicated solely by artists has never obtained in Australia, the position of artists vis-à-vis other 'players' in the art field has been weakened in several respects. They have been increasingly displaced from lead positions in State and Federal arts bureaucracies by arts management professionals, a tendency that was linked to the growth of arts schools and their absorption (until recently) into the university sector (Grishin 2013; De Lorenzo, Mendelssohn, and Speck 2011). The representation of artists and curators on the governing boards of galleries has similarly been weakened relative to that of representatives of the corporate sector.[2]

The key formal and institutional developments since the mid-1980s have consisted in the displacement of the modernist paradigm by the more flattened out temporalities of contemporary art. Terry Smith (2009) traces the emerging ascendency of contemporary art to the late 1980s, when the promotion of the Young British Artists by new galleries as part of the 'extended exhibitionary complex' (Smith 2012) broke increasingly with the White Cube conventions that governed modernist exhibition paradigms. The parallel development of installation and media art and the associated shift of emphasis away from easel painting that dominated twentieth century modernist conceptions of art history (Nagel 2012; Morphy 2009) have resulted in a radically altered set of institutions for the exhibition of art. In focusing its attention on the NGA, *Creative Nation* did not anticipate the range of new galleries – Sydney's Museum of Contemporary Art (MCA), Queensland's Gallery of Modern Art (GOMA), the Australian Centre for the Moving Image in Melbourne and Hobart's privately funded Museum of Old and New Art (MONA) – which, in the attention they have accorded to new art practices (contemporary, abstract and video art, installation and performance art), have been the most significant institutional drivers of change.

The increasing influence of these new institutional actors has been closely tangled up with that of biennales and art fairs. From their origins in the 1890s, biennales have offered a counterpoint to the curatorial visions of national museums and galleries, albeit initially retaining the tradition of national pavilions associated with earlier international exhibitions of arts and industry. The more decisive break, Carolyn Jones (2016) argues, came with the 1951 Sao Paulo biennale which both excluded national pavilions and initiated the move from figurative traditions, articulating regionalist or national values, toward abstraction as the key formal signature of a new set of internationalist art world values. The 1960s saw a further shift in the conception of biennales as their role in providing general overviews of art gave way to guest-curated thematic programs, a tendency accelerating in momentum from the 1980s with Australia participating largely via the Sydney Biennale, first held in 1973 (see Stevenson, this volume).

These developments have undoubtedly weakened the Euro-centric organization of the international art world that prevailed until the mid-twentieth century.

That said, the extent to which they have done so should not be exaggerated. As Monica Sassatelli (2015) notes, the Biennale Foundation estimated that, by 2014, there had been over 150 biennales, of which 44 per cent were in Europe, 32 per cent in Asia, 21 per cent in the Americas, 9 per cent in Africa and 3 per cent in Oceania. Chin-Tao Wu's (2013) analysis of artists exhibited at Kassel's *Documenta* between 1968 and 2007 also demonstrates the continuing predominance of Western art centres in Europe and North America, with the vast majority of those artists either being born in or having moved to those centres in consequence of their gravitational pull. The pace of change here is, however, rapid with the relative size and influence of biennales shifting in favour of those held in the Asia Pacific and Latin America in which, by 2014, artists from those regions predominated (Zarobell 2016, p. 127).

While, as a part and parcel of these developments, there have been significant changes in the international positioning of Australian art, these too should not be exaggerated. There has been some shift in the importance of its relations to Asian art fields relative to those of Europe and America while, within these, the importance of America has – following the trajectories initiated in the late 1940s – continued to increase relative to Europe. The Asia Pacific Triennial of Contemporary Art, established in 1993, has contributed to re-positioning Australian art in the Asia-Pacific region. The growth of China as a significant art market has also been important. Noah Horowitz (2011) estimates that, by 2006, China accounted for 20 per cent of the global market for contemporary art sold at auction, with Hong Kong now the world's third largest art market after New York and London (see also Zarobell 2017, p. 54). At the same time, Horowitz cautions against reading too much into such figures, noting that the distribution of buying power has remained firmly centred on the US and Europe, accounting for 86 per cent of 2006 contemporary art purchases transacted via Sotheby's, while collectors from China, Russia and India only mustered 0.2 per cent of such purchases between them. The pattern for the sale of Australian art overseas via international auction houses similarly remains strongly oriented to European and American markets (Acker 2016).

These new economic and institutional forms of art's internationalization have, in Jones's assessment, generated new forms of 'critical globalism' albeit, she argues, that these have to be viewed as both working alongside and being pitched against the increasingly close tethering of art to global capital. Other studies go further, suggesting that it is the 'rules of art' themselves that have now become marketized through their connections to the practices of distinction of transnational corporate and cultural elites. Olav Velthius (2014) has thus shown how international art fairs, commercial galleries and the Internet marketing of art all tend to operate in accordance with the 'anti-economy' which Bourdieu attributed to art markets. Commercial galleries, he argues, are inclined to be indifferent to the nationality of artists in conformity with the rules of art that art values are the only ones that count; the design of art fairs typically operates to exclude all information that would detract from the art's aesthetic value; and Internet displays of art on gallery websites as well as by Internet sales companies like Artnet also typically show only the art itself. These presentations of art as autonomous, in the sense of being disconnected from indicators of economic or social value, increase its symbolic value and, thereby, its market value through its capacity to generate symbolic returns of distinction on financial investments in art works.

These various tendencies have contributed to a shift in the organization of practices of distinction. Julian Stallabrass (2004) argues that it is the very lack of a distinguishing style for contemporary art – its break with the modernist logic of the historical succession of temporally marked styles – that allows its varied forms to be eclectically integrated into lifestyle markers. This is not to suggest that the more traditional role of art in providing unique or rare objects whose singularity allows them to function as investment and symbolic assets for the wealthy is no longer relevant. To the contrary, the development, since the 1970s, of art investment funds has constituted a purely instrumental approach to owning art as an asset which, seen initially as a hedge against inflation, now functions both as a secure source of accumulation against the turbulence of financial markets and as a luxury collectible (behind only private jets, yachts and high-end cars) for High Net Wealth owners (Horowitz 2011). This trend has, indeed, become a more significant aspect of the relations between art fields and the economic field in view of the marked increase in inequalities that has characterized Australia, alongside other developed economies, since the 1980s. The changing structure of these inequalities, owing less to inequalities of income than to inequalities of wealth derived largely from inheritance but complemented by the recruitment of a super-elite of highly paid CEOs, is equally important.[3]

The consequences of these developments are manifested in the increasing reliance of artists on the commercial sector and in the tendency for investment in new art to be increasingly focused on a small number of artists. They are also manifested in the continuing tendency for art gallery visitors to be recruited disproportionately from higher class positions. The Australian Cultural Fields (ACF) data, for example, show rates of visiting different kinds of art gallery varying – at the extremes – between members of the higher professional, management and owning classes being about twice as likely to visit state galleries and about three times more likely to visit contemporary art galleries than routine workers. The divisions are even more pronounced when expressed in terms of level of education: 60 per cent of those with tertiary qualifications had visited museums of contemporary art, compared to 20 per cent of those who had only completed secondary schooling, with the equivalent figures for State galleries being 83 per cent and 25 per cent. Involvement in art fairs and festivals is even more strongly tilted toward higher class and education positions. These figures tally with comparable findings that 75 per cent of MONA's visitors in 2013–2014 were tertiary educated and 77 per cent were professionals or managers (Franklin and Papastegiadis 2017, p. 678), and with Judith White's report that 76 per cent of the members of the Art Gallery Society of New South Wales at this time had at least one university degree, and that 37 per cent had two (White 2017, p. 180). Nor has the Internet made much difference to these patterns. The ACF data shows that those occupying lower class positions and with lower levels of education are no more likely to use the Internet for any purpose connected with the art field than they are to visit art galleries of any kind (Bennett and Gayo 2018). The visual arts in Australia are, in short, still very much a class thing.

It's a black, white and class thing

I come back now to the most distinctive development that has singled out the Australian art field from other national art fields: namely, the range of positions that Indigenous art practices have come to occupy within it. To place these in the context of the developments reviewed above would require engagement with a number of longer histories:[4] the changing relations, throughout the post-war period, between Indigenous, ethnographic and aesthetic conceptions of art; the initiation of government support for Aboriginal art, mainly through the newly established Australia Council in the 1970s; the overseas exhibitions of Aboriginal art which served to boost its national presence in Australia; and the post-war emergence of the discourses and practices of abstraction, abstract expressionism and, later, contemporary art in providing a set of local coordinates with which different strands of Indigenous art practice might resonate.[5] The *Creative Nation* statement was also significant, in Laura Fisher's (2016) estimation, in marking a moment when a whole range of Indigenous cultural practices were brought into an officially sanctioned zone of intercultural dialogue focused on the role that Indigenous culture might play in overcoming the heritage void that postcolonial critiques of the bicentenary celebrations of 1988 had left in their wake.

Placing the subsequent development of Indigenous art practices in the context of these longer-term histories affords a means of both amplifying and qualifying Knell's (2016) assessment of the productive tensions between art and nation associated with the NGA's exhibition of Aboriginal art. I shall, in doing so, add a couple of riders to the contention of Indigenous artist Richard Bell (2002) that Aboriginal art is 'a white thing'. Bell's point was not to deny that it was also a 'black thing' emanating from, and of cultural and political significance for, Indigenous Australians in renegotiating their relations with mainstream Australia. Rather, it was a pointed statement of the number of white people who were involved in the array of government policies and processes, commercial operators, and art institutions through which Aboriginal art was commissioned, classified, valued, transported, criticized and curated in being exhibited as art.[6] What I want to add to this is a sense of the ways in which, as a white thing, Aboriginal art has also been a class thing in ways that have lent specific inflections to its functioning as both a black and a white thing. Fred Myers's work has been insightful in this regard. As one of a number of anthropologists who have been closely associated with the repositioning of Aboriginal art as a distinctive component of the contemporary Australian art field, and as a key mediator of its relations to the New York art world, Myers has consistently stressed the distinctive class characteristics (mainly those of the professional middle classes) of the white people who – whether as collectors, key mediators in the relations between Indigenous art producers and art institutions, or gallery publics – have been most actively engaged with the 'high art' end of the Indigenous art practices spectrum.[7]

The ACF data also illuminate more broadly based patterns of engagement with Indigenous art practices. The general category of Aboriginal art is, after landscapes, the second most popular genre in the survey, included in the most liked genres of 26 per cent of the 1202 members of the main sample. There is relatively little class differentiation in this preference which is, indeed, lower among the two higher-class positions – owners and higher-level managers, and higher professionals, who were more likely to prefer Impressionism, Renaissance art and modernism – than among a range of lower-class positions (intermediate, semi-routine and lower supervisory and technical workers, for example). However, this pattern is reversed when – in contrast to the many interpretations that might be placed on the category of Aboriginal art (from its 'high art' forms to tourist kitsch) – respondents were asked whether they had seen and liked specific Indigenous artists. While 53 per cent of high-level professionals had seen and liked the work of Albert Namatjira, for example, this was true for only 37 per cent of routine workers.

Fisher (2016) engages with some of the consequences of these classed characteristics of white engagements with Aboriginal art in the contrast that she draws between Indigenous conceptions of 'art for culture's sake' – that is, the use of Aboriginal art within Indigenous communities as a means for the rediscovery, remaking and cross-generational transmission of the relations between culture and country, and as a civic-cum-pedagogic bridgehead into white Australia – and white interpretations of Aboriginal art within the aesthetic register of 'art for art's sake'. She is particularly concerned with the consequences that the inter-mixing of earlier ethnographic framings of Aboriginal art with Western art historical and aesthetic interpretations and with Indigenous conceptions of creativity have had for the kinds of aesthetic 'purification' associated with white consumption of Aboriginal art.

The relations between ethnographic and art historical interpretations of Aboriginal art have a long and complex history, and one that has never complied with a strict ethnographic/art history binary. Indeed, in the immediate post-war period, it was often anthropologists who first stressed the distinctive aesthetic qualities of Aboriginal art, while the initial shift in institutional framing associated with its collection and exhibition in art galleries, rather than in ethnographic or natural history museums, had little impact on its interpretation. While State galleries led the way here, the works that they acquired were, prior to the 1980s, exhibited mainly as 'curiosities with no place in the historical narratives that structured the collections' (McLean 2011, p. 46). Although the 1966 Lindsay Report had advocated that the NGA should collect and exhibit Aboriginal art for its aesthetic rather than its ethnographic value, its record in this regard was indifferent until, prompted by the exhibition of Papunya Tula acrylic desert art at the 1981 Australian *Perspecta*, director James Mollison committed the Gallery to a systematic program of collecting contemporary Aboriginal art. The subsequent inclusion of Aboriginal art within Australian art historical frameworks has, however, been accompanied by concerted efforts on the part of those anthropologists who have played significant mediating roles between art producers in remote Aboriginal communities and art institutions to adjust the aesthetic registers of art history and its temporal horizons to accommodate the collective forms of creative agency and the extended temporalities to which Aboriginal art practices testify (Morphy 2009).

The fact that such interpretations of Aboriginal art have, with some notable exceptions,[8] been developed mainly with regard to the art produced in remote Aboriginal communities has prompted perceptions of marginalization on the part of the much smaller number of Indigenous artists working in urban settings and often practising more individualized forms of art production that bring Indigenous motifs into a critical relationship with Western art practices. The 'ubiquity and authority of non-Indigenous experts on remote Aboriginal art,' (Fisher 2016, p. 128) argues, has produced a 'hierarchy of legitimacy that subordinates artists from urban areas to such an extent that some would rather be located outside that paradigm', resulting in critiques of the concept of Aboriginal art on the part of such artists wary of the forms of Indigenous essentialism that it can sometimes imply.

Fisher's second point relates to the modes of consumption of Aboriginal art by white art consumers that are produced by the mingling of the different regimes of value that are brought together in anthropologically revised art historical frameworks in which Aboriginal conceptions of the sacred are often conjoined with Western aesthetic perceptions. While not unifying the responses that this mingling generates, Fisher argues that the forms of aesthetic purification that have accompanied the production of an Aboriginal high art have given rise to three forms of distancing that now accompany its consumption. First, the circuits through which the works of a select set of remote Indigenous artists are brought to the fine art market, where they are validated as Indigenous versions of art-for-art's sake, distances them from the commercial art dealers whose purchase and distribution of more routinized forms of art production on the part of a wider range of Indigenous artists make a more systemic contribution to the economies of remote communities. Second, these same processes have enabled a critical distancing from what had, by the 1980s, become a developed commercial arts and crafts sector for the production of 'Aboriginalia' for the tourist industry, and from the unlicensed appropriation of Indigenous designs and motifs for mass-produced commodities and the circulation of Indigenous imagery in popular culture. Third, Fisher (2016, p. 64) argues that if Aboriginal art has become 'one of the most potent and amenable means of circulating positive images of Aboriginality in the public domain,' this is partly attributable to the purifications which its aestheticization effects in distancing it from less palatable aspects of Indigenous presence in contemporary Australia: claims to sovereignty and to land; unassimilable traditions, such as punishment via ritualized spearing; and levels of trauma and disadvantage that are unimaginable from the point of view of urban middle-class life. And, it might be added, a distancing from increasingly strong reminders of the violence of Australia's frontier history.

This brings me back to Knell's contention that the Aboriginal art exhibited at the NGA has, in standing partly within the national narrative but also separate from it, functioned as a locus for ethical dialogue and as a marker of contentious political mutuality between Indigenous and non-Indigenous Australians.

Simultaneously 'leading actors in the high art of nation making', Knell argues, Indigenous artists have also placed 'a disquieting political voice in the most aesthetic of objects in the most serene of symbolic spaces' (Knell 2016, p. 214). Although it is not an example that Knell cites, *The Aboriginal Memorial* has been the most emblematic of the NGA's Indigenous installations in this regard. Commissioned in 1987, displayed initially at the Sydney Biennale in 1988, included in the NGA's first major exhibition of Aboriginal art in 1989, and placed, in 1991, at the NGA's entrance, *The Memorial* has since operated as a symbolic marker of the NGA's continuing commitment to the collection and display of Aboriginal art (Caruana 2003). The work of 43 Ramingining artists curated by John Mundine, *The Memorial* comprises 200 log coffins *in memoriam* for each year of Indigenous deaths inflicted during the ongoing history of invasion from 1788 to the bicentennial celebrations of 1988. The extensive history of commentary governing its subsequent interpretation has, Nigel Lendon (2016) argues, been mostly directed toward art audiences. As such, it has placed *The Memorial* within a range of conflicting aesthetic registers – a canonical work of Australian art, a modernist masterpiece, an instance of contemporary art expressing an anti-modernist temporality – just as the material context of its exhibition has increasingly assimilated it to the NGA's other art objects. In drawing attention to the history of its production, however, Lendon peels away the aesthetic accretions that have accumulated around *The Memorial* to restore the horizons of its significance that stand outside them: its relationship to the longer histories of collective forms of Indigenous cultural production as a means of intercultural socio-political agency; its significance for Indigenous Australians as a memorial to the unacknowledged war dead of the frontier wars; and its repudiation of individualist forms of aesthetic innovation derived from the collective Yolngu artistic traditions on which *The Memorial* draws.

Although occasioning some disquiet, the initial exhibition of this memorial to Aboriginal deaths on the colonial frontier at the NGA contrasted markedly with a key episode in the 'history wars' that was prompted by the National Museum of Australia's inclusion of an exhibition featuring scenes of violence and resistance along the colonial frontier when it opened in 2001 (Attwood 2015). Its reception also stands in marked contrast to the controversies that have been generated in response to suggestions that Australia's frontier conflicts should be re-categorized as acts of war against Australia's Indigenous peoples (Reynolds 2013), and that the Indigenous warriors who were killed in resisting such intrusions should be included among the war dead who are commemorated at the Australian War Memorial.[9] It is a testimony to the purification effected by art's aesthetic registers that the 'history wars' have not been accompanied by any 'art wars'. I do not say this to diminish the significance of the NGA's installation of *The Memorial* any more than, in calling attention to the class registers of Aboriginal art's reception, I mean to imply that they account for all that eventuates in the encounters with Aboriginal art that are mediated by art world values. As many studies have shown, the aesthetic dispositions associated with such registers are no more singular than the professional middle class is without internal divisions into different class fractions (Daenekindt and Roose 2017). There is no doubt that, considered more closely, the relations between these class fractions and tastes for different kinds of Aboriginal art would prove to be connected to a wide range of social, civic and political effects. My purpose has, rather, been to suggest the respects in which the complex relations between the different authorities that adjudicate the place and value of the position of Aboriginal art within the Australian art field mean that it sometimes falls prey to the rules of art and is sometimes over-determined by them in the process of challenging them. At other times, however, it side-steps or reaches through them in ways that have significantly re-shaped the ground upon which the cultural relations between Indigenous and non-Indigenous Australians are negotiated.

Beyond nation, beyond art? Not quite, and certainly no more than they are beyond class. But there is no doubt that the complexities of Indigenous art practices have confounded these categories and the relations between them.

Notes

1 Most of the literature examining the relations between Australian art practices and institutions draws on the terminology of art worlds. This has a variable currency, referring to a distinctive set of art discourses (Danto 1964) or to the agents and institutions – galleries, markets, dealers, critics, etc. – that make the production and circulation of artworks possible (Becker 1982). Bourdieu (1996, pp. 34–35) argued that the key difference between this conception and his concept of the art field consisted in its lack of any account of the relations between the agents comprising the art world and the functioning of broader economic, social and political fields. While I shall use both terms, this qualification should be borne in mind.
2 Judith White (2017) argues that the Sydney Modern project of the Art Gallery of New South Wales has derived its main impetus and support from the corporatization of its board.
3 Piketty (2014, pp. 174, 177–178) shows how the fall in income inequalities relative to the returns on capital applies to Australia alongside other developed economies. The Australian Council of Social Services (2015) confirms the growing role of disparities in wealth in the increasing rate of inequalities in Australia since 2010.
4 See McLean (2011) for the fullest discussion and Bennett (2015) for an interpretation of these developments in the context of art field theory.
5 The NGA's 2017 travelling exhibition *Abstraction: Celebrating Australian women abstract artists* foregrounds the significance of abstraction in connecting Indigenous women artists like Emily Kam Kngwarray to the turn to abstraction by other Australian women artists.
6 This is still the case. Acker (2016) cites a 2014 report estimating Indigenous involvement in these institutions and processes at only 10 per cent.
7 Myers (2006) assesses the role that the class values of Tim and Vivien Johnson played in their mediation of the relations between Aboriginal artists and the Australian art field; Myers (2013) discusses the class value informing the work of influential American collectors of Aboriginal art; and Myers (2002) discusses the predominance of the professional middle classes as consumers of Aboriginal art.
8 McLean (2016) is distinctive in aligning Indigenous art with modernist termporalities.
9 The Australian War Memorial's first exhibition commemorating the service of Indigenous soldiers in Australian wars overseas was in 2016. A petition presented by Indigenous elders asking for similar commemoration of the victims of the Frontier Wars was not granted. Director Brendan Nelson stated that the Australian War Memorial was not appropriate for this purpose.

References

Acker, T., 2016. *Somewhere in the world: Aboriginal and Torres Strait Islander art and its place in the global art market*. CRC-REP Research Report CR017, Alice Springs: Ninti One Limited.

Attwood, B., 2015. The international difficult histories boom, the democratization of history, and the National Museum of History. *In*: A. E. Coombes and R. B. Phillips, eds. *Museum transformations*. Chichester: Wiley-Blackwell, 61–84.

Australian Council of Social Services, 2015. *Inequality in Australia: A nation divided*. Sydney: Australian Council of Social Services.

Australian Government, 2013. *Creative Australia: National cultural policy*. Canberra: Commonwealth of Australia.

Becker, H., 1982. *Art worlds*. Los Angeles: University of California Press.

Bell, R., 2002. *Bell's theorem: Aboriginal art – it's a white thing!* [online]. Available from: www.kooriweb.org/foley/great/art/bell.html [Accessed 19 July 2017].

Bennett, T., 2015. Adjusting field theory: Art fields in settler societies. *In*: L. Haniquet and M. Savage, eds. *Handbook in cultural sociology*. London and New York: Routledge, 247–261.

Bennett, T. and Gayo, M., 2018 [forthcoming]. For the love (or not) of art. *In*: M. Quin, D. Beech, M. Lehnert, C. Tulloch and S. Wilson, eds. *The persistence of taste: Art, museums and everyday life after Bourdieu*. London and New York: Routledge.

Bourdieu, P., 1996. *The rules of art: Genesis and structure of the literary field*. Cambridge: Polity Press.

Caruana, W., 2003. The collection of Indigenous Australian art: Beginnings and some highlights. *In*: P. Green, ed. *Building the collection*. Canberra: National Gallery of Australia, 192–209.

Daenekindt, S. and Roose, H., 2017. Ways of preferring: Distinction through the 'what' and the 'how' of cultural consumption. *Journal of Consumer Culture*, 17(1), 25–45.

Danto, A., 1964. The artworld. *Journal of Philosophy*, 61, 571–584.

De Lorenzo, C., Mendelssohn, J. and Speck, C. 2011. Curated exhibitions and Australian art history. *Journal of Art Historiography*, 4, 1–15.

Department of Communication and Arts, 1994. *Creative nation: Commonwealth cultural policy*. Canberra: Commonwealth of Australia.

Fisher, L., 2016. *Aboriginal art and Australian society: Hope and disenchantment*. London: Anthem Press.

Franklin, A. and Papastegiadis, N., 2017. Engaging with the anti-museum? Visitors to the Museum of Old and New Art. *Journal of Sociology*, 53(3), 670–686.

Grishin, S., 2013. *Australian art: A history*. Melbourne: The Megunyah Press.

Horowitz, N., 2011. *Art of the deal: Contemporary art in a global financial market*. Princeton and Oxford: Princeton University Press.

House of Representatives Standing Committee on Expenditure, 1986. *Power, patronage and the muse: Inquiry into Commonwealth assistance to the arts*. Canberra: Australian Government Publishing Service.

Jones, C. A., 2016. *The global work of art: World's fairs, biennials, and the aesthetics of experience*. Chicago and London: University of Chicago Press.

Knell, S., 2016. *National galleries: The art of making nations*. London: Routledge.

Lendon, N., 2016. Relational agency: Rethinking. *The Aboriginal Memorial. emaj*, 9, 1–28.

McLean, I., ed., 2011. *How Aborigines invented the idea of contemporary art*. Sydney: Institute of Modern Art, Power Publications.

McLean, I., 2016. *Rattling spears: A history of Indigenous Australian art.* New York: Reaktion Books.

Morphy, H., 2009. Art theory and art discourse across cultures: The Yolngu and Kunwinjku compared. *In*: C. Volkenandt and C. Kaufmann, eds. *Between Indigenous Australia and Europe: John Mawurndjul.* Canberra: Aboriginal Studies Press/Reimer, 75–102.

Myers, F., 2002. *The making of an Aboriginal high art.* Durham and London: Duke University Press.

Myers, F., 2006. Collecting Aboriginal art in the Australian nation. *Visual Anthropology*, 21(1–2), 116–137.

Myers, F., 2013. Disturbances in the field: Exhibiting Aboriginal art in the US. *Journal of Sociology*, 49(2–3), 151–172.

Nagel, A., 2012. *Medieval modern: Art out of time.* London: Thames and Hudson.

Piketty, T., 2014. *Capital in the twenty-first century.* Cambridge, MA: Harvard University Press.

Reynolds, H., 2013. *Forgotten war.* Sydney: New South Books.

Sassatelli, M., 2015. The biennalization of art worlds: The culture of cultural events. *In*: L. Haniquet and M. Savage, eds. *Handbook in cultural sociology.* London and New York: Routledge, 277–289.

Smith, T., 2009. *What is contemporary art?* Chicago: University of Chicago Press.

Smith, T., 2012. Shifting the exhibitionary complex. *In*: *Thinking contemporary curating, perspectives in curating.* New York: Independent Curators International, 57–99.

Stallabrass, J., 2004. *Art incorporated: The story of contemporary art.* Oxford: Oxford University Press.

Van den Bosch, A., 2005. *The Australian art world: Aesthetics in a global market.* Crows Nest, NSW: Allen and Unwin.

Velthuis, O., 2005. *Talking Prices: Symbolic Meanings of Prices on the Market for Contemporary Art.* Princeton and Oxford: Princeton University Press.

White, J., 2017. *Culture heist: Art versus money.* Blackheath, NSW: Brandl & Schlesinger.

Wu, C., 2013. Biennals without borders? *In*: Z. Kocur and S. Leung, eds. *Theory in contemporary art since 1985.* Malden, MA and Oxford: Wiley-Blackwell, 56–63.

Zarobell, J. *Art and the global economy.* Oakland: University of California Press.

3 The Australian art field
Fairs and markets

Deborah Stevenson

Introduction

For a week in September 2015, Sydney was the location for three very different art fairs, the highest profile of which was the second staging of the biennial Sydney Contemporary that showcased works from over 90 leading galleries from 14 countries. There was also a boutique event called SPRING 1883, which was held in the Establishment Hotel in central Sydney, and 'The Other Art Fair' that featured artists unrepresented by agents or dealers and was held at an up-market, high-density residential development on the edge of the central business district. In the same week, the Artspace Visual Arts Centre in the inner suburb of Woolloomooloo held an art market focused on art books. These events highlight the diversity of the contemporary art fair and point to their different relationships to the art market and to the Australian art field.

The major art fair may be a relatively recent phenomenon in Sydney, but the Melbourne Art Fair has been held biennially since 1988, and art fairs are very well established internationally, where there are now more than 180, generating approximately AU$10 billion worth of sales. Art fairs are central aspects of the commerce of the visual arts, as well as key events through which major cities seek to assert their global status as a 'cultural capital' and enmeshment in the international art marketplace. Art fairs are also proliferating at regional and local levels, being held in towns and cities across Australia. Alongside identity-focused events such as the Cairns Indigenous Art Fair, these more local fairs also play a part in shaping the art field, if only because they disrupt the established (mediated) relationship between producer and consumer and create markets that previously did not exist.

This chapter examines the art fair as an increasingly important aspect of the art field in Australia. It points to their differential scale, including the key cleavage that has become evident between those art fairs that are 'curated' and show high-level content as extensions of the gallery-centred national and transnational art marketplace and those that are relatively unmediated spaces where artists sell their work directly to the public, but which also have the potential to challenge, if only at the margins, the structures of commerce and value that comprise the art field. Indeed, primary and secondary networks and hierarchies of markets are emerging that warrant investigation as part of an examination of the art fair as an element of an art world that is transnational, commercial and implicated in the reconfiguring of regimes of value and taste. And although the nation and the processes and governmentality of 'nationing' are clearly enmeshed with art as cultural symbol and object of policy, art fairs are largely outside these interrelationships and influences. The chapter also suggests that not only can different types of art fair be understood in terms of Bourdieu's analysis of taste hierarchies, but many also operate as symbolic markers of economic and social status and controlled spaces of exchange for the elite.

Values of exchange

Until the mid-nineteenth century, the production, distribution and consumption of art occurred within a framework of patronage whereby work was produced in response to direct commissions from wealthy patrons, including the aristocracy and the Catholic Church (Inglis 2005). With the decline of the patronage system of support, artists increasingly produced works for sale in the marketplace, a process that came to be mediated through an art dealer often associated with a commercial gallery. As David Inglis (2005, p. 25) explains, as well as depending on intermediaries, it is necessary for the artist also to have their work exhibited in galleries so that they can attract the attention of potential buyers, be they individuals, private organizations or, much less commonly, public collecting institutions. Indeed, having work displayed in a public art museum is a particularly strong statement of the attainment of excellence and can considerably increase the value and collectability of works by exhibited artists. The acts of acquisition and display by public art museums are also strongly linked to the processes of 'nationing' because these galleries, as curators of the markers of national significance and identity, occupy an unassailable role in the provision, protection and legitimization of a nation's cultural heritage (see Waterton, this volume). They also collect within the policy and funding frameworks of governments. So, while public galleries, from the major to the local and regional, see themselves as working largely outside the art marketplace and often having a role as bulwarks against the commercialization of the art world, they are, in fact, highly influential operatives if only because, although they do not sell work, they buy and display it. Also, playing a central role in the art market is the art critic, whose endorsement of artists and their work, usually through the art media, is critical to the achievement of status and to the marketability of work. Indeed, the influence of the critic in the commercialization of the art world is also well established (see, for instance, Van den Bosch 2005).

Bourdieu (1993) points out that symbolic goods have both cultural and commercial value and, while the emergence of a seemingly independent market for art may have 'liberated' artists from benefactors, collectors and commissions, it also ('paradoxically') rendered them submissive to the demanding 'laws of the market of symbolic goods' (1993, p. 114). The artist, according to Bourdieu (1993, p. 114), is regularly 'reminded of this demand through sales figures and other forms of pressure, explicit or diffuse, exercised by publishers, theatre managers, art dealers'. At the core of the contemporary art field is the interplay of value and exchange; indeed, it is in the marketplace that art comes to be legitimated as 'Art'. This marketplace (both secondary and primary circuits) has since the 1950s been dominated by the major auction houses (including Sotheby's and Christies), leading galleries, and art dealers (Van den Bosch 2005, p. 9). The other key players, as discussed above, are the buyers (collectors in particular), curators, the art media, and critics. In various combinations, these people comprise what the sociologist Howard Becker (2008, p. 34) calls 'art worlds'.

Art worlds are made up of those 'whose activities are necessary to the production of the characteristic works which that world, and perhaps others as well, define as art' (Becker 2008, p. 34). They are spheres of networks and interdependencies as well as of negotiation and struggle (as Bourdieu (1993) demonstrates) over what may be classified as art – and desirable art in particular. The art world is the space of production, distribution and consumption (Inglis 2005); it is where regimes and processes of value, commercialization, nationing and transnationalization are simultaneously interdependent and in tension. For Becker, there is not one single art world. Rather, art worlds are multiple, intersecting and competing. In this respect, it is possible (and useful) to understand art worlds as a series of dynamic spaces played out within the broader framework of the art field although, as Inglis (2005, p. 27) and Tony Bennett (in this volume) point out, there are some significant differences between Becker's concept of the art world and Bourdieu's art field. Bennett notes that Bourdieu's conception of the cultural field is broader than that of the art world, and brings into play the economic, social and political fields that exercise significant influence on it. Inglis, in particular, suggests that where Bourdieu highlighted the importance of tensions between the different groups that comprise the field (such as emerging and established artists), Becker's principal concern is to trace the '"gatekeeping" functions' of the 'institutions, persons and practices', with a key function being the power to determine or classify what is and what is not 'art'. In other words, artists are just one (albeit important) set of actors who comprise an art world and rarely do they have the power to determine the aesthetic status of their work. According to Becker:

> Works of art ... are not the products of individual makers, 'artists' who possess a rare and special gift. They are, rather, joint products of all the people who cooperate via an art world's characteristic conventions to bring works like that into existence.
>
> (2008, p. 35)

But, at the same time, the contemporary art market trades on the reputations of artists and their celebrity. In her analysis of the Australian 'art world', Annette Van den Bosch (2005) talks about the emergence from the 1980s of the 'superstar' contemporary artist, which she argues was directly connected to the domination of the art market by a 'small group of dealers whose New York galleries were associated with a string of multi-national subsidiaries' (p. 116). The objective of these dealers was to 'maximise the investment value of contemporary art' (p. 4) and to this end to set about creating the necessary conditions of scarcity. Central to this endeavour was an 'ever-diminishing circle of reputations' (p. 116), whereby selected artists came to be acclaimed as 'brilliant', which in turn rendered their work highly marketable. When coupled with an increase in speculation in contemporary art through the financial markets at this time, the outcome was a significant change in both the nature of the art market and the role of dealers and collectors in shaping it. More buyers entered the market but the opportunities tightened for artists, with the focus being on the works of 'well-known' artists. One significant consequence of this development was the increasing internationalization and transnationalization of the art field and its networks and the consolidation of certain cities as key nodes in these networks. Art worlds may be multiple, but this multiplicity does not mean that they are equivalent; another outcome of the reshaping of the art field was thus a reshaping of the hierarchies of art worlds and their places.

It is in this context that the current proliferation of biennales and art fairs should be understood. While it is art fairs that drew me to this subject, it is difficult to talk about one in isolation from the other. Biennales and art fairs may not be interchangeable but they are certainly overlapping. Both are major urban events, markers of a city's (and nation's) art world status as well as sites for the consumption of contemporary art and the negotiation and assertion of value. But they have a different relationship to the market and, intriguingly, what increasingly links them are the covert strategies developed to negotiate this difference. Where biennales have strong connections to processes of nationing and, supposedly, eschew the market, art fairs are squarely in the realm of the transnational and the commercial. The Australian government, for instance, either directly or through the Australia Council, provides financial and symbolic support for Australia's participation in the Venice Biennale as an aspect of a broader agenda to promote Australia through its art. The Australia Council is also responsible for overseeing the selection of artists to 'represent Australia' at the Venice Biennale. In contrast, the staging of an art fair, such as Sydney Contemporary, is an outcome and assertion of the transnational; and, even though this particular event takes place in a facility, Carriageworks, that is owned by the NSW government and receives funding from both federal and state governments, being a venue for the art fair is a commercial transaction, and sits outside the cultural nationalist agenda of arts policy.

The urban art event

Biennales, or biennials, are significant urban as well as cultural events organized around the exhibition of contemporary art. They are curated events, usually themed and involving numerous galleries often from around the world (Sassatelli 2015). Biennales are most often staged every two years (as the word indicates), but there are other, regularly staged major contemporary art events that occur less frequently but which have similar structure and status, such as the Asia Pacific Triennial of Contemporary Art (the Queensland Art Gallery and Gallery of Modern Art's contemporary art event that is held every three years), Documenta (held in Kassell Germany every five years) and Skulptur Projekte Münster (every ten years). The key point is not what they are called or how often they are held but that they recur according to a set timetable. Biennales may have become major events but, as Jeannine Tang (2011) explains, they are not new, having been staged since 1895. It has been since the 1990s, however, that art fairs and biennales have proliferated, partly as an outcome of trends in global financial capitalism. Now, in any one year, something like 35 biennales are held in cities around the world. This proliferation also coincided with an increasing interest globally in cultural tourism and in the role that the arts can play in urban redevelopment and revitalization strategies, particularly for cities dealing with deindustrialization (Stevenson 2014). Biennales are regular features of the cultural and events calendar of host cities, and play an important part in many place marketing and tourism strategies (Sassatelli 2015). It is interesting, for instance, to note that, in 2017, the Venice Biennale, Documenta and Skulptur Projekte Münster all took place in the same (northern) summer. This coincidence of timing made it possible for them to be packaged and marketed as the 'Grand Tour of the 21st Century',[1] as they were when the staging of these three events and the Basel Art Fair also coincided in 2007. Significantly, the focus of the marketing for the packaged events was to 'attract visitors' and, in particular, tourists (the 'leisure-class art collectors', as Alexandra Peers (2007) has dubbed them), and there were links to accommodation, travel agencies and transport on the 'tour' website. Reflecting in 2004 on the emerging circuits of biennales and art fairs, Simon de Pury (who at the time was chairman of auction house Phillips de Pury (now Philips)) reportedly observed that, '[t]he art world has become a traveling circus' (quoted in Peers 2007, n.p.) where 'you run into the same people again and again – and never see the art'. But, as Julian Stallabrass (2004, p. 26) points out, the 'being there' of the biennale has become an important marker of status, 'another way to confirm social distinction' (see also Bennett in this volume).

The highest profile and largest of the biennales is held in Venice which, modelled on the phenomenon of the World Expo, involves exhibitions from more than thirty nations. The link between the Art Biennale in Venice and the nation is an important one, and the event is used as a showcase for exhibiting nations to assert their status as part of the premier international circuit of cultural capital, while within the Biennale space, a hierarchy of nations can be discerned if only by the location and permanency of pavilions. Venice is an exercise in cultural nationalism and an element of, in the case of Australia, the federal government's cultural diplomacy agenda. For instance, Australia's permanent pavilion was opened in May 2015 by the federal Arts Minister George Brandis (even though AU$6.5m of the $7.5m that the pavilion cost came from private benefactors) with the claim that the opening marked 'yet another step in the emergence of Australia as a culturally accomplished nation' (Chadwick 2015, n.p.).

When it was first staged in 1895, the ambition of the Venice Biennale was both to showcase contemporary art and establish a market for it. This dual function ended in the 1960s when the overt selling of art was no longer permitted and the focus instead became the exhibition and the event. This dual concern is the case with all biennales and a key feature distinguishing them from art fairs. A biennale is regarded as a premier exhibition space for showcasing cutting edge work that has been selected by the event curator according to established criteria and themes. In spite of this veneer of the non-commercial, however, art is being showcased for sale at a biennale, just not overtly: '[D]eals' are done at the event which are 'consummated later' (Peers 2007). Not 'every work' is necessarily for sale (despite Vince Chadwick's (2015) assertion in his *Sydney Morning Herald* report on the opening of the Australian pavilion at the Venice Biennale), but this is precisely the point. Artwork on display does not have price tags nor is it marked as being 'for sale', and there are no red stickers indicating that something has been sold. What this means is that, in order to purchase works through the biennale, a potential buyer must have specialist knowledge of the processes and codes of the event and the (unadvertised) protocols to be followed in order to enter into a sales transaction. They would need to know, for instance, should the work of the Australian artist Fiona Hall be of interest, that it would cost them between $35,000 and $600,000. In other words, to purchase work in the biennale space, very specific forms of cultural capital operate which (along with the economic capital) even quite experienced art consumers may lack. As Jeannine Tang (2011, p. 77) explains:

> Biennales are underwritten by the joint efforts and relationships between collectors, gallerists and curators. However, the *visibility* of this network remains determinedly understated. Overt selling appears gauche.

While the visual consumption of art is clearly an attraction, it is highly likely that many, perhaps most, biennale visitors are there for entertainment, to consume the event and the spectacle rather than the art, while potential buyers occupy a parallel space of viewing and negotiation.

The ambivalent relationship between biennales and commercialization is further played out through the connections many biennale participants have with art fairs; for instance, galleries that have artists included in a biennale will often capitalize on that exposure by participating in a concurrent or subsequent art fair. The blatant selling of art may be taboo at a biennale, but this is certainly not the case at an art fair, which exists primarily for this purpose. As the Director of a regional Australian art gallery said to me, it is possible to walk out of an art fair with a 'pile of art' under one's arm (personal communication, 24 November 2015). Art fairs and biennales are also important elements of global culture circuits but, where biennales are international in that they serve national cultural agenda in some way, art fairs are elements of a marketplace that is transnational and highly commercialized. Art fairs are privately owned and operated, although, in common with the biennale, their hosting can increasingly be regarded as a marker of a city's status and be the impetus for the staging of coterminous events that further animate place and raise the profile of a city. Indeed, biennales and art fairs are often held in a city at the same time and may be connected through marketing strategies, along the lines of the above-mentioned 'grand tour', and through the dual participation of audiences/consumers, galleries and other influential brokers who comprise an art world. If biennales are intended to be mediated spaces for the display of 'excellence', art fairs are largely unmediated events where inclusion is an outcome of a participant's capacity to pay for a space and not of any theoretically informed curatorial judgement.

Fun, fairs and finance

Writing in the Australian edition of the *Guardian* in 2013, Andrew Frost suggested that the 'launch' of Sydney Contemporary in September of that year marked the moment when Sydney got is first 'credible art fair'. The use of the word 'credible' is important and points to implicit values and power relations at the heart of the art fair and the art world of which it is a part. Based on the structure and agenda of Sydney Contemporary, it would appear that a 'credible' art fair is one that serves as an outlet for established galleries, as well as having some curated works and a program of talks and tours. In the case of the 2015 fair, the objects of curatorship were 'contemporary video, installation art and performance' alongside talks on such topics as gender and art and tours presented by 'industry leaders'.[2] The curatorial and talks dimensions are important markers of the status (achieved or desired) of the event because, as Jeannine Tang (2011) explains, the major art fairs Art Basel, Frieze and Shanghai Contemporary routinely commission work from leading artists (installations, performance and films), as well as 'playing host to and attempt(ing) to foster dialogues and discussions' (p. 76).

The origins of the art fairs have been traced to the fifteenth century (Thompson 2011) but, as in the case of the biennale, they have multiplied in recent years. Don Thompson (2011, p. 59), for instance, describes the 'start of the twenty-first century [as being] the decade of the art fair'. This proliferation shows no signs of abating, and the art fair is now firmly entrenched as an integral part of the art marketplace as well as the urban agenda. It is not unusual for an art fair to be linked with city imaging, and even non-metropolitan areas are embracing them either as integral to a creative cities agenda or as a way of showcasing and selling the work of local artists and craft workers. Art fairs range in size and scale from the high profile (such as the Frieze Art Fairs, which are held annually in Regent's Park, London and on Randall's Island in New York) to the much smaller scale including, for instance, the Hawkesbury Art Fair in the New South Wales town of Windsor, which is organized by the council-run art gallery and involves local artists, designers and 'artisans' as well as local creative collectives; and the three Art Bazaars run annually in Newcastle, Maitland and Lake Macquarie by the Hunter Arts Network (an incorporated body that was established with the assistance of Newcastle City Council). In between, there is a raft of such events in towns and cities across Australia and around the world, all organized to provide a space for selling artwork. Gallery owners, in the case of the large fairs, and artists themselves (often supported by local government and collectives) at the local level occupy a space at the fair in which to show works from their collections or portfolios. Unlike at a biennale, they choose what to exhibit and, where the large fairs will sell to collectors and galleries, works at local fairs are marketed principally to local residents and visitors.

Sasha Grishin (2015) reported being told by representatives of two prominent London commercial galleries that, in 2014, 60 per cent of their business occurred through art fairs, 25 per cent of sales were online, and only 15 per cent was directly attributed to attendance at the gallery. This is a big shift in the structure of the art market, which has historically been gallery/exhibition-focused, whereby galleries select the artists that they want to represent, and then rely on exhibitions in the gallery space to reach potential buyers. Of course, art critics and the art media also played, and continue to play, pivotal roles in this process.

In 2014, '[t]he top 180 major art fairs … generat[ed] 40% of all dealer sales and about 20% of the total global art market' (Grishin 2015). Art fairs are now big business as well as big events (30,000 people attended Sydney Contemporary in 2015), which significantly affects the shape of the art market as a result. Being challenged in particular, is the role of gatekeepers in determining priorities and, most importantly, what constitutes art and what is regarded as valuable/collectable. What is occurring with the reconfiguring of the art market is a considerable shift in of the positioning of the commercial gallery within it. Grishin (2015, n.p.), for instance, asserts that it is becoming evident that commercial galleries are no longer 'delivering a product that the art consuming public wants'. They are increasingly being forced to attend art fairs in order to remain relevant and retain their place in the art world, but it would seem that this participation comes at a cost. As Andrew Frost (2013, n.p.) points out, most of the participating galleries at the inaugural Contemporary Sydney would not have broken even because a 'space at the fair cost $20,000 to $60,000' and 'most reports put the average gallery take at just $15,000'. Reports suggest that total sales at the event were in the order of AU$14m, which is an increase of AU$4m on 2013. As the art fair is an increasingly transnational phenomenon, Australian commercial galleries will also seek spaces at fairs internationally, in particular in Asia, which also comes at a cost.

The New York art critic Jerry Saltz (2005) infamously dismissed art fairs as unimportant and lacking spaces for debate and introspection. He described them as being:

> adrenaline-addled spectacles for a kind of buying and selling where intimacy, conviction, patience, and focused looking, not to mention looking again, are essentially nonexistent. They are places where commerce has replaced epistemology, and the unspoken contract that existed between artists, dealers, and collectors has been scraped. As one private dealer gleefully told The New York Times recently, 'It's one-stop shopping. The mall experience … fashion, parties, and fun all wrapped up in one'.

Here, it is asserted that art fairs are fun to attend but not places for the serious display and contemplation of 'Art'. Art critics such as Saltz prefer the more traditional curated events, biennales and gallery exhibitions to the confusion of the art fair. The reasons for this position are fairly obvious: the art critic has a central place in the art world as a gatekeeper, mediating between the gallery and art patrons through their reviews, and influencing the value and marketability of particular works. They thus have a clear interest in the *status quo*.

The argument of the critics is that art fairs undermine 'Art' and the established hierarchies of value that comprise the field because they are not spaces for detachment and social criticism. The art critic – as judge, arbiter of artistic value, 'mediator between the art experience and the true believing audience' (Gleason 2012, n.p.) – thus sits uncomfortably in the context of the art fair because these events are not organized around the viewing and contemplation of art but its sale. As discussed above, there is a strong connection historically between criticism and the assessment of a work of art as 'Art'. Van den Bosch (2005, p. 3) explains that 'criticism has become so central to reputation formation that any concept of disinterested judgement is untenable in the contemporary art world'. Art fairs disrupt this relationship. In addition, they are not organized around the (often exclusive) exhibition of works, which, as suggested above, is a key aspect of the assignation of market (and hence symbolic) value, and are not necessarily spaces for encountering the new or the curated (unlike a biennale). There is, for instance, a view that collectors come to art fairs to purchase works by artists with whom they are already familiar and that it is simply more convenient to buy in this context rather than in the gallery space. The same is true of the online art market, which is also often unmediated. So clearly, there is an important relationship between what is sold at the art fair and for how much and the value and marketability ascribed through other spheres of the art field/market.

The Australian art market is increasingly enmeshed in a series of exchanges that are transnational as well as local. Thirty per cent of the exhibitors at Sydney Contemporary were from international galleries, while Australian galleries and artists are ever eager to be a part of fairs and markets overseas. The way in which this transnationalization is changing the Australian art market is yet to become evident, but it is possible (a bit like removing tariffs) that it may undermine the value of Australian artists and their works. Sasha Grishin (2015, n.p.) puts the problem this way:

> A drawing by [British artists] Damien Hirst or David Hockney costs about the same as a drawing by [Australian artist] Brett Whiteley, but a drawing by Whiteley can be sold only in Australia, whereas a drawing by Hirst or Hockney can be sold anywhere in the world.

Grishin may be slightly overstating the threat, but it is doubtless the case that the internationalization of the art market, in part through the hosting of art fairs, may well serve to reshape the Australian art field and its regimes of value in unanticipated and not necessarily welcome ways.

Conclusion

In examining any aspect of the art world, including its marketplaces, it is always important to ask whose interests are being served, and this is no less true of art fairs. They are not neutral spaces floating free of the complexity of art worlds, and their associated power structures and regimes of value. The display of art through sanctioned exhibitions is a critical element of the art market and the assignation of value. The exhibition of work by emerging artists or new works by those who are more established usually occurs in commercial galleries which have long played an important role in the determination of value, both symbolic and economic. The starting point for this chapter was the emerging place of the art fair (at its different scales) in the Australian and international art field, and the consequences of this increasing importance for the ways in which art markets are shaped and value is ascribed. It is evident that art fairs are presenting a challenge to the position of the commercial gallery and undermining the established nexus between artist, gallery, critic and buyer as influential gatekeepers and key arbiters of value. While at the local level, the role of artist collectives and, more recently, of artist-run initiatives in this process have developed as important.

It is also relevant that art fairs have emerged as major urban events as well as key spaces for purchasing art work. Art fairs take place in public and private spaces, including galleries, parks and gardens. They attract thousands of people, most of whom are probably there to consume the spectacle and assert their cultural capital rather than to purchase art. This situation is in stark contrast to the number of people who historically frequent commercial galleries. It is now common for commercial and public galleries and even auction houses to time their own events and exhibitions to coincide with an art fair in order to capitalize on the popularity and general hype. Many art fairs not unusually now also run alongside a biennale, while several art fairs may be held simultaneously in the same city. The emergence of the multi-city art fair/biennale trail or tour (the 'grand tour' of 2007 and 2017) is another noteworthy development in generating maximum interest and creating a critical mass of activity. They also assert the place of particular cities in the global circuits of cultural capital. It is clear that the art field in Australia is undergoing a substantial reconfiguration and perhaps democratization. At its core are fundamental changes in the regimes of gatekeeping and power that comprise its art worlds. It is difficult to regard art fairs, irrespective of their location and scale, as anything other than spaces of commercialization and, in the case of the mega-art fair, central elements in an art world that is increasingly transnational and where the marketability of a work of art is a product of its situation in the flows of value and taste that transcend the nation and, potentially, challenge the national. In this context, it could well fall to government to play a very direct role in supporting the production and consumption of Australian art to ensure the sustainability of art worlds that are distinctly Australian.

Notes

1 See 'Welcome to Grand Tour of the 21st Century' available at: http://www.e-flux.com/announcements/40555/welcome-to-the-grand-tour-of-the-21st-century/
2 See 'Sydney Contemporary' available at: http://sydneycontemporary.com.au/about-sydneycontemporary/

References

Becker, H., 2008. *Art world's: 25th anniversary edition, updated and expanded*. Berkeley: University of California Press.

Bourdieu, P., 1993. *The field of cultural production: Essays on art and literature*. Trans. and ed. R. Johnson. New York: Columbia University Press.

Chadwick, V., 2015. Australian pavilion at the Venice Biennale opened by George Brandis and Cate Blanchett [online]. *The Sydney Morning Herald*. Available from: www.smh.com.au/entertainment/art-and-design/australian-pavilion-at-the-venice-biennale-opened-by-george-brandis-and-cate-blanchett-20150505-ggulnj.html [Accessed 26 November 2015].

Frost, A., 2013. Seven things we learned about Australian art in 2013 [online]. *The Guardian*. Available from: www.theguardian.com/culture/australia-culture-blog/2013/dec/30/seven-things-we-learned-about-australian-art-in-2013 [Accessed 21 October 2015].

Gleason, M., 2012. Why art critics really hate art fairs [online]. *The Huffington Post*. Available from: www.huffingtonpost.com/mat-gleason/why-art-critics-really-hate-art-fairs_b_1541555.html?ir=Australia [Accessed 1 November 2015].

Grishin, S., 2015. Friday essay: The art market is failing Australian artists. *The Conversation* [online]. Available from: https://theconversation.com/friday-essay-the-art-market-is-failing-australian-artists-51314 [Accessed 1 December 2015].

Inglis, D. 2005. Thinking 'art' sociologically. *In*: D. Inglis and J. Hughson, eds. *The sociology of art: Ways of seeing*. Houndsmills: Palgrave Macmillan, 11–29.

Peers, A., 2007. The return of the Grand Tour: A nineteenth-century aristocratic habit gets the art-world makeover [online]. *New York Magazine*. Available from: http://nymag.com/news/intelligencer/32405/ [Accessed 7 August 2017].

Saltz, J., 2005. Feeding Frenzy [online]. *The Village Voice*. Available from: www.villagevoice.com/arts/feeding-frenzy-7138665 [Accessed 1 November 2015].

Sassatelli, M., 2015. The biennalization of art worlds: The culture of cultural events. *In*: L. Hanquinet and M. Savage, eds. *Handbook of the sociology of art and culture*. London: Routledge, 277–289.

Stallabrass, J., 2004. *Art incorporated: The story of contemporary art*. Oxford: Oxford University Press.

Stevenson, D., 2014. *Cities of culture: A global perspective*. London and New York: Routledge.

Tang, J., 2011. Biennalization and its discontents. *In*: B. Moeran and J. Strandgaard Pedersen, eds. *Negotiating values in the creative industries: Fairs, festivals and competitive events*. Cambridge, UK: Cambridge University Press, 73–93.

Thompson, D., 2011. Art fairs: The market as medium. *In*: B. Moeran and J. Strandgaard Pedersen, eds. *Negotiating values in the creative industries: Fairs, festivals and competitive events*. Cambridge, UK: Cambridge University Press, 59–72.

Van den Bosch, A., 2005. *The Australian art world: Aesthetics in a global market*. Crows Nest, Australia: Allen and Unwin.

4 The 'music nation'

Popular music and Australian cultural policy

Shane Homan

Introduction

Of all the arts and cultural pursuits, popular music has displayed consistent popularity with Australians. A 2017 national survey found that 97 per cent of participants listened to recorded music (the highest for any art form); 15 per cent had 'creative participation' in music; 27 per cent had attended a music festival; while 54 per cent had attended a live music performance (Australia Council 2017). In professional terms, Australia has enjoyed remarkable success in international markets of late, leading to claims of a 'golden generation' of acts breaking overseas (Brandle 2016). While the number of Australians watching bands, listening to music radio or enjoying lives as amateur, semi-professional or professional musicians remains impressive and relatively stable, the history of government support for *popular* music (as distinct from art or classical music) is a more complex one. This chapter examines the two defining cultural policy documents (indeed, the *only* policy documents approaching a coherent vision), *Creative Nation* and *Creative Australia*, and subsequent developments to trace overlapping ideas of nation, culture and economy.

Popular music studies have always been interested in formations of identity and nation, the uses and national adaptations of global technologies and related cultural and media policies. Malm and Wallis's (1992) *Media Policy and Music Activity*, examining the music industries and policies of Jamaica/Trinidad, Kenya, Tanzania, Sweden and Wales, is an important work in how 'peripheral' nations confront the relentless needs of national self-esteem and economic growth through their music industries. Their concerns with how nation-states retain legal, cultural and political sovereignty in the face of technological and industrial change are relevant within contemporary times. Subsequent, sporadic assessments of national music policy systems (e.g., Bennett et al. 1993; Breen 1999; Cloonan 2007; Scott 2013; Homan et al. 2016) have to some extent been understandably overwhelmed by preoccupations with global, digital music economies (e.g., Anderson 2014; Collins and Young 2014).

Historic foundations are important in policy settings. Australia shares with other Commonwealth nations the governmental and arts machinery of British structures, including an Arts/Cultural Minister within national government, and an overarching arts body (in this case, the Australia Council) as primary funder.

52 Shane Homan

These historic structures are worth noting for two reasons. Firstly, Australians have experienced some support of popular music since the 1970s with the election of the Whitlam Labor government. Secondly, such expectations of federal funding from industries, state governments and audiences have been at least partially revisited in recent times. The North American belief that government should 'abstain from cultural policy altogether, leaving a society's cultural life in the hands of free market forces' (Lewis 2000, p. 80) means that 'floating unresolved ... is the conception of culture as a whole way of life and the consequences of that idea for policy makers at all levels of government and in the commercial and non-profit sectors' (Wallach 2000, p. 8). While Australian settings have never shared the first approach, the conditions and rationales for popular music to play a role in Australian cultural policy is experiencing change which cannot simply be reduced to current centre-right government preoccupations.

Further, discussions of nation in this policy context must contend with the broader shift from cultural to creative industries policy in reshaping different governments' thinking in the past twenty years. In short, it has meant moving away from simpler subsidy models of support to 'combining the arts with market-driven, commercial ventures and employment' (Cunningham 2008, p. 265) as part of broader national economies. This shift has had implications not just for nation-states, but for cities. The 'creative class' (Florida 2002) thesis has informed cultural/creative city policies to a remarkable degree, with Australia not immune both to Richard Florida's prognoses and remedies. In arguing that there has been a withdrawal of the nation-state (in historic terms), the chapter will also examine the increasing role of Australian cities in popular music policy. Overall, though, I am chiefly interested in assessing how (and whether) the 'nation' retains some ideological and practical purchase.

From *Creative Nation* to *Creative Australia*

As the nation's first cohesive cultural policy since the 1950s,[1] *Creative Nation* prefigured the British turn to culture as important economic and national branding exercises after the election of the Blair Labour Government in 1997. Its *Creative Industries Mapping* report marked an important shift in reconfiguring arts and culture within an emerging creative/cultural industries (see Oakley 2004). It is understandable, too, as a document crafted by a Labor Party headed by a Prime Minister, Paul Keating, fond of both classical and popular music, and a government keen to continue the arts policies of the 1970s Whitlam era. At the same time, globalization and technological change were evident as pressing concerns. Consequently, the Keating Labor Government merged the Communications and Arts ministries, acknowledging the then-looming 'information superhighway' (Commonwealth of Australia 1994, n.p.). Pop history gained a place within plans to connect national heritage with contemporary technologies to produce the CD-ROM, *Real Wild Child! Australian Rock Music: 1950s–90s* (Powerhouse Museum 1994; based on the Museum's exhibition of the same name) as part of the national focus on cultural histories. For artists, there were increases in national touring and recording grants through the Australia Council, acknowledging the difficulties of live performance and production in a large country with long distances between central live venue hubs. As documented elsewhere in this book, culture was to play its part in the broader economic agenda. Continuing the Whitlam themes of promoting 'the identity of the nation, communities and individuals', the policy was 'also an economic policy ... The level of our creativity substantially determines our ability to adapt to new economic imperatives' (Commonwealth of Australia 1994, Introduction, n.p.). At the urging of Labor Victorian backbencher Pete Steedman, the Keating Government also found funding for the establishment of Ausmusic, a training and advisory body for popular music (see Breen 1999).

The election of the conservative Howard coalition Government in 1996 led to many of the *Creative Nation* programs being diluted or abandoned altogether. Ausmusic lost its funding, although touring and recording activity continued to be supported. The return of Labor in 2007 prompted more work in assessing popular music's role, and that of the cultural industries more generally, culminating in the publication of the *Strategic Contemporary Music Industry Plan* (Commonwealth of Australia 2010) and the *Convergence Review* (Commonwealth of Australia 2012). Both shared concerns with how Australian cultural production would retain national and global visibility, but with different solutions: funding support to place Australian music on global media platforms (*Strategic Contemporary Music Industry Plan*) and a content production fund to pay for increased local music content (*Convergence Review*). The mild utopianism evident in *Creative Nation* about participation in the global, mediated marketplace had been replaced by the practical problems associated with the erosion of traditional industrial structures and the negotiation of competition with larger nations (and with larger music-media corporations) (see Homan 2013).

These issues were certainly evident in *Creative Australia*, the policy homage to *Creative Nation* by Arts Minister Simon Crean within the Gillard Labor Government, released in 2013. As a post-Global Financial Crisis document, little new funding was evident, although AU$3m was provided for 'contemporary music'. Notably, the music export program, Sounds Australia, received significant additional funding, with a total of AU$1.75m over four years (Australian Government 2013, p. 18). Beyond the continuation of touring and recording structures, the Australia Council funded a recording grant for 'indie' recording labels, acknowledging their unique role for emerging artists. It also established a National Live Music Office to address issues of national/state venue regulations and to provide a clearinghouse for the music industry to deal with different levels of noise, planning and licensing governance (Australian Government 2013, p. 66).[2]

Amidst these innovations, *Creative Australia* was underscored by a belief that 'the impact of global economic change will not fall evenly – some parts of the [cultural] sector will thrive and others will grapple with new business models and competitive pressures' (Australian Government 2013, p. 36). It re-asserted the primacy of the state in cultural management, and returned to the twin preoccupations of national identity and economic productivity in 'the centrality of the arts to our national identity, social cohesion and economic success' (Australian Government 2013, p. 2). The central problem of the new music media platforms, identified in the previous music and media industry reports, was again relegated to the idea of an 'online production fund' (Australian Government 2013, p. 82). Despite the injection of new funding and other initiatives for popular music, the policy settings for classical music, which receives 60 per cent of Australia Council music funding, remained unchanged (Homan 2013). As with *Creative Nation*, many of the central plans within *Creative Australia* were not fully implemented following the return to a conservative Abbott Coalition Government in September 2013. The idea of a nationally funded structure to support and promote music content on global media platforms died with the Prime Minister Gillard, and her replacement, Kevin Rudd, in subsequent Labor Governments.

Do all 'the levers' still work? Questioning settled national structures

According to his biographers, Prime Minister Paul Keating believed that politicians' power was founded in knowing how 'to operate the levers and pulleys' of policy (Edwards 1996, p. 304). As I and fellow authors have noted elsewhere (Homan et al. 2016, p. 1), this was a useful metaphor for Labor governments keen to correct historic beliefs that conservative governments are better economic managers, even while Labor exhibited a curious mix of deregulation and subsidy across cultural and media policies. It also accords with conventional Labor government predilections towards different mixes (depending upon the era) of social equity and industry support based upon state interventions. However, whether conservative or left/centrist, some fundamental concerns about music industry structures and their relationships with other media and cultural sectors are now being raised beyond governmental preoccupations and policies of ideological faith.

This is evident in several issues across Australian music. Firstly, local broadcast content laws for Australian music, in existence since 1942, have been questioned in recent years. Radio broadcasters have always quietly grumbled about the amount of 'free' promotion of recording company product (e.g., Federation of Australian Radio Broadcasters 2001). Arguing that the federal government had abandoned local content quotas for new digital television stations in 2010, Commercial Radio Australia sought the same outcome while expressing its displeasure with older analogue content laws. Arguing that the content quotas should be reviewed every three years, the CEO of Commercial Radio Australia explicitly linked the debate to a 2010 battle with the Phonographic Performance Company of Australia over an attempt to increase the 1 per cent cap on radio broadcasting royalties (Sexton 2010). The understanding – expressed in the radio Code of Practice that content quotas assist in increasing production and promotion of Australian recordings – was now seriously under review with the dominance of digital platforms and the view of the broadcasters that older royalty fee structures were not sustainable. For the authors of the 2012 *Convergence Review*, the traditional broadcast content laws were to remain and to apply to digital broadcasting once the sector had matured (Commonwealth of Australia 2012, p. 1). In similar arguments about the role of media ownership laws in the digital era, the radio sector believes that local quotas are redundant in the global mesh of Internet stations. In submissions to the *Convergence Review*, several industry bodies pointed to fair use of the radio spectrum, the quota's role as part of the value chain and the broad popularity of quotas with Australians. Historically, Australians have not fared well on their own national charts. The Australian Recording Industry Association (ARIA)'s end of year charts for 2016 revealed that local artists comprised only 15 of the top 100 singles and 31 of the top 100 albums (ARIA 2017).

Secondly, intellectual property laws remain locally contentious (both *Nation* and *Australia* reaffirmed government commitments to 'strong' copyright laws to 'protect' Australian artists). The *Copyright and Digital Economy* report of 2014, commissioned earlier by Labor, was delivered to the Abbott Coalition Government with little fanfare. Ignoring the more contentious recommendations, such as fair use provisions, then Attorney-General (and Arts Minister) George Brandis instead promised reform on illegal content uses, with the *Copyright Amendment (Online Infringement) Bill 2015* granting copyright holders the right to seek Federal Court action in blocking overseas websites that have the 'primary purpose' of infringement (Grubb 2015). 'Safe harbour' laws providing some immunity for ISPs from users' illegal downloading remains the core concern. Yet, the fair use debate refuses to go away. A subsequent 2016 Productivity Commission report, *Intellectual Property Arrangements*, charged more broadly with how copyright could be reformed to 'encourage creativity, investment and new innovation' (Australian Government 2016, p. v), advocated the narrowing of copyright terms for content, the need for a fair use provision and widening of acceptable uses of content and allowing geo-blocking (prohibiting access to content based on location) for Australian consumers. The local music industry was uniform in their dismissal of these key recommendations. Hosing down suggestions that the copyright terms might be reduced, the Government has yet to provide a meaningful response to the report's other key recommendations.

The Australian industry has joined other territories in the royalty arrangements exercised by the larger aggregators of music content, with YouTube as the chief offender exploiting 'safe harbour' laws within the United States' 1998 *Digital Millennium Copyright Act*. The 'value gap' between the low royalties paid by YouTube and other video-on-demand services and the music content's worth remains the dominant concern for the call for reform to recoup returns from unlicensed content:

> The value gap is a striking example of how wealth has shifted from those who create content – our artists and their partners – to the large companies that build their platforms on that content. Creators are worse off today than they were when digital came into their lives. This is disturbing and was avoidable. Policy makers now have the opportunity to rebalance the framework in such a way that creators are fairly compensated.
> (Graham Henderson, CEO of Music Canada, cited in Recording Industry Association of America 2016)

Yet, policy-makers seem impotent to act against the larger corporations, which also increasingly dictate royalty terms to recording companies for digital sales and streaming.

The forms of industrial protectionism and promotion of local content discussed here, broadly imagined as traditional governmental machinery in the name of cultural nationalism, are remarkable now for the extent to which Australian federal governments are either reluctant participants in, or bystanders to, wider global changes. These sites of tension are reflected in Music Australia's *National Contemporary Music Plan*, which lists digitization, globalization and diminishing artist returns as the three chief challenges for local music (Music Australia 2016, p. 10). Its proposed solutions are a mix of traditional arts support (tax offsets for recording companies; strengthening of local content quotas; funding for audience development; amending music education) with some recognition of the new industrial landscape (funding for micro-businesses and artist development; increased funding for export assistance) (Music Australia 2016, pp. 12–31).

In contrast, conservative federal governments have reduced the budgets for the Australia Council, protecting flagship arts organizations while reducing opportunities for small-to-medium enterprises (Mendelssohn 2015; Letts 2015; Belot 2017). Beyond discussions about copyright reform, the past two Coalition governments have refused to meet to entertain broader issues and means of support for the *National Contemporary Music Plan*, liable to be redundant in meeting current needs before the next technological shifts. The most entrepreneurial of programs – the Sounds Australia Export Scheme – has been subject to different attempts to abolish it as federal governments continue to seek an 'efficiency dividend' within arts funding.

De-nationing: the 'music city'

As the challenges of the 'internationalization' of music, coupled with increasingly sophisticated digitalization, become too great and the federal government departs the field (at least for the moment), intra-state policies have shouldered much of the policy burden, particularly in the rise of 'music city' policies. Interest in how cities come to define particular sounds, genres and scenes (e.g., Bennett et al. 2004) is now accompanied by studies in how popular (and classical) music can define city economies and identities (e.g., Grodach 2012). Cities as diverse as Bogata, Adelaide, Toronto, Kingston and New York have 'music city' strategies tied to plans for growth in employment and tourism, live music regulation and resultant branding. In global terms, the music city phenomenon has its consultancy/conference firm, Sound Diplomacy; and its policy primer, *Mastering of a Music City* (International Federation of the Phonographic Industries/Music Canada 2015). Supplemented with case study policies, the report argued that the contemporary music city is defined by 'Artists and musicians; a thriving music scene; access to spaces and places; a receptive and engaged audience; and record labels and other music-related businesses', supported by strong funding, infrastructure and education programs (International Federation of Phonographic Industries/

Music Canada 2015, p. 13). This policy approach required practical responses from local and provincial governments for 'music-friendly and musician-friendly policies; a Music Office or Officer; a Music Advisory Board; engaging the broader music community to get their buy-in and support; access to spaces and places; and audience development' (International Federation of Phonographic Industries/ Music Canada 2015, pp. 13–15).

However, Australian cities have been grappling with infrastructure and related issues since the 1980s. The acute problems of noise for suburban music venues, coupled with the Australian reluctance to allow cultural/entertainment precinct zoning, has seen licensing reforms that are globally innovative: the controversial Fortitude Valley entertainment precinct (Brisbane); the *Live Music and Performance Action Plan* and Small Bar Licence reforms (Sydney); the 'Agent of Change'[3] principle in noise disputes (Melbourne); and the recent promised AU$3m Creative Music Fund and licensing/planning reforms (Perth) (City of Sydney 2014, pp. 48–50; Crittenden 2017). In December 2015, Adelaide was granted UNESCO City of Music status for their mix of festivals, classical and popular musicians, and levels of global collaboration between genres and artists (ABC News 2015). Remaining concerns about the role of alcohol and music in night-time leisure were evident in industry protests against broad accusations of venue 'alcohol-fuelled violence' in 2010 in Melbourne; and the 'lockout law' debate in Sydney in 2014 that reduced venue trading hours in its CBD entertainment precincts after deaths from 'one-punch' assaults (Homan 2016, 2017).

The establishment of the nationally funded Live Music Office in 2013 has played a role in providing a sounding board for governments and in bringing many local councils up to best practice in licensing, planning and noise regulations. Among the many state government initiatives, the Victorian government AU$22m 'Music Works' funding package is worthy of mention. It consists of a music history/heritage program; an exports program; funding to improve live venue acoustics and urban relationships; and capacity-building grants (Creative Victoria 2017). Funds were also granted for the Music Vault, a physical and digital repository of music artefacts and a Hall of Fame (Francis 2016). However, this activity is founded upon an expected Return on Investment. Notably, Arts Victoria has been re-badged as Creative Victoria, and situated within the Department of Economic Development, Jobs, Transport and Resources. There is no doubt that the 'Music Works' program is expected to strengthen music employment amidst a broader Creative Industries Strategy of 'Strengthening the creative industries ecosystem ... to stimulate entrepreneurship and develop a stronger capacity to commercialise ideas and capture economic returns' (Victoria State Government 2017).

The Australian narrative here – of increasing governmental resources and planning across heritage, cultural, industrial and economic planning – reflects other music city narratives globally (e.g., Stahl 2014; Holt and Wergin 2013; Botta 2016). However, the success and extent of their traction in localized industrial ecosystems remains contingent upon highly localized 'political opportunity structures' (Silver 2013, p. 261), where cultural/political histories inform contemporary action. The relative depth of cultural funding in Melbourne from state and local governments, complemented by an activist local industry structures (the combined strength of advocacy/advisory bodies Music Victoria, FairGo4LiveMusic and SLAM (Save Live Music Australia)), has been successful in translating community concerns into music city policies.

The Australian experience reflects other global concerns in whether the practised meanings of 'liveable' cities, and related notions of diversity and sociability, are conversant with industrial and economic ambitions. Austin, Edinburgh and London are useful examples where relationships between land use, zoning and planning regulation have been at least partially examined for the effects of gentrification upon local music venues and related infrastructure (City of Austin 2015; City of Edinburgh 2015; Greater London Authority 2017). The flight of cheap residential and commercial properties out of the music city is easy to identify while solutions are more difficult; but the fear of the loss of the 'subcultural entrepreneurs' (McRobbie 2012, p. 80), those disposed to managing the 'indie' label and venue, the local rehearsal and recording studio, or the emerging artist, is well founded. One increasingly popular solution – city councils commissioning (usually disowned) CBD spaces for rehearsal, songwriting or performances – reflects the failure to address the structural basis of the problem, where the state remains reluctant to intervene to ensure a diversity of commercial (and non-commercial) uses.

Conclusion

The construction of national settings is never easy; for example, two prominent popular music studies academics in Scotland attempted to garner cross-party support for a 'Music Manifesto' for that country's 2011 election, but with little success (Frith and Cloonan 2011). In the Australian context, there is no appetite federally for any kind of 'manifesto'; indeed, as the challenges of the 'internationalization' of music becomes ever greater, the federal government has vacated the policy field. The policy reviews on copyright and media convergence in the past decade have not provoked government responses that properly consider the consequences for Australian artists and fans. The earlier fears of music/media companies 'floating up above sovereign national states' (Malm and Wallis 1992, p. 2) remain. The ability of YouTube, Google, Apple and Spotify to dictate contractual terms with recording companies and publishers, and to openly defy national copyright and taxation systems, is all too real. Relatedly, the promise of merged government portfolios to formulate policy reflecting multi-platform industries and convergences has not been realized.

This problem is also evident in the ways that settled mechanisms of industry support are now under question. While remnants of the national 'cultural hearth' exist (e.g., the ABC music video program *Rage*, which celebrated its thirtieth year in 2017), substantial broadcasting and media policy changes have altered the ways in which local popular music is audible/visible. The regular skirmishes between the broadcasting and music industries indicate that older 'nationing' instruments (such as local content quotas) are under assault, both from other countries seeking trade parity, and media company beliefs that they are outdated. This is not to dispense with the space of the 'national' in terms of its regulatory, legislative and discursive powers; yet in popular music we can see the ways in which consolidated music-media companies are enabled to reach past prior national structures within new circulations of music markets embedded in digital networks. The nation-state is now more interested in managing at the margins of cultural policy: ameliorating the effects of ticket touting, smoothing touring visa processes, providing limited touring/recording funding for emerging artists and so on.

One of the few areas where the state has increased its financial and discursive investment is in music export strategies. Canada, Brazil, South Korea, Britain and France (among others) have significantly increased funding for excursions into other markets (as discussed, Australia is also an international presence despite its scheme, Sounds Australia's enmeshment in broader arts funding cuts). This interest, backed by relatively substantial funding, accords with broader visions of the entrepreneurial state putting its most innovative artists in front of the world.[4] Yet, for the reasons outlined above, nations have been far less effective in managing both macro- and micro-policies that consider the best conditions for facilitating the creative musician; and they remain largely silent about whether it is important that musicians also make a living wage.

It is striking that the 'music city' has resonated more strongly in contemporary eras than ideas of the 'music nation'. The dissonance between industrial and governmental aspirations has been partially redeemed through State and local government initiatives. Increased funding across city incubator strategies, exports, training, touring and heritage has become increasingly important to local cultural identities and economies. In Australia, something like Creative Victoria's 'Music Works' program, then, is the contemporary link to the 1994 promise of *Creative Nation* in its willingness to back industry ambitions, with sharp expectations of an economic lift accompanied by a distinctive cultural branding. The music city concept offers more though, than the sum of industry policies, perhaps as a crucible where 'culture lives a hybrid life as a creature of the state, commerce, and civil society' (Durrer et al. 2018, p. 3). In this sense, debates (in different cities at different times) about music precincts, zoning laws, noise regulations or busking policies re-introduce a very localized politics removed from abstract national and international issues. This carries its own risks. For example, the music city is mostly defined through live music venue practices and regulations, 'brick-and-mortar' cultural policy that can be contained within municipal and regional boundaries. At the same time, the remarkable extent of global discussions of policies, animated by city music policy networks, has seen a broad consensus of policy concerns anchored in implicit 'right to the city' narratives, despite persistent and obvious narratives of branding and city/regional competition.

The Labor government policies of *Creative Nation* and *Creative Australia* have been useful to this chapter in tracing the place and role of popular music in the development of creative industry strategies and to see where cultural nationalism remains influential in narratives of national identity. I have also argued that local histories and practices remain important in explaining the nature and framing of particular music policies. With the exceptions of copyright and exports, it is difficult, as I have described, to see how a future national project similar to *Creative Australia* will have purchase with conservative or Left/liberal governments. The traditional domain of national cultural policies (heritage, identity, belonging), for popular music at least, has shifted (at least temporarily) to a more driven localism, most evident in the emergence of the music city idea. In similar ways in which cities canvassed common concerns and solutions, there is a need to more closely follow national music policy formations, particularly as digital globalization further complicates industrial and social structures. This, perversely, can enable national structures to sharpen their differences with an increasingly global music corporatism that raises new questions about culture and power.

Notes

1 Piecemeal assistance had been provided by national governments after World War Two, such as funding of the Elizabethan Theatre Trust established in 1954. The major art forms were brought together with the Whitlam Labor Government's Australia Council in 1975 (Gardiner-Garden 1994, pp. 4–6).
2 The author completed an Australia Council report, *The Music Recording Sector in Australia: Strategic Initiatives* (2012), which included the recommendation of production grants for small, independent labels and increased funding for Sounds Australia. The Live Music Office funding derived from a series of meetings that then Arts Minister Tony Burke (replacing Crean) held with music industry figures in Sydney and Melbourne a few months before the Gillard government lost office. The author attended the Melbourne meeting with Burke.
3 The Agent of Change principle means that 'that a new residential planning proposal close to a live music venue will need to include appropriate noise attenuation measures. Similarly, if a live music venue seeks to expand, the owner/operator will be responsible for attenuating any noise effects that are caused by that change' (Music Victoria 2017).
4 The attendant export activities by which such initiatives are measured indicate the increasing role of the 'attention economy' (Davenport and Beck 2001) in economic success beyond the usual metrics of performances, tours and recording sales. As one Canadian report emphasizes, showcases, streaming, licensing/publishing, business meetings and media promotional tours are equally important export activities (Canadian Independent Music Association 2016, p. 7). Contemporary export strategies thus call for smarter combinations of traditional business activities (the strategic, corporate 'meet-and-greet') and digital media exposure.

References

ABC News, 2015. Adelaide gains UNESCO city of music recognition. 11 December. Available from: www.abc.net.au/news/2015-12-12/adelaide-unesco-city-of-music/7023412 [Accessed 13 July 2017].

Anderson, T., 2014. Popular Music in a Digital Music Economy: Problems and Practices for an Emerging Service Industry. Abingdon and New York: Routledge.

Australia Council, 2017. Connecting Australians: National Arts Participation Survey, June. Available from: www.australiacouncil.gov.au/research/connecting-australians/ [Accessed 16 August 2017].

Australian Government, 2013. *Creative Australia: National cultural policy*. Canberra: Office for the Arts.

Australian Government, 2016. *Intellectual property arrangements: Productivity Commission inquiry report No. 78*, 23 September. Canberra: Commonwealth of Australia.

Australian Recording Industry Association, 2017. ARIA announces 2016 end of year charts. ARIA web site, 6 January. Available from: www.ariacharts.com.au/news/2017/aria-announces-2016-end-of-year-charts [Accessed 13 June 2017].

Belot, H., 2017. Mitch Fifield abolishes arts fund Catalyst after community feedback. ABC News, 18 March. Available from: www.abc.net.au/news/2017-03-18/mitch-fifield-abolishes-arts-fund-catalyst/8366012 [Accessed 12 August 2017].

Bennett, T., Frith, S., Grossberg, L, Shepherd, J. and Turner, G., eds., 1993. *Rock and popular music: Politics, policies, institutions*. London: Routledge.

Botta, G., 2016. *Invisible landscapes: Popular music and spatiality*. Munster and New York: Waxmann.

Brandle, L., 2016. Australia's new generation of global stars: Lars Brandle studies the form guide. Music Australia, 1 April. Available from: http://musicaustralia.org.au/2016/04/australias-new-generation-of-global-stars-lars-brandle-studies-the-form-guide/ [Accessed 17 August 2017].

Breen, M., 1999. *Rock dogs: Politics and the Australian music industry*. Sydney: Pluto Press.

Canadian Independent Music Association, 2016. *Music in motion: An analysis of exporting Canadian independent music*. Toronto: Nordicity.

City of Austin, 2015. *The Austin music census: A data-driven assessment of Austin's commercial music economy*. Austin: Titan Music Group.

City of Edinburgh, 2015. *Desire lines: A call to action from Edinburgh's cultural community*. Edinburgh: City of Edinburgh Council.

City of Sydney, 2014. *Live music and performance action plan*, March. Sydney: City of Sydney.

Cloonan, M., 2007. *Popular music and the state in the UK: Culture, trade or industry?* Aldershot: Ashgate.

Collins, S. and Young, S., 2014. *Beyond 2.0: The future of music*. London: Equinox.

Commonwealth of Australia, 1994. *Creative nation: Commonwealth cultural policy*, October. Canberra: Department of Communications and the Arts.

Commonwealth of Australia, 2010. Strategic contemporary music industry plan. Canberra: Department of the Environment, Water, Heritage and the Arts.

Commonwealth of Australia, 2012. Convergence review final report [online]. Canberra: Department of Broadband, Communications and the Digital Economy. Available from: http://www.dbcde.gov.au/__data/assets/pdf_file/0007/147733/Convergence_Review_Final_Report.pdf.

Crittenden, J., 2017. WA premier Mark McGowan to cut red tape for live music, Music Australia, 14 March. Available from: http://musicaustralia.org.au/2017/03/wa-premier-mark-mcgowan-to-cut-red-tape-for-live-music/.

Creative Victoria, 2017. Music Works. Available from: http://creative.vic.gov.au/funding-and-support/programs/music-works [Accessed 17 August 2017].

Cunningham, S., 2008. *In the vernacular: A generation of Australian culture and controversy*. St Lucia: University of Queensland Press.

Davenport, T. H. and Beck, J., 2001. *The attention economy: Understanding the new currency of business*. Harvard: Harvard Business Review Press.

Durrer, V., Miller, T. and O'Brien, D., 2018. Towards global cultural policy studies. *In*: V. Durrer, T. Miller and D. O'Brien, eds. *The Routledge handbook of global cultural policy*. London and New York: Routledge, 1–16.

Edwards, J., 1996. *Keating: The inside story*. Ringwood: Penguin.

Federation of Australian Radio Broadcasters, 2001. *Final submission by Federation of Australian Broadcasters Limited to House of Representatives Standing Committee on communications*, 23 May. Canberra: Transport and the Arts, Inquiry into the Adequacy of Regional Radio.

Florida, R., 2002. *The rise of the creative class and how it's transforming work, leisure and everyday life*. New York: Basic Books.

Francis, H., 2016. Australian music vault to tell the whole story at Arts Centre Melbourne. *The Sydney Morning Herald*, 13 December. Available from: www.smh.com.au/entertainment/music/australian-music-vault-to-tell-the-whole-story-at-arts-centre-melbourne-20161213-gt9tm3.html [Accessed 18 August 2017].

Frith, S. and Cloonan, M., 2011. A music manifesto for Scotland. Available from: www.gla.ac.uk/media/media_193054_en.pdf [Accessed 13 June 2017].

Gardiner-Garden, J., 1994. *Arts policy in Australia: A history of commonwealth involvement in the arts*. Canberra: Department of the Parliamentary Library. Available from: www.aph.gov.au/binaries/library/pubs/bp/1994-95/94bp05.pdf [Accessed 24 October 2017].

Greater London Authority, 2017. *Rescue plan for London's grassroots music venues: Making progress*. London: Greater London Authority, Nordicity and Sound Diplomacy.

Grodach, C. 2012. Before and after the creative city: The politics of urban cultural policy in Austin, Texas. Journal of Urban Affairs, 34(1), 81–97.

Grubb, B., 2015. Australian senate passes controversial anti-piracy, website-blocking laws. *The Sydney Morning Herald*, 22 June.

Holt, F. and Wergin, C., eds., 2013. *Musical performance and the changing city: Postindustrial contexts in Europe and the United States*. New York and Abingdon: Routledge.

Homan, S., 2013. From coombs to crean: Popular music and cultural policy in Australia. *International Journal of Cultural Policy*, 19(3), 382–398.

Homan, S., 2016. SLAM: The music city and cultural activism. *Law, Social Justice and Global Development*, 1, 1–12.

Homan, S., 2017. 'Lockout' laws or 'rock out' laws? Moral panics, governing the night-time economy and implications for the 'music city'. *International Journal of Cultural Policy*. Available from: DOI: 10.1080/10286632.2017.1317760

Homan, S., Cloonan, M. and Cattermole, J., 2016. *Popular music industries and the state: Policy notes*. Abingdon and New York: Routledge.

International Federation of Phonographic Industries/Music Canada, 2015. *The mastering of a music city: Key elements, effective strategies and why it's worth pursuing*. Toronto: IFPI and Music Canada.

Letts, D., 2015. The Brandis Heist. Music Trust, 2 June. Available from: www.musictrust.com.au/2015/06/the-brandis-heist/ [Accessed 17 August 2017].

Lewis, J., 2000. Designing a cultural policy. *In*: G. Bradford, M. Gary and G. Wallach, eds. *The politics of culture: Policy perspectives for individuals, institutions and communities*. New York: The New Press, 79–93.

Malm, K. and Wallis, R., 1992. Media Policy and Music Activity. Abingdon and New York: Routledge.

McRobbie, A., 2012. Key concepts for urban creative industry in the UK. *In*: I. Elam and L. Tunbjörk, eds. *Artists and the arts industries*. Stockholm: The Swedish Arts Grants Committee, 78–129.

Mendelssohn, J., 2015. Arm's length? Forget it – it's back to the Menzies era for arts funding. *The Conversation*, 13 May. Available from: www.theconversation.com/arms-length-forget-it-its-back-to-the-menzies-era-for-arts-funding-41743 [Accessed 10 May 2017].

Music Australia, 2016. National Contemporary Music Plan. Sydney: Music Australia.

Music Victoria, 2017. How to: Agent of change. Available from: www.musicvictoria.com.au/resources/agent-of-change-explained [Accessed 17 August 2017].

Oakley, K., 2004. Not so cool Britannia: The role of the creative industries in economic development. *International Journal of Cultural Studies*, 7(1), 67–77.

Powerhouse Museum, 1994. Real Wild Child! Australian Rock Music & Culture 1950s – 90s [curated exhibition]. Sydney: Powerhouse Museum.

Recording Industry Association of America, 2016. Value gap growing, according to new UK figures, 5 May. Available from: www.riaa.com/value-gap-growing-according-to-new-uk-figures/ [Accessed 17 August 2017].

Sexton, E., 2010. Sound and fury over Copyright Act cap. *The Examiner*, 13 October. Available from: www.examiner.com.au/news/national/national/general/sound-and-fury-over-copyright-act-cap/1967126.aspx?storypage=1 [Accessed 13 June 2017].

Scott, M., 2013. *Making New Zealand's pop renaissance: State, markets, musicians*. Aldershot: Ashgate.

Silver, D., 2013. Local politics in the creative city: The case of Toronto. In: C. Grodach and D. Silver, eds. *The politics of urban cultural policy*. London and New York: Routledge, 249–262.

Stahl, G., ed., 2014. *Poor, but sexy: Reflections on Berlin scenes*. Bern: Peter Lang.

Victoria State Government, 2017. Creative industries strategy. Available from: http://economicdevelopment.vic.gov.au/significant-projects/creative-industries-strategy [Accessed 17 August 2017].

Wallach, G., 2000. Introduction. In: G. Bradford, M. Gary and G. Wallach, eds. *The politics of culture: Policy perspectives for individuals, institutions and communities*. New York: The New Press, 1–10.

Whiteley, S., Bennett, A. and Hawkins, S., eds., 2004. *Music, space and place: Popular music and cultural identity*. Aldershot: Ashgate.

5 Television

Commercialization, the decline of 'nationing' and the status of the media field

Graeme Turner

Introduction

This chapter deals with the media field by focusing on Australian television. Television is currently the most important location for the concerns examined in this book, and at the time of writing it is going through a transformation of its cultural and commercial functions that is possibly unprecedented. Currently, television in Australia is transitioning from what was predominantly a broadcast mass communication environment to a hybrid operating environment comprised of broadcast, narrowcast, online and networked platforms and portals. It is becoming more transnational in composition as regulatory arrangements from the broadcast era prove inadequate to maintain national control over access to the Australian market in the digital era. Australian television is nowhere near the end of this transitional process yet, but even now, it is clear that it has led to structural changes in the industries concerned and is likely to lead to significant changes in the behaviour of audiences and consumers. There are also significant shifts in the regulatory domain, with the transition away from a nationalist cultural policy context for Australian television and towards a more globalist industry policy context in which commercial, rather than cultural, considerations prevail.

Today, in Australia, the role of television as an instrument of the nationing agenda of the state, and indeed, as we demonstrate throughout this book, the level of the state's interest in nationing itself, has significantly changed. In what follows, I outline the internal dynamics of the Australian television sector over the period under consideration: noting the changing points and patterns of consumption as the mass media's structural dominance declines, and the manner in which the media industries, and, to a lesser extent the state, have responded to these changing circumstances. This is terrain that shifts almost weekly as I write, and despite the fact that many of these changes are surveyed and calculated with great frequency by the television ratings agencies, our understanding is complicated both by the sector's overall volatility and by the welter of industry accounts which routinely take signs for wonders. We are inundated with self-interested corporate prognoses of media futures upon which it would be unwise to rely. A further complication is the fact that the media field has become more diverse and extensive than it was in the pre-digital era; we now have not only the publics of the mass media, and the taste fractions targeted by narrowcast media such as pay-TV, but also the networks created by connective media (van Dijck 2013). These are not distinct or autonomous zones of activity, but intersect with each other in a complicated interface. Not only does this extensiveness reconfigure what might once have been thought of as something like a common national culture, it also forces us to reconsider traditional assumptions about the status of the media field. Is it any longer legitimate, we should ask, for us to think of the media as a single, relatively autonomous field? Or, rather, do the media now constitute an overarching meta-field, with the power to shape or influence the internal activities of other cultural fields as well as the construction of social space more generally? How we answer such questions carries implications for our understanding of contemporary media power and, for our purposes here, in particular for the media's participation in projects of nationing.

I start, then, with the shifts in the dynamics of the television sector of the media field in Australia over the period since the Australian government's release of the *Creative Nation* policy paper in 1994. At that time, television was broadcast only; apart from the limited development of networked subscription services within particular locations and industries, pay TV was still a few months off. There was little need for the Australian television industry to worry too much about transnational influences other than those which governed the competition for exclusive rights to content within international markets. There was an established regulatory agenda and, despite the upheavals in television ownership of the preceding decade, a renewed stability in the structure and performance of the ommercial television industry (although not in the funding environment of the public broadcasters). Assessing the status of the television industry at that time could have been largely contained within a national context; television was a relatively discrete national industry run by primarily nationally-based proprietors with a healthy revenue base in the local advertising market. The long history of debates about broadcasting regulation, the protection of local content, restrictions on ownership, content classification and so on also meant that access to the television market, its contribution to cultural diversity, and the connection between local television content and national cultural identities were all located within the domain of national cultural policy (there never has been either a broadcasting or a media policy in Australia). Within the discipline of media studies at the time, tellingly, television was routinely described as a media institution as well as a cultural and commercial industry.

To discuss the Australian situation in 2017, however, takes us away from the sheltered domain of national cultural policy and into the complex of industrial and technological developments that have shaped the media 'globally'[1] over the last decade or two. Internationally, albeit to varying degrees, the content and structure of the media across all systems and platforms of delivery have become dramatically more diverse – paradoxically, at the same time as the forces framing how and in whose interests they operate have become more focused and concentrated. There has been a clear convergence of economic imperatives, as is evidenced by the thoroughgoing programs of commercialization visible in so many, and some quite unlikely, locations: China, Singapore and Malaysia, for instance (Tay and Turner 2015). In some locations (such as Mexico), the political influence consequent upon the commercial power of local media has rivalled, even outstripped, that of the state. That said, it is important to stress that much of the media's commercialization appears to be politically agnostic. It is widespread across the full spectrum of state systems: in highly centralized, socialist and authoritarian states, in transitional democracies and in capitalist liberal democracies. Such developments usually constitute, in varied ways, modes of modernization that are primarily aimed at enabling better access to, and participation, in global markets.[2] To be clear, I am using the term 'commercialization' here to reference both the introduction of a marketized system serving alongside the state's existing mechanisms of political control (which is how one might describe the system in China, for instance), as well as the marketizing tendency within (neo)liberal democracies where virtually all sections of the media (including the news media, but in some cases excluding publicly funded media) identify themselves as commercial entertainment industries with strategic interests of their own (Madaniou 2013), rather than, as the more traditional formulation would have it, as central national institutions serving the public good by providing for the nation's information and cultural needs as well as its entertainment (Turner 2016).

In terms of transnational trends that are now finally starting to bite in the Australian context, the most important is the strength of the challenges to the dominance of free-to-air (FTA) broadcasting networks. As subscription platforms have proliferated, and as subscription video on demand (SVOD) services exploit their transnational potential to challenge both FTA services and cable, the range of choices on offer to television consumers has dramatically expanded. In most places, consequently, what Dayan (2009) calls 'televisions of the centre' (national broadcast networks, both commercial and public) have lost ground. Televisions of the centre are seen as playing a fundamental role in constructing a national community, in creating the common ground upon which democratic politics can function, or alternatively as the platform upon which governments of a more authoritarian persuasion control information and construct their claims for legitimacy. Televisions of the centre were intimately connected, first and to varying political ends, with the state, and only secondarily, as a rule, with the economy. Their decline begins to disarticulate television from the state, leaving the sector free to align itself in a comparatively uncomplicated way with economic forces. In Australia, the FTA broadcasters have not only lost ground in the battle for audiences for traditional forms of content, but also face serious challenges from the increasing diversity of the patterns of production and distribution of television and video, and the multiplication of platforms and devices through which they can be consumed.

Not to exaggerate the scale of this tendency, of course, it needs to be acknowledged that in the last quarter of 2016, 86 per cent of television viewing in Australia was still via FTA TV (Davidson 2017), with news, reality programming and sport the top-rating genres. However, things are changing. In 1994, the year of *Creative Nation*, 17.1 per cent of Australians were watching broadcast television at any one minute across the day (Productivity Commission 2000, p. 71), but in 2015, that figure was 12.5 per cent. Over 2016 alone, the FTA audience declined by 5 per cent, the size of the advertising pie over which they compete has shrunk by 4 per cent (Chenoweth 2017), and there is a clear division emerging in the audience demographics (traditional TV is losing the 18–39s) (Davidson 2017). It has been claimed that as many as one in seven Australian consumers will watch no FTA TV at all on a normal weekday (that leaps to one in five for the under-35-year-olds), and that Australians watched 80 minutes less television per week in 2016 than in 2015 (A. Turner 2016). The FTA networks' once indomitable hold on television viewing in Australia has significantly loosened, spreading something like panic among the FTA broadcasters and generating calls for government intervention. The 'gamechanger', according to them, has been the arrival of the US-based streaming service Netflix (G. Turner 2016b; Given et al. 2015).

The Netflix disruption

Netflix, like several of the US-based SVOD providers, had an informal subscription base in Australia for some years before its official Australian launch in 2015. It is reputed that something of the order of 200,000 Australians used virtual private networks (VPNs), BitTorrent and other methods to access the Netflix catalogue and to view downloads well before this time. The high-quality profile of Netflix and HBO drama productions such as *House of Cards* and *Game of Thrones*, respectively, had made such content a significant component of the television viewing habits of the younger market in Australia – 18–39-year-olds – as has been the case elsewhere. Neither has ever screened on FTA TV in Australia. When Netflix was finally introduced to Australia, it picked up 10 per cent of the market within three months (Thomsen 2015)! At the time of writing (2017), after two years, it has a reach of close to six million, which amounts to 2,223,000 households, or 29 per cent of the market (Morgan 2016a). This share now edges out that enjoyed by linear pay TV (27%) (Morgan 2016b). Most significantly, while there had been relatively little change in viewing habits in response to pay-TV over its 22 years in the market, Netflix already seems to be having an effect. Linear viewing is in decline across all platforms, and so-called 'binge-viewing' is now a fundamental component of the SVOD experience. We are beginning to see changes in the configuration of platforms in the ordinary household: a highly customized combination of FTA, SVOD, pay-TV, YouTube, Facebook and social media feeds. Furthermore, while the demographics of the FTAs skew towards older viewers, the demographics of Netflix subscribers skew young – one of the factors that worries the FTA networks as a sign that they will face even greater disruption in the future. As part of the larger research project from which this book emerges, a survey of cultural consumption was conducted and followed up with a series of interviews. The survey was conducted before the arrival of Netflix, but the follow-up interviews came after it. In the interviews, we found a striking number of the respondents who had cited free-to-air as their major television platform told us, one year later, that they no longer watched FTA at all. They used Netflix or a combination of streaming services as well as a range of mobile devices – mobile phones, tablets, Xbox, everything but the TV set in the living room (although mine was a small sample, this was true of *all* the interviewees I dealt with who were under 25 years old). Several of the younger interviewees also told us that they no longer got their news from television; rather, it came to them via their Facebook feed. Small though it is, this group provides some insight into the changes which lie ahead for the broadcasting sector.

A couple of years ago, the FTA broadcasting networks responded to competition from pay-TV, and in particular from Foxtel (the main pay-TV provider in Australia), by copying the UK's Freeview consortium, which promotes affiliated digital FTA channels as if they constituted a single platform, mimicking the pitch for pay-TV. The introduction of the secondary digital channels multiplied the total amount of content available by drawing upon fresh content from overseas, but those channels are also widely used for recycling content already broadcast and 'encore' presentations of high-profile drama and reality TV. The most substantive and systemic expansion of content to flow from the Freeview channels is the capacity of networks with rights to major sporting events to screen them on their digital channels; although they are meant to screen the events first on their standard definition primary channel, it has proven quite easy to get ministerial permission to relax this rule. Not only does this change address the political problem associated with the Australian anti-siphoning regulations (which nominate certain sporting events as of national importance and cultural significance, and thus are required to be screened by, or at least offered first to, the broadcast networks), but it also enables the FTA channels occasionally to compete with the Foxtel sports channels. Now, however, there is more than Foxtel for them to worry about. The rising presence of the digital, the hybridizing of consumption via mobiles, laptops, tablets and so on, and the opportunities for seeking video content online through aggregator platforms such as YouTube, with no corporate connection to the television industries, have influenced the commercial strategies preferred by the television industry in significant ways – all of them focused on securing commercial survival against the multiple challenges coming from new platforms for the production, circulation and retailing of video content.

Elsewhere (Turner 2016a), I have argued at some length that the informational/ institutional role of the national media has declined, not only in terms of its influence on their operations, but also regarding how the media now conceive of themselves. This decline is also reflected at the level of state media or communications policy in many locations around the world (although I should acknowledge that there are significant exceptions to what is essentially a tendency towards deregulation). As I noted earlier, in Australia that tendency is evident in the gradual extraction of television from the domain of national cultural policy. The current government media reforms (Australian Government 2017), represented as liberalizing the regulatory environment for broadcasters, are focused upon reducing the costs to licensees while assisting in the production of economies of scale across the existing commercial networks. Both strategies are aimed at improving the commercial viability of these businesses against online competition for audiences and advertisers. The days of television's 'nationing', its mission of seeking to address or construct a national public, are not over; the special place accorded to the public broadcaster, the ABC, by the Australian public provides regular evidence of that. However, while that mode of address was a crucial component of the broadcast era, it is not a significant characteristic of the digital era, built as it is upon technological affordances within which the individual rather than the community is privileged (Marwick 2013; Banet-Weiser 2012). At best, even though many would claim an interest in building community, the platforms of the digital era are designed to construct networks rather than publics. The importance of social networks to the changing patterns of media consumption generally amongst younger viewers will, if maintained, constitute a major shift. There are repeated claims that 14–24-year-olds are the largest market sector to derive most of their news and current affairs from preference-driven, customized menus delivered online via PCs, laptops, tablets and mobiles and circulated through social media.

While television is far from dead, then, it will not necessarily continue to play the same nationing role in the future that it has performed in the past. Partly, as we have seen, this change is due to the fact that the national audience has started to break up into fractions: as digital and mobile entertainment platforms attract a greater share of the younger audience (in the survey held as part of our larger project, 65 per cent of the 18–24-year-old respondents claimed to watch no TV at all), FTA TV audiences skew older every year. Furthermore, in the post-broadcast era we have now entered, there is no longer a common menu of choices available to, and accessible by, the whole nation. To complicate matters further, and as far as we can tell, today's audiences are not necessarily fragmenting around class or gender or ethnicity or even around taste. The fragmentation seems to be more volatile and contingent than that. Television is the most vigorously surveyed of industries. While this is not the case with any of the other cultural fields discussed in this book, we know almost everything we need to know about the FTA television audience: we know their program preferences, and how they are distributed by age and gender. We know how many televisions they have, how many are in use at a particular time and when they change channels or turn them off. There is also now a wide range of sources from which we can extract information about the popularity of individual media celebrities and so on. We don't know much, though, about certain things that the FTA ratings can't measure – such as what FTA content is consumed via the SVOD platforms, for instance – but which now constitute significant interventions in the state of the media field. In my view, the issue which most requires investigation is the role played by the choice to use other kinds of platform and device to watch video content initially screened on or produced for television. Why is this so important? Because it would reveal the considerations which now drive audience behaviour and, in turn, help us to understand what might drive the behaviour of the media industries into the future.

Digital devices are notable for their almost infinite capacity to deliver highly targeted menus of choices and affordances into niche markets that are further individualized by the habits of use, at which point they often interface with the world of connective media. What determines the patterns of access to these platforms has an economic dimension, of course, but that is not the only (or maybe even the most significant) factor in play: there are lifestyle, social and cultural identity considerations and issues of availability and quality of service, patterns of fashion and subculture, the role of social networks and so on. Those responding to the proliferation of devices now used to view television – tablets, PCs, laptops, smartphones, game consoles, etc. – as well as the range of platforms upon which 'television' now appears, are in a sense platform agnostic. Audiences can source their entertainment from more than just broadcast television; indeed, that is the basis for a raft of emerging and established production industries in Australia and elsewhere. Video, sometimes made for TV, sometimes not, can be found in news blogs, on the official sites of print media, in links on social media such as Facebook, on aggregator sites such as YouTube, on-demand streaming sites such as Netflix or Stan, playing on out-of-home sites such as bars, gyms, shopping complexes and entertainment venues, on mobile apps and so on. While the traditional television set remains by far the most commonly used device to access broadcast and other platforms, it is noticeable, for instance, how certain areas of video production have targeted the mobile as the preferred platform for viewing. How long that strategy continues remains to be seen, although there are plenty of countries where the mobile is already the dominant device used not only to consume video, but also to access the Internet. By the end of 2016, 84 per cent of Australians possessed a smartphone (Multi-Screen Report, Q3, 2016). It is the most customizable communications device there is, and customization appears now to be a highly important consideration in both the production and the consumption of media products. So, the construction of a national audience or community looks to be something that is no longer easily located among the affordances of the technologies which are now coming to dominate the digital era and which are now driving its social and cultural functions.

The status of the media field

This point takes me to the second issue that I want to consider in this chapter: the growing pervasiveness of the media field, a pervasiveness which some suggest now challenges the validity of its conceptualization as a separate field. Nick Couldry (2003) has argued that it is probably no longer of greatest interest to examine the changes internal to the media field, but rather to examine how the media field now influences the internal dynamics of other fields. While sympathetic to what field-based research can tell us in general, Couldry suggests that 'field-based accounts of media', even as they attempt to differentiate the media field from others, 'are irrevocably pushed towards a type of explanation that spills out beyond the field model, largely because of the scale of activity now accessed through the media's symbolic power'. Specifically, he goes on, this is a form of 'definitional' power which has effectivity across the whole of social space (Couldry 2003, p. 669). He proposes a number of empirical questions which we could ask that might enable us to investigate this matter, such as whether media exposure is a significant or even a predominant form of symbolic capital in a particular field.

It would be hard to deny that such exposure is significant in the music field, for instance, or in the literary field. One could certainly argue that professional sport is more or less non-viable without media coverage. Couldry goes on to suggest that we understand media power as a form of 'meta-capital', through which the media exercise power over other cultural, political and economic fields. While this form of social capital is constructed through the media and is transportable across fields, it is only fully negotiable through the media dimensions of those other fields. The media, then, is a 'meta-field' with a shaping role over all others to the extent that the non-media fields have become dependent upon the forms of visibility and publicity that the media provide.

Such claims for the media's social influence and pervasiveness are not just confined to debates within field theory. There are similar arguments coming from the proponents of theories of 'mediatization'. Andreas Hepp (2013), for example, has argued that it is now important to be as attentive to the *indirect* consequences of the function of the media in our society as to the consequences of direct encounters with media. He argues that our view of social reality is 'moulded' by the media and presents a similar line to Couldry on the lack of boundaries between the media and other configurations of social space. Some of the examples that he suggests are a little more instrumentalist than this construction would demand, such as his summary of how mobile phones have changed social relations, but nonetheless, he presents a compelling proposition for a more extensive view of the social function of the media field and for a recognition of a more widespread mediatization of everyday life than the focus on the media as a distinct and autonomous cultural field would allow.

Some have begun to think about how the trade in meta-capital from the media field into non-media fields might actually be accomplished. Olivier Driessens (2013) proposes that celebrity might be considered as serving such a function. He defines celebrity itself as a form of capital, describing it as 'accumulated media visibility through recurrent media representations, or broadly as recognizability' (p. 556). Celebrity is clearly tradeable across fields, particularly when in its purest form it is simply constituted at a level of visibility and availability that is not necessarily connected to any specific skills or arena of performance. It is not hard to see how celebrity might indeed operate as a form of symbolic capital, although Driessens argues that celebrity is not a subset or special category of symbolic capital but rather 'a substantially different form of capital' (p. 557). I'm not entirely persuaded of this argument as yet, but there is no question that celebrity has become a key means of moving brands across national boundaries, that it has been widely used to brand social campaigns, such as in relation to health issues, and so it does seem a plausible vehicle for the kinds of trade across cultural fields that Couldry proposes.

There is a point of connection between this critique of claims of the relative autonomy of the media field and the first part of my discussion of television, nationing and commercialization. The changes that I outlined in the television sector of the Australian media field are not entirely driven from within the sector. In part, they reflect significant transnational influences that are driving changes in the structure of the production industries regarding the interdependencies of globalizing markets. Most importantly, however, they reflect something that I noted earlier: a significant change in how the media industries view themselves. In *Reinventing the Media*, I talked about the manner in which the production of news has increasingly become subject to the commercial interests of the media organization concerned and thus has increasingly identified itself as part of the entertainment industry (Turner 2016a). In many cases, it is journalists and news proprietors themselves who are at pains to draw attention to the consequences of these commercial interests upon what the public might legitimately expect from the news media today. This point reinforces the observation that the commercialization of the media in general, not just television and not just news, significantly changes its social role; at the simplest level, it means that the commercial media should no longer be examined as if they were cultural institutions – or maybe even social institutions. They are industries, businesses.

At the same time, while the social and cultural remit of these organizations may have narrowed, their influence has increased. Couldry and Hepp are far from alone in making their arguments for the media's capacity to define social space or 'mould' social reality. In other areas of enquiry, such as around reality TV, there are rich literatures about the manner in which television, in particular, intervenes in the construction of the social, producing and framing identities and playing a key role in the staging of debates around politics and values (Skeggs and Wood 2012; Bratich 2007). Paradoxically, then, television's potential for 'nationing', even as it seems to be sliding off the cultural policy agenda, has probably never been more substantial. In Australia today, the continuing audience for locally produced television and the resilience of audiences for the ABC are among two indicators of a continuing sense of belonging that is implicated in what people choose to watch on television. It is possible that Netflix will put a dent in this belonging, at least temporarily, but it is also possible that there are further internal changes open to the local industry. Local production, for instance, is beginning to be talked about as a key competitive advantage to be exploited by the leading local telco, Telstra; pay provider Foxtel (co-owned by Telstra and News Corporation Australia) has suddenly taken a leading role in developing high quality Australian drama; and YouTube has begun running newspaper ads for crowd-funding Australian-based comedy and documentary series.

Conclusion

There are, however, (at least) two reasons to have reservations about such developments. The fragmentation of audiences, platforms and publics also carries another possibility: the fragmentation of community, of any sense of identity that goes beyond one's own set of preferences or established social network. Cass Sunstein (2009), in *Republic.com 2.0*, has warned of the dangers of the 'cyber-balkanisation' that comes from the complex of developments that we have talked about, and which he places within a context of nation formation. In my view, that fragmentation is of particular concern in relation to the consumption of news, and the US is the perfect laboratory case to demonstrate what happens to political debate in such circumstances. The second reservation is that, even if it is the case that the extensiveness of the influence and power of the contemporary media does carry with it enhanced potential for the production and maintenance of the national community, this influence and power is now overwhelmingly located in organizations which no longer consider themselves to be part of the communications architecture of a liberal democratic state. Rather, they are simply competing for a profitable share of the market. There is now great potential for conflict between the interests of the nation – the interests of nationing, broadly conceived – and the commercial interests of media organizations. The decline in the state's interest in regulation probably makes such a conflict inevitable and the likely outcomes worrying.

Notes

1 The scare quotes indicate that I am using this term reservedly, without going into the problems attendant upon the many versions of how it might be used.
2 There is a large literature dealing with this set of issues in a wide range of contexts, including Anderson and Chakars (2015); Milhelj (2011); Pertierra and Turner (2013); Tay and Turner (2015); and Volcic and Andrejevic (2015).

References

Anderson, S. and Chakars, M., eds., 2015. *Modernization, nation-building and television history*. London: Routledge.
Australian Government, 2017. Australian media reforms passed by Parliament. 15 September. Canberra: Department of Communication and the Arts. Available from: www.communications.gov.au/departmental-news/australian-media-reforms-passed-parliament [Accessed 27 March 2018].
Australian Multi-Screen Report, Quarter 3, 2016. Regional Tam, Oztam, Nielsen. Available from: www.nielsen.com/au/en/insights/news/2016/more-screens-more-options-to-view.html [Accessed 16 March 2017].
Banet-Weiser, S., 2012. *Authentic: The politics of ambivalence in a brand culture*. New York: New York University Press.
Bratich, J., 2007. Programming reality: Control societies, new subjects, powers of transformation. *In*: D. Heller, ed. *Makeover television: Realities remodelled*. London: I.B. Taurus, 6–22.
Chenoweth, N., 2017. For Seven, Ten, and Nine: It's the end of the party. *Australian Financial Review*, 17 February. Available from: www.afr.com/business/media-and-marketing/tv/for-seven-ten-and-nine-its-the-end-of-the-party-20170216-guemu5 [Accessed 16 March 2017].
Couldry, N., 2003. Media meta-capital: Extending the range of Bourdieu's field theory. *Theory, Culture and Society*, 32, 653–677.
Davidson, D., 2017. Seven, Ten, Nine red ink the signal for television reform. *The Australian*, 24 February. Available from: www.theaustralian.com.au/business/media/opinion/seven-ten-nine-red-ink-the-signal-for-television-reform/news-story/cb4e56cede79b-262de7d578dc45da436 [Accessed 24 February 2017].
Dayan, D., 2009. Sharing and showing: Television as monstration. *Annals of the American Academy of Political and Social Science*, 625, 19–31.

Driessens, O., 2013. Celebrity capital: Redefining celebrity using field theory. *Theory, Culture and Society*, 42, 543–560.
Given, J., Goggin, G., Brealey, M. and Gray, C. 2015. Television:2025: 20 Questions, 24 Viewpoints. Swinburne: Swinburne University of Technology.
Hepp, A., 2013. *Cultures of mediatization*. London: Polity Press.
Madaniou, M., 2013. Ethics of mediation and the voice of the injured subject. *In*: N. Couldry, M. Madaniou and A. Pinchevski, eds. *Ethics of media*. London: Palgrave Macmillan, 178–197.
Marwick, A., 2013. *Status update: Celebrity, publicity, and branding in the social media age*. New Haven and London: Yale University Press.
Milhelj, S., 2011. *Media nations*. London: Palgrave Macmillan.
Pertierra, A. C. and Turner, G., 2013. *Locating television: Zones of consumption*. London and New York: Routledge.
Productivity Commission, 2000. *Broadcasting, report no. 11*. Canberra: AusInfo.
Roy Morgan Research, 2016a. Second wind lifts Netflix to over 5.75 million Australians – but not everyone actually watches it. Article No. 7077, 1 December. Available from: www.roymorgan.com/findings/7077-netflix-subscriptions-and-viewership-time-australia-november-2016-201612011017 [Accessed 10 December 2016].
Roy Morgan Research, 2016b. More Australians now have SVOD than Foxtel. Article No. 6957, 8 September. Available from: www.roymorgan.com/findings/6957-svod-overtakes-foxtel-pay-tv-in-australia-august-2016-201609081005 [Accessed 10 December 2016].
Skeggs, B. and Wood, H., 2012. *Reacting to reality television: Performance, audience and value*. London: Routledge.
Sunstein, C., 2009. *Republic.com 2.0*. Princeton: Princeton University Press.
Tay, J. and Turner, G., 2015. Television histories in Asia: Nation-building, modernization and marketization. *In*: J. Tay and G. Turner, eds. *Television histories in Asia: Issues and contexts*. London: Routledge, 1–19.
Thomsen, S., 2015. Netflix just cracked 10% of the Australian market. *Business Insider Australia*, 15 October. Available from: www.businessinsider.co.au/netflix-just-cracked-10-of-the-australian-market-2015-10 [Accessed 2 August 2016].
Turner, A., 2016. Is Netflix hurting Aussie broadcasters? Depends who you ask. *The Age*, 11 March. Available from: http://theage.com.au/technology/gadgets-on-the-go/is-netflix-hurting-aussie-broadcasters-depends-who-you-ask-20160331-gngcvq.html [Accessed 30 June 2016].
Turner, G., 2016a. *Re-inventing the media*. London: Routledge.
Turner, G., 2016b. Surviving the post-broadcast era: The international context for Australia's ABC. *Media International Australia*, 158(1), 17–25.
van Dijck, J., 2013. *The culture of connectivity: A critical history of social media*. Oxford: Oxford University Press.
Volcic, Z. and Andrejevic, M., eds., 2015. *Commercial nationalism: Selling the nation and nationalizing the sell*. London: Palgrave Macmillan.

6 A history of heritage policy in Australia
From hope to philanthropy

Emma Waterton

Introduction

The publication of *Creative Nation* in 1994 lies roughly at the midpoint between two key government interventions into Australia's heritage field: the *Report of the Committee of Inquiry into the National Estate* (henceforth 'the Hope Report') published in 1974, and the *Australian Heritage Strategy*, commenced in 2012 and released in December 2015 (henceforth 'the Strategy'). Commissioned by the Whitlam government, the first incursion into the field opens with the words of Gough Whitlam who, borrowing from US President John F. Kennedy, invokes a vision that seeks to link heritage with a broader Commonwealth mandate, through which the Australian government might come to 'see itself as the curator not the liquidator of the *national estate*' (The Hope Report 1974, p. 5, emphasis in original). Although he does not use the phrase, Whitlam is clearly referencing the heritage field and points to a time in which the growth of popular and governmental interest in 'the past' was exponential. Significantly, the Hope Report represents the first – and most rigorous – attempt by any Australian government to comment upon the definition, conservation and presentation of heritage, with all engagements prior dismissed as an 'almost wilful official unconcern with preservation, which is so much at variance with the opinions of the public that it can only be concluded that many politicians are seriously out of touch with the wishes of the electorate' (Ian Grant, cited in The Hope Report 1974, p. 136). It also represents the first time that an Australian government sought to collate a sense of heritage via consultation with 'ordinary citizens'.

The second incursion, some 40 years later, arrived under the leadership of Julia Gillard's Labor Party and saw the Australian government once again seek public input into defining and managing heritage. Three observations about the resultant Strategy are important for this chapter: first, it was based on an evocation of heritage with which almost half the population might struggle to identify, given its prioritizing of Anglo-European history prior to the 1970s; second, it imagined the field as reliant on voluntary community initiatives and was underpinned by a rhetoric that required heritage to justify investment and provide a return in terms of economic regeneration; and third, it reversed the Hope Report's vision of state intervention, presenting instead a clear retreat from governmental investment in, and responsibility for, heritage. Clearly, a lot happened in the intervening years.

Using the Hope Report as my starting point admittedly pushes at the historical parameters of this volume. I do so necessarily as the Hope Report signifies a pivotal moment in the field's emergence – a 'time of hope', as Sharon Veale (cited in Sullivan 2015, p. 114) puts it. In drawing attention to the interrelatedness between the heritage field 'then' and 'now', my purpose is to probe at the degree to which the federal government's commitment to heritage, and the mechanisms that it employs to manage the field, have diminished across the past four decades. In terms of specific discussion, I will examine some of the more forceful influences of the Hope Report, before turning to consider the concept of 'the nation' and its employment. I then move to isolate some of the key themes emerging from the Strategy, before thinking through the role played by more general ideological uncertainties surrounding the viability of public investment in heritage. At various junctures throughout, I also contemplate the ways in which the field has been shaped by its own transnational spaces, including developments occurring in other nation-states, as well as those at the supranational level.

A time of hope

In a context wholly dissimilar to that surrounding the publication of *Creative Nation*, the Committee of Inquiry into the National Estate, formed in the early 1970s, operated at a time when issues of the environment – natural and cultural – were only just emerging in Australian politics. It was during this time that serious attention was first given to the possibility of creating a national heritage agenda, which occurred in Australia far later than in Britain, Europe and the US (Ashton and Cornwall 2006). This turn to heritage was a response to numerous influences, including: extravagant increases in National Trusts membership and the emergence of numerous resident action groups; a growing interest of trade unions in conservation matters and the subsequent implementation of green bans on development sites across Melbourne and Sydney; increased environmental concerns; and a rapid growth in urbanization, with 85.5 per cent of the population living in areas that could readily be labelled 'urban' by 1971 (The Hope Report 1974). Importantly, it was also a context earmarked by swift technological advancements, increased leisure time and the awakening of a national conscious – or the 'new nationalism' of the Labor Party's Whitlam government (Davison 1991, p. 6).

Appointed by the Whitlam government in April 1973, the Committee reported jointly to the Minister for the Department of Urban and Regional Development (DURD) and the Minister for the Department of Environment and Conservation (King 1975). Over 650 submissions were received in response to the inquiry, coming from government departments and agencies, as well as National Trusts, conservation societies, professional groups and members of the public (The Hope Report 1974). The resultant report composed a number of recommendations that have had a profound effect on the heritage field, including: the establishment of a principal advisor to the Australian Government on heritage matters, the Australian Heritage Commission (now the Australian Heritage Council), established in 1976; the enactment of federal heritage legislation, including the *Australian Heritage*

Commission Act of 1975 (repealed by John Howard's Liberal-National Coalition government and replaced by the *Australian Heritage Council Act* of 2003) and the *Environment, Protection and Biodiversity Conservation Act* of 1999; and the development of the Register of the National Estate (1974–2004). By 1978, two years after its establishment, the Australian Heritage Commission had proposed the addition of more than 6,000 places onto the Register. The same period also saw the emergence of Australia ICOMOS (the International Council on Monuments and Sites, founded in 1976) and its associated conservation guidelines, the *Australia ICOMOS Guidelines for the Conservation of Places of Cultural Significance ("Burra Charter") 1979*.[1] Both continue to be incredibly influential.

The Hope Report can thus be credited with sponsoring three central movements in Australia's heritage field: an emerging agitation for a national role in the management of heritage; the development of 'the National Estate'; and a belief in the need for government to respond to, and support, voluntary heritage organizations. While the term 'the National Estate' had already edged its way into view prior to the publication of the report, it is often attributed to then Prime Minister Gough Whitlam and defined as those 'things that you keep' (p. 20).[2] Introduced to provide an encompassing basis for all human-environment interactions, 'the National Estate' draws on four elements: (i) the natural environment; (ii) the cultural environment; (iii) archaeological or scientific areas; and (iv) cultural property.[3] Aboriginal artefacts and sites are specifically aligned with the latter two (iii and iv). Prior to, or in the immediate aftermath of, its publication, all states implemented legislation to protect Aboriginal sites and relics, early examples of which include the 1955 *Native and Historical Objects Preservation Ordinance* in the Northern Territory and the 1972 *Aboriginal Heritage Act* in Western Australia. The Committee saw in the Hope Report an opportunity to change attitudes to Aboriginal and Torres Strait Islander people and their culture, and stressed consultation and cooperation, recognizing that:

> Aboriginal sites and artefacts [had] been preserved chiefly for the scholarship of European man [sic], and not in any direct way for the benefit of the Aboriginal. Further, implicit in all aspects of the Committee's activities, the National Estate is primarily seen as that of European man [sic] in Australia. It seems likely that an Aboriginal may well find the current concept of the National Estate deficient in this respect.
>
> (The Hope Report 1974, p. 170)

Any intentions of the Committee to contribute to debates about Indigenous rights were, however, curtailed by their own loose definition of the National Estate, which, as Ashton and Cornwall (2006, p. 56) point out, 'ultimately and incorrectly came to be seen as describing a collection of places of "national significance" '. Thus, while all manner of objects, places and sites could be included in the report's expansive definition, decisions over *how* they might come to find their place on the Register were left open to judgements of taste – inevitably an elitist and exclusive set of judgements (King 1975). This predisposition was ultimately shared by those places included on the Register in the decades that followed its enactment: colonial/pioneer homes, architecturally impressive buildings, historic churches and monuments found a place there, but the same cannot be said of Aboriginal, industrial, working-class, multicultural and women's heritage (Byrne 2017). Indeed, Aboriginal heritage in large part continued to be registered on a separate list, and in many sectors was considered to be synonymous with the natural environment or prehistory. Thus, tangible objects detailing a European past, such as fine buildings and their remains, pastoral estates, war memorials, monuments, places of colonial significance, artefacts and works of art, became the central obsessions of the heritage field, largely because of their assumed use in identity-making and nationhood. By the time *Creative Nation* was published, only 112 places with significance for migrant groups had been added to the Register and these were seen as forming a separate category of 'migrant heritage' (Byrne 2017). As Byrne argues, this category of heritage might better be understood as a form of differential inclusion, 'insofar as, in separating off immigrant heritage places into their own realm, they never quite penetrate or disturb the terrain of the majority culture' (p. 6).

In the years following the release of the Hope Report, numerous state Acts and heritage registers were established, with the New South Wales' *Heritage Act* arriving in 1977 and the *Queensland Heritage Act* in 1992, one year after Western Australia's *Heritage Act* (Ashton 2009). Yet, while the report made recommendations for state and local involvement in Australia's National Estate, it agitated most vociferously for legislation that could afford uniform protection on a national basis. This it did largely to avoid 'sectional development interests [that] may affect preservation issues', arguing that the national level was where 'the force of a conservation or a development viewpoint [could] be assessed in the nation's best interest' (p. 274–275). A central recommendation of the Committee was that it ought to be the Australian government that provided the 'adequate funds for effective preservation and conservation' (p. 277); and it would do this via the Australian Heritage Commission, which was established not only with the power to register heritage places, but also to make available federal money for conservation processes (Freestone 1995). As Freestone (1995, p. 85) has argued, '[a]ccess to these funds provided a major impetus for both state and local governments to start taking heritage conservation seriously for the first time'.

While the report was unapologetically framed to implement a national heritage agenda, allowances were nonetheless made for both international and local influences. The report made clear references to many developments shaping heritage globally and specifically named Britain, Canada and the US. Such mentions are unsurprising, as these were the countries to which the Committee looked for examples of good practice. These transnational flows are visible in the detailed passages dealing with debates surrounding the preferred use of the term 'conservation' over 'preservation', which draws heavily on the UK context. They are also visible in recommendations pointing to the possibilities of establishing a system of 'English' national parks and in arguments for the adoption of an administrative structure similar to the National Parks Service of the US Department of the

Interior and to the National and Historic Parks Branch of the Canadian Department of Indian and Northern Affairs (see pp. 275–282).

Additionally, the report made reference to a range of international charters and conventions, such as the *Venice Charter for the Conservation and Restoration of Monuments and Sites* (1964) and the *Convention Concerning the Protection of the World Cultural and Natural Heritage* (1972; henceforth the World Heritage Convention), as well as prominent international agencies including ICOMOS, the International Union for the Conservation of Nature (IUCN), the United Nations Educational, Scientific and Cultural Organization (UNESCO) and the Rome Centre. Australia had become a member of IUCN shortly before the report was written, and formed *Australia ICOMOS* shortly after in 1976. It was also one of the first countries to ratify UNESCO's World Heritage Convention in 1974. This decision, as the report itself forecast, would have important consequences at a national level, as the Convention confers to the Commonwealth the power to legislate in respect of matters of heritage throughout Australia, by virtue of the requirement of signatories to give the Convention's provisions legal effect. The report also points to transnational trends framed around Australia's interests in its offshore components, with a brief interlude to Papua New Guinea that makes recommendations that the Australian Government initiate discussions with PNG in order to offer financial or technical help (or both) to 'revise its own National Estate and decide preservation priorities' (The Hope Report 1974, p. 252). These global networks brought into existence that which the report termed 'an "external affair" of Australia' (p. 209), pushing heritage forward as something that might be understood as an international obligation, all the while with the capacity to affect the internal dynamics of the Australian field.

After Hope: the intervening years

In the aftermath of the Hope Report, the heritage field became professionalized and institutionalized, culminating in a complex of multi-level legislative frameworks operating across local, state/territorial, national and international levels. Such frameworks were accompanied by continued government investment in heritage planning, and the concomitant expansion of the management role played by state and local governments. It was also mirrored in the participation practices of the Australian public which, as Kate Clarke (2012) observes, saw some 95 per cent of Australians engaging in at least one heritage-related activity per year. Yet political interest in heritage, on the whole, waned; indeed, it has never since received the depth of support of the 1970s.

The expansive definition of the National Estate envisioned by the Hope Report receded and, while increasing recognition of intangible and social values is evident within professional circles, the political environment – particularly at the national level – narrowed its focus, settling on a resilient antiquarian imagining (Griffiths 1996, p. 3; see also Veale and Freestone 2012). By the time of *Creative Nation*, heritage had settled into three distinct parcels: natural heritage, historic heritage (essentially European buildings and places) and Aboriginal heritage. While they were legislatively bundled together, there was, effectively, a 'siloing' of the three in practice. The latter two parcels, concerned with what scholars and practitioners in the field might refer to as 'cultural heritage', became the responsibility of architects, who took primary responsibility for built or historic heritage on the one hand, and archaeologists, who oversaw Aboriginal 'pre-contact' heritage (Byrne 2003) on the other. This division continues to operate within current heritage legislation, where Australia's heritage remains displaced and segregated.

The National Estate continued to play an influential role in the field during the intervening years, albeit one perhaps not originally envisioned by the Hope Report. But a role it played (and continues to do), commencing a process in which specific places would be drawn into a newly formalized system that 'overtly and covertly' shaped what constitutes heritage (Ashton 2009, p. 388). As Mulvaney (2008, p. 59) puts it, inclusion on the Register 'implied that each item listed was a place *Australians* wanted to keep' (emphasis added). By the time the Howard government repealed the *Australian Heritage Commission Act*, amended the *Environment Protection and Biodiversity Act 1999* and terminated the Register (which by then included over 13,000 places) in the mid-2000s, the federal approach to heritage was almost entirely implicated in the representation of a national past that conferred an Anglo-European identity, the visible symbols of which were exemplified by various lists and taxonomies. By then, the tides had started to turn against heritage and moves were made to limit the Ministerial independence of the Heritage Commission. In 2004, ironically the Year of the Built Environment, the Register was replaced by three new lists – (i) the National Heritage List, (ii) the Commonwealth Heritage List and (iii) the List of Overseas Places of Historical Significance to Australia – which, with their narrower focus, transitioned from focusing on 'places of the heart' to 'jewels in the crown' (Ireland and Blair 2015, p. 11; see also Clarke 2017). Heritage, as a tool of 'nationing' under Howard's government, was as alive in Australia as it had been in Europe in the eighteenth century, and showed no clear signs of decline (Winter 2015a; see also Clarke 2012). Yet, all the while, the broader heritage sector was in the process of being devalued, serving as a useful reminder of the ties that bind heritage with nation-making, which Allcock (1995, p. 109) sums up thus:

> By designating features of the past specifically as 'heritage', the items in question are endowed with an elevated status reminiscent of Emile Durkheim's concept of 'sacredness'. 'Heritage' does not just refer to elements of our past: it designates things towards which we have an *obligation*. That obligation holds because the item in question is regarded as peculiarly important in defining an aspired identity. The identification of heritage therefore involves an attempt to create a sense of there being a moral bond which draws together a given community ... around the object in question ... and sets it off in significant respects from others.

As the composition of these newly formed lists made clear, historic buildings, churches, cemeteries and war memorials had become exemplars of an obsessive materiality and 'thingness' at work. This obsession can be glimpsed in the stock of colonial homes owned by National Trusts, which are responsible for their upkeep and presentation. While many of these places continue to be the subject of attention by historians and tourists, they have simultaneously become a core part of the nation's cultural fabric, and are imagined as symbols of an enduring national past and cohesive national identity. They have been variously taxonomized, preserved, conserved and interpreted as aesthetic, national objects and, in that guise, have admitted few other readings of their significance. In the post-Hope context, and under the conservative regime of John Howard, this nationalization of the past came to represent the very term 'heritage'. It was connected with the assumed inherent value of the artefact-object (which is still institutionalized in legislation) and with the terms of reference of official agencies and conservation organizations (such as the 2015 Strategy). The object of heritage had, in other words, become an object of respect and veneration. At the same time, the imperative to realize the value of such objects as capital assets turned them into attractions and leisure spaces that could generate cultural meaning in subtle reciprocity with authorized narratives of a national past and of national identity. Heritage, at essence, had become very much a thing of the present rather than the past to which it constantly alludes.

Who cares for heritage?

While 'the nation' continues to drive the field forward, the recent publication of the Australian Heritage Strategy is indicative of the emergence of new foci in the field, the most obvious of which is a move away from federal and state government investment in care and management of the past (Ireland and Blair 2015). This move has seen the introduction of severe cuts to the heritage field, and a consequent turn towards both philanthropy and 'seeing the "community" as holding the responsibility to care for its heritage' (Ireland and Blair 2015, p. 10). Overseen by the Department of Sustainability, Environment, Water, Population and Communities (now the Department of the Environment and Energy), the production of a new strategy commenced with a consultation document released in April 2012, accompanied by a series of ten commentary essays commissioned from academics and professionals working in the field (Department of Sustainability, Environment, Water, Population and Communities 2012). The consultation received 97 submissions by its close in June 2012. A revised paper, *A Strategy for Australia's Heritage: Draft for Consultation*, was released for comment in April 2014, closing in June 2014 with 124 public submissions received. Together, the 2012 and 2014 public responses equate with roughly one-third of the submissions received for the 1973/4 public consultation, and culminated in the 2015 Strategy.

Key themes to emerge across the consultation periods and resultant publication were that of an increased need for cooperation across state boundaries and a desire for the Commonwealth to assume what was seen as an essential leadership role (this emerged in the 2014 draft as a key element of 'National Leadership'). The decline in government support for heritage across Australia was also heavily discussed, particularly a reduction in financial support from governments, as was the need to more comprehensively understand community participation; these issues emerged in the 2014 draft as key elements of 'Innovative Partnerships' and

'Community Engagement'. The latter two themes were, in part, brought together through the newly formed Community Heritage and Icons Programme, a key component of the Government's *A Plan for a Cleaner Environment* framework, released in October 2013 and intertextually linked to the 2015 Strategy. All documents associated with the Strategy are replete with references to the field's continuing 'nationing' role, with heritage highlighted as that which 'underpins our sense of place and national identity', contributing 'significantly to our national story and sense of who we are' (Department of the Environment 2015a, p. 15). In many ways, the language employed to speak of heritage, and, in turn, the need for national leadership, differs little from that used in the Hope Report.

There are also significant similarities between the two periods when it comes to envisioning Australia's contributions to international standards and 'best practice'. The difference, however, is that Australia's leadership had already started to dwindle amidst sophisticated global alternatives by the time the national heritage review commenced in 2012 (Sullivan 2015). Indeed, there is a marked difference between Australia's current reputation and the position of formidable influence that it once enjoyed, evidenced at the time by the global popularity of the Burra Charter (published in 1979) and Australia's acknowledged role within the architecture of the World Heritage Committee. Likewise, Australia ICOMOS and the Australian Committee of IUCN seem today to play less of a leading role. As Sharon Sullivan has observed, 'the Australian Government (to some extent regardless of the political party in power) appears to have withdrawn from a leadership role in this area' (cited in Winter 2015b, p. 24). However, as recommended in the 1974 Hope Report, Australia has recently offered to support the wider Asia-Pacific region's engagement with the social, cultural and economic benefits of aligning with the World Heritage Convention. This role has not seen a diminishing of the nation-state; rather, such interventions have taken the form of bilateral aid programs, like those undertaken in PNG, Fiji and the wider Pacific and South, East and West Asia in recent decades (Winter 2015b).

Additional evidence of transnational trends can be drawn from the confluence of nationing and commercial influences established via tourism (see Gibson this volume) or, as the Strategy puts it, via Australia's 'tourism brand' (p. 38). Australia's 'brand' is dealt with in the Strategy under the mantle 'Outcome 2: Strong Partnerships' and is geared towards fostering 'greater collaboration between the heritage and tourism sectors' (Department of the Environment 2015a, p. 15; see also Objective 8). The intersection of heritage with tourism inevitably draws in processes of commoditization and exchange, and on a global scale. International tourists, in particular those interested in Australia's heritage, are earmarked as significant contributors to both national and regional economies, with such tourists expected to contribute to the largest average annual growth within the sector (Tourism Research Australia 2008). In monetary terms, attractions such as the Great Barrier Reef, which is both a World Heritage and a National Heritage Site, contribute over $3 billion to the Australian economy each year (Department of the Environment 2015a, p. 38). This commercialization of heritage mirrors that occurring internationally, with heritage tourism marked out as a category that will continue to expand (Light 2015). As Light (2015) argues, demand for heritage tourism is increasing, in part because of an expanding pool of newly affluent consumers, particularly those from Brazil, Russia, India and China. Studies conducted by Tourism Research Australia in 2009 and 2012 suggest that around half of all overseas visitors to Australia participate in some form of cultural and heritage tourism, which brings to bear a strong element of cross-border flows (of bodies, images, information, desires, policies, finance capital and so forth) on the field, all of which are exceptionally dynamic and uneven. Heritage, in this context, is thus produced through a greater range of spaces and sites than ever before. Indeed, thinking about heritage at the scale of the nation now relies on a range of bodies, objects and sites that are *beyond* the borders of the state.

Of course, transnational forces have always registered in some way in the heritage field, albeit with national undertones; colonial contact and processes of cross-cultural exchange are clear examples. Another straightforward example of such transnational forces is that of Australia's military heritage and subsequent attempts at a 'nationing' role outside Australian territory, pursued with vigour by the Howard government in the early 2000s and illustrated by the subsequent establishment of the List of Overseas Places of Historical Significance to Australia in 2007. These efforts say as much about what Australia has attempted to do in (and how it sees its ownership extending across) other peoples' territories as they do about what happens *within* Australia. Much can be gained, then, from exploring what is going on in France and Belgium with the Australian Remembrance Trail, for example, and the development of the Sir John Monash Centre at the Australian National Memorial at Villers-Bretonneaux; or the extension of Australia's influence into Turkey via Anzac Cove and the wider Gallipoli peninsula; or, more recently, in the Asia Pacific theatres of war, such as the Kokoda Trail and Museum in Papua New Guinea. The latter two examples are included on the List of Overseas Places, along with Florey's Laboratory in the UK – they remain the only places inscribed on that List. Other international sites and places in which the Australian government has expressed an explicitly national interest (rather than a shared, mutual interest) include the Sandakan Memorial Park in Malaysian Borneo, Hellfire Pass in Thailand, Changi Prison in Singapore, Kuta Bali in Indonesia and Lords Cricket Club in the UK (Clarke 2017).

Interestingly, these transnational flows are supported more and more by social media platforms, which bring official and user-generated content together within the heritage field. Websites and social media sites such as Facebook, TripAdvisor, Flickr, VirtualTourist, Fotki, Fotolog, Instagram, Pinterest and YouTube sit alongside, from the heritage tourists' perspective, their own photographs as records of their experience of 'being there'. This kind of symbolic value can be expressive of a variety of cultural attributes with which the consumer may want to be associated, especially in a period when people identify and express themselves so thoroughly in terms of what they consume, produce or do for a living (Bauman 2007). Together, then, this merging of digital platforms with more traditional modes of engaging with heritage conjures a semiotics of presence that, in itself, generates and organizes meaning that both reflects and refracts the representational practices associated with the 'supply side' and consumption of heritage, and how these practices might relate to a concept of selfhood. Surprisingly, though social media and issues of digitization are already in the process of significantly rupturing the ways in which the heritage field operates (economically, socially, politically), they were seldom mentioned in the 2012 consultation documents. In the 2015 publication, however, the prospect of 'social media led crowd-funding' is raised, as is the potential of digital media platforms, specialized apps and smartphone capabilities (Department of the Environment 2015a, pp. 34, 44). Such platforms, apps and associated capabilities are seen as democratizing tools and a way to wrest attention away from the interests of the elite and upper classes. Several public responses to the 2014 draft also drew attention to the need for the sector to recognize and invest in the digitization of heritage resources and to develop new media platforms for tourism purposes (whether through digital preservation, 3D reconstructions of heritage sites and objects, digitization of collections, computer aided modelling and so forth). In the Strategy, the field is also encouraged to grasp the inevitability that geospatial discovery tools will soon 'become major heritage information sources on the Internet as people travel Australia both physically and online' (AIATSIS 2014, p. 8). The question of how these digital technologies will transform the field, however, remains open. As Byrne has observed, while '[i]t seems safe to predict that the replicability of heritage objects and their digital consumption will form one dimension of heritage's future', it is 'equally safe to say that we cannot know where this will take us' (cited in Sullivan 2015, p. 116).

Perhaps the most significant alteration to the field over the period under scrutiny can be found in the language used to discuss domestic and international tourism economies, and which mark out a clear shift in the field since the 1970s. The increasing incorporation of, and reliance on, 'voluntary', 'active' or 'engaged' communities into the management process has seen the simultaneous incorporation of terms such as 'revitalisation' and 'regeneration'. Again, the work of National Trusts is exemplary here in their expansion from the provision of custodianship to 'recovering costs, raising revenue and making profit' (Freestone 1995, p. 88). The Community Heritage and Icons Programme is a case in point, bringing together a financial commitment of $1.4 million over three years (in the 2014/15 round) in support of improving community engagement with the improvement of the 'conservation, restoration and interpretation of Australia's National Heritage Listed Places' (Department of Environment 2015b, p. 7). Heritage and economic development, it would seem, are being brought together in ways never conceived by the authors of the Hope Report, with the former (heritage) providing all manner of places with distinctiveness and competitive advantage (Watson and González-Rodríguez 2015).

Australia's heritage field transformed?

Following the heyday of the 1970s, the past few decades have seen a diminishing of federal investment in heritage in Australia (Sullivan 2015, p. 111). Indeed, across that timeframe, Australia's heritage field has seen the onus of responsibility move from federal to local government to a significant degree, where it is now supplemented by the promise of community involvement and a growing expectation that heritage should duly attract its own capital investment, principally through tourism. The sum total, to borrow from Watson and González-Rodráguez (2015, p. 461), has been a strengthening belief in a 'heritage economy', which can perform its part not only within the wider environmental 'crusades', but as something that 'makes money and regenerates moribund places'. At the same time, its continued ability to *make* the nation remains one of its key features. Fulfilling that need is achieved through a process of careful selection and display and the ascription of national significance and meaning to those places concerned. This selectivity is of course self-fulfilling and remains essential for both the production of tourism commodities as well as a crucial mechanism in the identity-making process at the level of the nation. In other words, for heritage objects and places to be effectively developed as marketable and identity-lending, it remains essential that they be linked (through their very selection and subsequent marketing) to pre-existing national narratives that they can reflect, be a part of, substantiate or provide material evidence for (Watson 2009). Thus, it remains those 'national' stories – linked to periods that are well known, and are easy to imagine and visualise – that continue to provide the active semiotic that supports the selection of new heritage places and the product development and promotion that goes with them. This makes the heritage field something of an outlier from many of the other fields examined in this collection: though it illustrates a powerful movement towards the commercialization of heritage and a somewhat inconsistent engagement with transnational influences, it is a field that has refused to withdrawal from the project of nationing.

Notes

1 The most recent version of the Burra Charter carries the slightly amended title of *The Burra Charter: The Australian ICOMOS Charter for Places of Cultural Significance, 2013*.
2 The term would later be replaced by that of 'heritage'.
3 Some parameters become apparent when considering cultural property held within museums, where the following qualification is issued: 'those responsible for certain areas of museum collections, e.g., art collections, may look more appropriately to other areas of government for support' (The Hope Report 1974, p. 192).

References

Allcock, J. B., 1995. International tourism and the appropriation of history in the Balkans. *In*: M. F. Lanfant, J. B. Allcock and E. M. Bruner, eds. *International tourism: Identity and change*. London: Sage Publications, 100–112.

AIATSIS, 2014. Submission to the draft Australian Heritage Strategy. Available from: http://www.environment.gov.au/submissions/heritage-strategy/draft/106-australian-institute-of-aboriginal-and-torres-strait-islander-studies.pdf [Accessed 23 February 2018].

Ashton, P., 2009. The birthplace of Australian multiculturalism? Retrospective commemoration, participatory memorialization and official heritage. *International Journal of Heritage Studies*, 15(5), 381–398.

Ashton, P. and Cornwall, J. L., 2006. Corralling conflict: The politics of Australian federal heritage legislation since the 1970s. *Public History Review*, 13(1), 53−65.

Bauman, Z., 2007. *Consuming life*. London: Polity Press.

Byrne, D., 2003. The ethos of return: erasure and reinstatement of Aboriginal visibility in the Australian historical landscape, Historical Archaeology, 37(1), 73–86.

Clarke, A., 2017. Heritage beyond borders: Australian approaches to extra-national built heritage. *Archaeologies: Journal of the World Archaeological Congress*, 13(1), 153–174.

Clarke, K., 2012. Essay: 'Only connect': The social, economic and environmental benefits of cultural heritage. Available from: www.environment.gov.au/system/files/pages/f4d5ba7d-e4eb-4ced-9c0e-104471634fbb/files/essay-benefits-clark.pdf [Accessed 28 November 2015].

Davison, G. 1991. A brief history of the Australian heritage movement. In: G. Davison and C. McConville, eds. A heritage handbook. Sydney: Allen and Unwin, 14–27.

Department of the Environment, 2015a. A strategy for Australia's heritage. Commonwealth of Australia. Available from: www.environment.gov.au/system/files/resources/426e089a-b460-4e21-b613-4b86eabd3127/files/heritage-strategy-apr14_1.pdf [Accessed 28 November 2015].

Department of the Environment, 2015b. Community heritage and icons grants 2014–15. Commonwealth of Australia. Available from: www.environment.gov.au/system/files/pages/7f1f99c2-82b0-4004-8e79-239c51b4bc62/files/chig-2014-15-guidelines-6mar2015.pdf [Accessed 28 November 2015].

Department of Sustainability, Environment, Water, Population and Communities, 2012. Australian heritage strategy: Public consultation paper, April 2012. Available from: www.environment.gov.au/system/files/resources/9e13eb60-12d2-45ac-a09d-4b0655fd74b7/files/australian-heritage-strategy-consultation.pdf [Accessed 28 November 2015].

Freestone, R., 1995. From icons to institutions: Heritage conservation in Sydney. *International Journal of Heritage Studies*, 1(2), 79–90.

Griffiths, T. 1996. Hunters and collectors: The antiquarian imagination in Australia. New York: Cambridge University Press.

The Hope Report, 1974. *Report of the National Estate: Report of the Committee of Inquiry into the National Estate*. Canberra: Australian Government Publishing Service.

Ireland, T. and Blair, S., 2015. The future for heritage practice. *Historic Environment*, 27(2), 9–17.

King, R., 1975. Hobbies, the National Estate and equity. *Meanjin Quarterly*, 34(1), 63–70.

Light, D., 2015. Heritage and tourism. *In*: E. Waterton and S. Watson, eds. *The Palgrave handbook of contemporary heritage research*. Basingstoke: Palgrave Macmillan, 144–158.

Mulvaney, J., 2008. Things we wanted to keep: Politics and the Register of the National Estate. *Dissent*, 26(Autumn/Winter), 59–60.

Sullivan, S., 2015. Does the practice of heritage as we know it have a future? *Historic Environment*, 27(2), 110–117.

Tourism Research Australia, 2008. Through the looking glass: The future of domestic tourism in Australia. Tourism Australia. Available from: http://apo.org.au/node/3654 [Accessed 28 November 2015].

Veale, S. and Freestone, R., 2012. The things we wanted to keep: The Commonwealth and the National Estate, 1969–1974. *Historic Environment*, 24(3), 12–18.

Watson, S., 2009. Archaeology, visuality and the negotiation of heritage. *In*: E. Waterton and L. Smith, eds. *Taking archaeology out of heritage*. Newcastle-upon-Tyne: Cambridge Scholars Publishing, 29–47.

Watson, S. and González-Rodríguez, M., 2015. Heritage economies: The past meets the future in the mall. *In*: E. Waterton and S. Watson, eds. *The Palgrave handbook of contemporary heritage research*. Basingstoke: Palgrave Macmillan, 458–477.

Winter, T., 2015a. Heritage and nationalism: An unbreachable couple? *In*: E. Waterton and S. Watson, eds. *The Palgrave handbook of contemporary heritage research*. Basingstoke: Palgrave Macmillan, 331–345.

Winter, T., 2015b. Heritage diplomacy and Australia's responses to a shifting landscape of international conservation. *Historic Environment*, 27(2), 19–28.

7 The sport field in Australia

The market, the state, the nation and the world beyond in Pierre Bourdieu's favourite game

David Rowe

Introduction: Bourdieu on the rugby field

In 1995 – the year after the publication of the national cultural policy *Creative Nation* (Commonwealth of Australia 1994) and in the same year as the first subscription television broadcast in Australia – rugby union, the last of the major amateur sports in Australia, went fully professional. This so-called 'hooligan's game played by gentlemen'[1] was a favourite sport of Pierre Bourdieu, the architect of social scientific field theory, who was a useful player in his youth and frequently mentioned rugby union in his discussions of cultural capital and class (Calhoun 2007; Grenfell 2015). In his landmark work on culture and taste, *Distinction*, Bourdieu (2010, p. 206) expresses his awareness of the variable position of rugby union, which he describes as an 'initial ambiguity', with regard to class relations and national contexts. The English tradition of rugby union that Australia inherited, he notes, is traditionally associated with elite class, male schooling, while 'in France it has become the characteristic sport of the working and middle classes south of the Loire [i.e., is regional rather than metropolitan] (while preserving some "academic" bastions such as the Racing Club or the Paris Université Club)' (pp. 206–208). Bourdieu sees a sport such as rugby, in contrast to the French folk sport of pétanque, as subject to dual processes (analogous to those involving dance and music – see also Rowe 1995): first, 'the transmutation of popular games into elite sports, associated with an aristocratic ethic and world view ("fair play", "will to win", etc.)', and then to a process of popularization 'which, in a second phase, transforms elite into mass sport, a spectacle as much as a practice' (p. 208).

Thus, for Bourdieu, the aggressive masculinity of rugby may have some appeal to the 'dominant fractions of the dominant class' who have made an 'aesthetico-ethical investment in the game', but its aristocratic association with '"heroic virtues"':

> encounters its limits in the reality of modern rugby, which, under the combined effects of modernized tactics and training, a change in the social recruitment of players and a wider audience, gives priority to the 'forward game' [physically attritional combat that is less aesthetically appealing than the free flowing 'three-quarter game'], which is increasingly discussed in metaphors of the meanest industrial labour ('attacking the coal-face') or trench warfare (the infantryman who 'dutifully' runs headlong into enemy fire).
>
> (p. 211)

Bourdieu here is describing developments that are widely spread across the globe through the modernization of sport and those that are specific to twentieth-century France and its preponderant non-metropolitan, working/middle-class foundation of rugby union. Although he does not cite Bourdieu, Dine (2014, p. 67) echoes him in tracking the ways in which 'the French unquestionably do things differently in the field of sport, and this is especially true of rugby football'. He notes, however, that after being imported from Britain, it 'has been embraced in a wide variety of locations [in France] and has gone through almost as many incarnations and their associated representations'. These changes included the attempted appropriation of the game by Gaullist and regional politicians, through which, '[i]n the wake of professionalization, and the intensification of the sporting "glocalization" which it encouraged, a new breed of media-aware rugby managers have sought novel ways in which to exploit the old game's traditional appeal'.

This chapter appraises the game's similar and distinctive transformations in the case of Australia, focusing on the last 30 years but recognizing the preceding historical factors that helped condition rugby union's corner of the Australian sport field. It has been highlighted for two principal reasons – the rough 'coincidence' of its professionalization with the release of *Creative Nation*, and the centrality of commercialization, crucially accompanied by transnationalism and 'nationing', to the changing nature and position of the sport. Of course, rugby union cannot represent the entire Australian sport field – itself, in any case, a phenomenon that is resistant to easy conceptual and empirical capture – but it can effectively illuminate a range of convergent and divergent processes that help constitute the sport field as a whole.

Commercializing rugby union in Australia

Rugby union in Australia, as briefly noted earlier, is historically associated with the 'gentlemanly' amateur ethos championed in elite private schools. Sports of similarly elite patrimony, such as cricket and tennis, had significantly professionalized across the world during the twentieth century, although not without confrontations, including the leading tennis players abandoning the amateur for the 'open' game in the 1960s (Steen 2014, pp. 209–210) and the cataclysmic 'Packer Revolution' in cricket in the 1970s (Haigh 2007). Other sports, such as association football (often called soccer in Australia), had commercialized early, but then experienced a series of disputes, ultimately resulting in industrial advancement, over the minimum wage in England or freedom of player contract and movement within the European Union (Goldblatt 2007). Of most direct relevance to this chapter was rugby league's breakaway from rugby union and professionalization in Australia in 1908, as had occurred in Britain a decade earlier (Collins 2006). That feeling was high on the subject of 'paying for play' is well expressed by the declaration in 1923 in Australia's weekly *Rugby News* that, '[w]hen rugby is played with the motive of financial advantage, none of its objects can be achieved: the [moral] lessons are lost' (quoted by Collins 2008, p. 1). As Collins (2008, p. 7) observes, to challenge rugby union and amateurism was presented by some as disrespecting the British Empire, in defence of which many players had lost their lives in World War I. He quotes James Baxter, manager of the British Isles team that toured Australasia in 1930, as answering a journalist thus when questioned over the popularity of rugby league in Auckland: 'Every town must have its sewer'. Here, the Bourdieusian linkage between rugby union and the 'dominant fractions of the dominant class' and the assertion of its amateur-derived, superior cultural capital could not be clearer.

Across the twentieth century, as a global sport industry emerged (Miller et al. 2001), it became progressively difficult to maintain the amateur 'purity' of major national sports such as rugby union, especially with the enormous influx of resources and interest from the media and corporate sponsors that saw a substantial convergence or interpenetration of the sport and media fields (Wenner 1998). The consequent emergence of the sporting component of the 'new international division of cultural labour' (Miller et al. 2001) saw athletic labour flow across national and sporting boundaries, with attendant media technologies enabling audiences to follow (Rowe 2011). At the same time, the state (in national, regional and civic forms), which had buttressed amateur sport in various ways through its formal and often compulsory role in the school educational system, municipal facility provision, health promotion programs, championing and subsidization of ostensibly amateur international sport and its major events, notably the multi-sport Olympic and Commonwealth Games, became less enamoured of sporting amateurism. The principal reasons for this change were the increasing difficulty of policing the remuneration of sportspeople, enhanced support for and recognition of sport as a key element of the burgeoning service economy and the intensified political and popular pressure for performative success in the international sporting sphere (Hargreaves 1986). A significant discursive shift occurred at this time, with the term 'amateur' acquiring an increasingly pejorative connotation in contrast to that of 'professional' and often being represented as inferior and inefficient. In a sport field subject to massive marketization, the idea of elite sport performers playing for the love of the game began to look quaint and outmoded, although it retained something of its former moral authority (Allison 2001).

In rugby union, in particular, this transition was highlighted by the weakening of its aforementioned appeal to the values of Empire. Other sports had adopted marketing and presentational techniques derived from American sports and media (Goldlust 1987). The stately presentation and hierarchical deference that permeated amateur sports like rugby union became increasingly anachronistic, while in a now-intensively competitive sports industry, the necessities of preventing incursion by other sports, such as the 'poaching' of unpaid rugby union players by professional rugby league, were increasingly evident. In countries such as France and New Zealand, so-called 'shamateurism' was rife, with coaches and players receiving substantial hidden payments, subsidies, private sponsorship and 'side' employment (Richards 2006). In Australia and Britain, where rugby union's establishment connections had previously enabled discreet support arrangements for leading domestic players and overseas recruits, there was mounting pressure to submit to the inevitable, aforementioned second phase according to Bourdieu – 'to transform[s] elite into mass sport, a spectacle as much as a practice'. Officially disapproved commercial practices, therefore, became increasingly common in both countries.

In the early 1980s, an attempt was initiated by the Australian Rugby Union (ARU) to capitalize on the game's substantial, if highly variable, international reach – a clear mark of comparative advantage over rugby league – by ushering in a World Cup. International sporting competition has a dual impact on the process of 'nationing' – it links national sporting jurisdictions and fosters the development of an international market in particular sports, while being suffused with a nationalistic ethos that is closely tied to expressions of national identity and, not uncommonly, assertions of national superiority (Billings et al. 2013). When the International Rugby Football Board (IRFB) rejected the proposal, an unsuccessful World Series Cricket-style 'coup' was initiated from within Australia by an entrepreneur (David Lord). The Australian and New Zealand Rugby Unions then successfully moved jointly to host the first World Cup in 1987. But there was continuing concern that, without full professionalization – rugby union was not declared 'open' by the IRU until August 1995 – the game would be taken over by a commercial party or subjected to a debilitating split. This rupture had occurred within rugby league which, as noted, had itself separated from rugby union many years before, during the 1995–1997 so-called Super League War between media proprietors Kerry Packer and Rupert Murdoch (Colman 1996).

An enriched rugby league would also threaten even more effective 'poaching' of rugby union players. Indeed, it appeared that a version of the Super League conflict could occur as, on the eve of the June 1995 World Cup Final in South Africa (famous for the role of President Nelson Mandela in the immediate post-apartheid era, as captured in the film *Invictus* 2009), Murdoch's News Corporation announced a ten-year television and radio broadcast deal with the newly formed SANZAR, the governing body consisting of the South African, New Zealand and Australian Rugby Unions. Almost immediately, the Kerry Packer-backed World Rugby Corporation (WRC) claimed to have signed over 400 players to its worldwide professional competition. Through a combination of financial inducements and threatened punishments, including bans from playing for official national teams, initiated by the national rugby bodies, Packer's Corporation did not assume control of world rugby, but his initiative accelerated the commercialization and transnationalization of the sport (FitzSimons 2003).

SANZAR's 'regional' operation of a franchise-based 'Super Rugby' club competition (later to include Argentina and Japan) and a four-nation Rugby Championship competition (with Argentina included) to supplement each rugby nations' domestic and international competitive activities enabled a mix of local, national, international and transnational arrangements. For example, rugby union players may in any one season play for their local club, a franchise club in another country, and also represent their nation in the Sevens and 15-a-side versions of the game. Such a mix of competitive sites and forms has long been a feature of sports, like association football and cricket, that are more commercially advanced. Here it can be seen that the evolving Australian rugby union market has been progressively integrated into international sports commerce and, especially, into a transnational labour market via its 'Super Rugby' franchise system that has hired players freely from across the rugby playing world. Australian rugby union's commercial partners range from the naming rights partner of the national Wallabies team, the nation-identified airline Qantas, to other major and official partners including @asics (Japan), Samsung (Korea) and HSBC (Hong Kong). But there are also government partners, both federal and state, which provide significant funding and other forms of support as part of rugby union's 'nationing' remit, as is evident in Australia's hosting of the Rugby World Cup (co-hosted with New Zealand in 1987 and sole-hosted in 2003), one of the world's largest sport events (Jackson 2014).

'Nationing' is signalled also in Australia's long-time involvement in the Hong Kong Sevens and, more recently, through the 2009 decision to restore, for the first time since 1924, rugby sevens, a shortened form of the game with fewer players, to the summer Olympics (but now both men's and women's). In the light of these developments in rugby union in Australia, and especially in the two decades plus following *Creative Nation* and the game's coincidental full professionalization, this chapter has registered its specific compression of processes of long duration alongside those evident in, and entwined with, a discourse of sporting commercialization, modernization and Americanization (see McKay and Miller 1991) across the entire Australian sport field.

Rugby union and the Australian sport field

The Australian sport field is one of the most 'crowded' and competitive in the world, not least because it uniquely contains four (male-dominated) professional codes of football: Australian rules football, rugby league, rugby union and association football. As discussed earlier, rugby union was the last of these codes to go professional, its dominant ethos of amateurism eroded by commercial competitive pressure in the sport market. This development was market- rather than nation-state driven – sport in general was not regarded as a form of national culture that required protection and development in *Creative Nation* and, indeed, was treated by it as a competitor for public and private resources with more 'deserving', aesthetically prestigious forms (Rowe 2016).

Rugby union, already a major sport capable of attracting large co-present and mediated audiences, substantial broadcast rights, and corporate sponsorship, was, as noted, in danger of being commercially dominated by rival, fully professional sports and rent asunder by competing media companies. Indeed, when SANZAR's resultant 'Super Rugby' club competition was formed, it was not covered by the federal government's so-called anti-siphoning provisions, which (as noted in Chapter 5) are deemed to be events of 'national importance and cultural significance' that must be offered first to free-to-air broadcasters, rather than exclusively captured by subscription television, in order to maximize audience access in the interests of national cultural citizenship (Rowe 2016). However, the national men's team, the Wallabies, and the sport's premier event, the World Cup, are present on the current anti-siphoning list as presented in Table 7.1 below.[2]

Table 7.1 Rugby union in the Australian anti-siphoning regime

New list	Change from previous list
	Removal of
International test matches involving Australia, played in Australia or New Zealand	International test matches involving Australia, played in South Africa or Europe
	Removal of
Matches of the World Cup involving Australia, and the final	Quarter-finals and semi-finals of the World Cup not involving Australia

Source: Australian Government, Department of Communication and Arts (2017)

The 'nationing' role of rugby union is clearly critical in the context of the cultural citizenship concerns of the anti-siphoning regime (Rowe 2016), but not in this case at the level of domestic or club-based sporting competition (as is also the case for association football). It indicates how representing the nation in the domain of international sport is an especially important contribution to national culture. It is at this inflexion point that the projection of symbols of nation meets the mediated commercial sport spectacle involving a sport that was formally amateur only a little over two decades ago.

Furthermore, the federal government provides significant support to rugby union in Australia through programs and targeted funding by the Australian Sports Commission (ASC) and its high-performance entity, the Australian Institute of Sport (AIS). Again, the key motivating factor is the sport-nation nexus as exemplified by elite international competition. The self-described 'game plan', *Australia's Winning Edge*, is

> a collaborative effort led by the ASC with key partners in the sport sector, and builds on the National Sport and Active Recreation Policy Framework (the Policy Framework) [signed by all state and territory governments] and National Institute System Intergovernmental Agreement.
> (Australian Government 2012, p. 5)

In explaining 'Why international sporting success matters', *Australia's Winning Edge* proposes a range of justifications, from pride in nation to economic development, and from the winning of medals at major international sporting competitions to grassroots activity:

> High performance success is not only good for our athletes and our sense of national pride, it also contributes to other important Government objectives in areas such as participation, economic development, health and education.
> While Australia's Winning Edge is focused on high performance sport, the connection this has to grassroots participation is well established. Participation will continue to be a key focus area for Australian, state and territory governments.
> (p. 3)

In the particular case of rugby union, the 2013–14 investment allocation almost doubled from the previous year (91.2 percent) in recognition of:

> the inclusion of rugby 7s in the Olympic Games and our women's team as the current world champions. Funding will be prioritised to the women's pathway and an additional one-off $500,000 investment will be provided to establish a National Centre of Excellence with the expectation that Australian Rugby Union will co-invest.
> (Australian Government 2013)

This public-private investment model, familiar in non-sporting arenas, connects two tiers of government with a national sports organization supported by a range of commercial sponsors and financial arrangements. It also involves a mobile elite sporting labour force in which athletes move between codes of football and/or countries (for example, in Australia Israel Folau has moved to rugby union from rugby league via Australian rules football, and Sam Burgess from rugby league in England and then Australia to rugby union in England and back to rugby league in Australia).[3] Attempts to inhibit player movement in the interests of national club and representative team quality (by requiring rugby union players to play in Australia in order to be eligible for the Wallabies) have met considerable resistance, and resulted in some relaxation of current eligibility requirements (Australian Associated Press 2015). These, though, are not decisions of government, but are exercised by the national sporting organization, the ARU, in consultation with the Chief Executive Officers of the Australian Super Rugby franchises. They are made in response to tensions within the sport field between transnational athletes (Carter 2011), nation-based sport organizations, national and state governments, trans/international capital (especially media) and sport fans.

Such power struggles within the Australian sport field are implicated also in those between and across fields – notably that of the media. Rugby union in Australia, therefore, can be viewed as not only shaped by its positioning in the 'space of sports' (Bourdieu 1988, p. 154), but in the relations between that space and those that overlap with and impinge upon it (including the spaces of pedagogy, finance, mediation and governance). Mapping these complex field coordinates enables trends, conflicts and strategic accommodation to be discerned, as has been proposed here between national representative sport and transnational media sport capital. These synergies and contestations are manifest within any conceptualization of the Australian sport field, but their diverse entanglements require corresponding empirical inquiry and evidentiary corroboration.

The 2015 Australian Cultural Fields survey provides some indications of the current socio-cultural positioning of rugby union in the country. Among survey respondents, 61.2 per cent never play organized sport, and only 21 percent play sport once a week or more. Sport club membership also involved a minority of the population (32.8 per cent). These data are consistent with longstanding patterns of sports participation and involvement, despite successive campaigns to raise them in the interests of population health and social cohesion (McKay et al. 2000). Within the minority of the population that is involved in organized sport

Table 7.2 Involvement in rugby union by sex

		No	Yes	Total
	Male	575	18	593
		97.0%	3.0%	100.0%
	Female	597	13	610
		97.9%	2.1%	100.0%
Total		1172	31	1203
		97.4%	2.6%	100.0%

Source: Australian Cultural Tastes Survey

(as participants or in non-playing roles such as coaching or committee membership), rugby union (2.6 per cent) comes last among the football codes – the most direct comparative reference points – behind association football (12.2 per cent), Australian rules football (10 per cent) and rugby league (4.5 per cent). This low sport involvement level is exacerbated when gender, education and income are taken into account. In rugby union, only 2.1 per cent of those surveyed were women involved in rugby union (see Table 7.2), compared with association football (7.6 per cent), Australian rules football (7.2 per cent) and rugby league (2.8 per cent). Among people who had completed their education at secondary level, 1.6 per cent were involved in rugby union, compared to 3.7 per cent with postgraduate education. Strikingly, only 1.5 per cent of those with an income below AU$40,000 were involved in rugby union, compared with 9.5 per cent of those with incomes above AU$200,000 (Table 7.3). Thus, in the Australian sport field, among the minority of those involved in sport, rugby union is even more of a minority, and is skewed towards affluent men.

Regarding watching rugby union live through the media (and its relationship to national cultural citizenship discussed earlier), 24.2 per cent of those who considered themselves to be working class did so, compared with 40.5 per cent of the self-described upper middle class (see Table 7.4). By comparison, 45.5 per cent of those who considered themselves to be working class watched rugby league, compared with 38.6 per cent of the upper middle class. While the fact that Super League matches are not available on free-to-air television may have depressed rugby union's working-class viewership on grounds of cost, it is notable that association football, which has little free-to-air television coverage in Australia, registered 39.8 per cent of the self-described working class among its viewership, alongside 42.7 per cent of the upper middle class in the survey. Therefore, by a range of measures, rugby union's status as a 'gentleman's game' has been maintained to a degree, although it is apparent that it has a substantial following among those who cannot be counted among Australia's social elite.

These data in the main confirm rugby union's traditional positioning – advanced by Bourdieu (1988, p. 156) among others, despite his determination 'to avoid the errors due to directly connecting a sport and a group, as suggested by ordinary intuition' – as a relatively 'upper-class', male-oriented sport. In this regard, there

Table 7.3 Total annual household income from all sources and involvement in rugby union (in Australian dollars)

	No	Yes	Total
–$29,999	133	2	135
	98.5%	1.5%	100.0%
$30,000–39,999	67	0	67
	100.0%	0.0%	100.0%
$40,000–59,999	122	3	125
	97.6%	2.4%	100.0%
$60,000–79,999	133	3	136
	97.8%	2.2%	100.0%
$80,000–99,999	137	2	139
	98.6%	1.4%	100.0%
$100,000–149,999	196	4	200
	98.0%	2.0%	100.0%
$150,000–199,999	107	2	109
	98.2%	1.8%	100.0%
$200,000	86	9	95
	90.5%	9.5%	100.0%
Don't Know	191	5	196
	97.4%	2.6%	100.0%
Total	1172	30	1202
	97.5%	2.5%	100.0%

Source: Australian Cultural Tastes Survey

has been some resistance or inertia in its transformation to popular spectacle after its professionalization. However, the men's national team attracts a substantial media viewership to major matches, such as the 2015 World Cup final in London between Australia and the New Zealand which, despite occurring in the early hours in the southern hemisphere, drew a live audience of 501,000 to the commercial Nine Network and 292,000 to pay-television channel Fox Sports 2 (Ward 2015) out of approximately eight million households. Just as in France (Bourdieu's homeland), where matches involving the national team in the 2015 World Cup averaged 8.5 million viewers (out of approximately 25 million households) in a much more viewer-friendly time zone (Ward 2015), the sport assembles a large, commercially attractive live audience to watch the nation compete with others in an event sponsored both by national governments and multi-national corporations.

Conclusion: continuities and discontinuities

Bourdieu's view of sport in general, and of rugby union in particular, is that of a fairly unidirectional passage from folk game to rationalized elite play to mass cultural form, while allowing for some national-contextual variations. It is unclear, though, whether changes to the sport field are caused by predominantly endogenous or endogamous factors – as noted earlier by Dine (2014), rugby union in

Table 7.4 Nominated social class and watching rugby union live through the media

	No	Yes	Total
Working class	338	108	446
	75.8%	24.2%	100.0%
Middle class	371	149	520
	71.3%	28.7%	100.0%
Upper middle class	78	53	131
	59.5%	40.5%	100.0%
Other class identity	74	23	97
	76.3%	23.7%	100.0%
Don't know class identity	7	1	8
	87.5%	12.5%	100.0%
Total	868	334	1202
	72.2%	27.8%	100.0%

Source: Australian Cultural Tastes Survey

France is a British import. It has been 'customized' there under local conditions but, as has also already been observed, national sport fields – including France's and Australia's – are profoundly influenced by transnational and global forces. Rugby union in Australia and elsewhere has changed dramatically since the mid-1990s in response to internal and external pressures, but it is essential to reflect on the historically conditioned continuities that may co-exist with the sport's transformations. For example, has rugby union retained its appeal to the 'dominant fractions of the dominant class' in spite of what Bourdieu sees as its industrialization, brutalization and, perhaps, proletarianization?

Certainly, its followers are still routinely described in the media as dominated by 'the leather patch brigade' (that is, as affluent, middle-aged men – see, for example, Massoud 2011). More kindly, this point was emphasized during the 2013 tour by the British and Irish Lions, with Andrew McEvoy, Managing Director of Tourism Australia, remarking that, 'There is research that suggests rugby fans are high-spending. So when they have time between matches you will see them in [wine tourism] places like the Hunter Valley in NSW and Mornington Peninsula outside of Melbourne' (in Stensholt 2013). Similarly, the Chief Executive of Destination NSW, Sandra Chipchase, said, 'The food and wine trail is very popular. This is a group that is used to eating well and drinking well' (Carroll 2013). Indeed, it can be argued that it was the creation of sporting spectacle facilitated by the sport's professionalization that has fostered such 'high-end', globally mobile sport tourism consumption (see Gibson's chapter (9) in this volume for a broader discussion of tourism and cultural taste).

Rugby union, a component of the Australian sport field that still retains elements of a diminishing elite amateur ethos, has in common with other sports a disconnection from the primary concerns of *Creative Nation*. Yet, in some regards it has travelled along a parallel path with other cultural fields, such as visual art, music and literature, that the national cultural policy did embrace and which are discussed elsewhere in this book. A settler-colonial import, at its apex rugby union signifies the nation, while being increasingly underpinned by the marketization and commercialization propelled by transnational and global forces. It is pervaded by a sense of crisis (Georgakis 2015) as it competes with agents in the national and international sports fields for athletic labour power, media attention and rights revenue, exemplary governance, corporate brand support, committed spectatorship, and government endorsement. Existential anxiety of this kind is inevitably produced by the abrasive process of contestation over power within and between cultural fields intricately cross-cut by the unforgiving demands of unstable markets and unsettled nations.

Therefore, only a little over two decades since it went fully professional, and despite hosting a highly successful Rugby World Cup in the early years of the new century, the game's position in the Australian sport field has become consistently associated with organizational pathology. As one veteran rugby union journalist has put it, 'Whatever crises other sports are going through lately, they at least can console themselves that they are not going as badly nor perceived as poorly as rugby union' (Smith 2017). Among its many problems is the decline of the game at the grassroots level and the ARU Board's decision to remove a franchise that it regards as unviable – the Perth-based Western Force. The latter action brought it into conflict with the mining billionaire Andrew Forrest, who threatened to establish a rival Indo Pacific Rugby Championship involving the Western Force and teams from Singapore, Malaysia, Sri Lanka, India, Hong Kong, China, South Korea, Japan, Fiji, Tonga and Samoa (Perry 2017).

This regional tension involving a national sport organization and a hybrid national/international competition is echoed in the sphere of the global mega media sport event, with the Council of World Rugby voting against an independent technical assessment and awarding the 2023 Rugby World Cup to France at the expense of the recommended host, South Africa – as already noted, host of the historic 1995 immediate post-Apartheid tournament – and the other host country competitor, Ireland. The principal reason, it was widely argued, was that:

> France's proposal reportedly guaranteed a net revenue return of [AU]$607 million for World Rugby to invest back into the game, compared to approximately [AU]$468 million from South Africa and Ireland.
>
> Wednesday's verdict has raised concerns that from now on, World Cups will become a matter of money.
>
> (Decent 2017).

This interconnectedness of culture and capital has significantly re-fashioned a sport that once celebrated its amateurism and its distinctive national sporting cultures into one that calculates the financial rates of return derived from deal-making within international peak bodies. It has necessarily implicated rugby union, as an important component of the Australian sport field, in the decision to take part in a major sport event in the northern hemisphere nation where, as noted, Bourdieu played and watched the game. As has been argued in this chapter, rugby union remains in some sense 'elite' while also being subject to the process of popularization described by Bourdieu. These characteristics are exhibited both within the Australian sport field and in its inter/transnational relations. In this respect, while sport is largely absent from *Creative Nation*, it has in common with other cultural forms the continuing need to juggle the awkward demands of 'nationing', inter/transnationalism, globalization and the commercial.

Notes

1 An aphorism attributed to various people, including Oscar Wilde and Winston Churchill, but judged by sport historian Sean Fagan (2013) to originate in a statement in the 1890s by the Chancellor of the University of Cambridge, who was seeking to distinguish rugby union and association football, with the latter implicitly called "a gentleman's game played by hooligans." (Fagan 2013)
2 The Coalition government introduced changes to the anti-siphoning list which removed matches played in South Africa or Europe and the quarter-finals and semi-finals of the World Cup not involving Australia. The Broadcasting Legislation Amendment (Broadcasting Reform) Bill 2017 gave effect to these changes through its final passage through both Houses on 16 October 2017 (Parliament of Australia 2017).
3 The substantial coverage of leading Australian rugby league player Jarryd Hayne's move to the US's National Football League, then to rugby Sevens with Fiji and back to rugby league in Australia, is one prominent case of wide-ranging sporting and geographical mobility (Meddows 2014; BBC 2016).

References

Allison, L., 2001. *Amateurism in sport: An analysis and defence*. London and New York: Routledge.
Australian Associated Press, 2015. ARU relaxes Wallabies eligibility rules, opens door to Matt Giteau for World Cup. *The Guardian*, 22 April. Available from: www.theguardian.com/sport/2015/apr/22/aru-relaxes-wallabies-eligibility-rules [Accessed 1 August 2015].
Australian Government, 2012. *Australia's Winning Edge, 2012–2022*. Canberra: Australian Sports Commission. Available from: www.ausport.gov.au/__data/assets/pdf_file/0011/509852/Australias_Winning_Edge.pdf [Accessed 1 November 2015].
Australian Government, 2013. *Australia's Winning Edge: Investment allocation*. Canberra: Australian Sports Commission. Available from: www.ausport.gov.au/__data/assets/pdf_file/0005/526154/Investment_Allocation_fact_sheet.pdf [Accessed 1 November 2015].
Australian Government, Department of Communication and Arts, 2017. Broadcast and content reform package. Available from: www.communications.gov.au/what-we-do/television/broadcast-and-content-reform-package [Accessed 29 November 2017].
BBC, 2016. Jarryd Hayne: Former NFL player returns to rugby league with Gold Coast Titans, 3 August. Available from: www.bbc.com/sport/rugby-league/36963783 [Accessed 20 November 2017].
Billings, A. C., Brown, N., Brown, K., Guo, Q., Leeman, M., Licen, S., Novak, D. and Rowe, D., 2013. From pride to smugness and the nationalism between: Olympic media consumption effects on nationalism across the globe. *Mass Communication & Society*, 16(6), 910–932.
Bourdieu, P., 1988. Program for a sociology of sport. *Sociology of Sport Journal*, 5, 153–161.

Bourdieu, P., 2010, 1984. *Distinction: A social critique of the judgement of taste*. London and New York: Routledge.

Calhoun, C., 2007. Pierre Bourdieu. *In*: G. Ritzer, ed. *The Blackwell companion to major contemporary social theorists*. Malden, MA: Wiley-Blackwell, 274–309.

Carroll, L., 2013. Lion pride: Thousands of rugby fans descend on city. *The Sydney Morning Herald*, 15 June. Available from: www.smh.com.au/national/lion-pride-thousands-of-rugby-fans-descend-on-city-20130614-2o9lw.html [Accessed 10 November 2015].

Carter, T., 2011. *In foreign fields: The politics and experiences of transnational sport migration*. London: Pluto Press.

Collins, T., 2006. *Rugby's great split: Class, culture and the origins of rugby league football* (2nd ed.). London and New York: Routledge.

Collins, T., 2008. 'The first principle of our game': The rise and fall of amateurism: 1886–1995. *In*: G. Ryan, ed. *The changing face of rugby: The union game and professionalism since 1995*. Newcastle: Cambridge Scholars Press, 1–18.

Colman, M., 1996. *Super league: The inside story*. Sydney: Pan Macmillan Australia.

Commonwealth of Australia, 1994. *Creative nation: Commonwealth cultural policy* (revised ed.). Canberra: Department of Communications and the Arts. Available from: http://pandora.nla.gov.au/pan/21336/20031011-0000/www.nla.gov.au/creative.nation/contents.html [Accessed 1 August 2015].

Decent, T., 2017. Money talks as France named hosts of 2023 Rugby World Cup. *The Sydney Morning Herald*, 16 November. Available from: www.smh.com.au/rugby-union/union-news/money-talks-as-france-named-hosts-of-2023-rugby-world-cup-20171115-gzme38.html [Accessed 26 November 2017].

Dine, P., 2014. Une certaine idée du rugby: Sport, media and identity in a 'glocalised' game. *French Cultural Studies*, 25(1), 54–69.

Fagan, S., 2013. A gentleman's game played by hooligans. *Saints and Heathens.com: Rugby#Australia#History*, 30 September. Available from: https://saintsandheathens.wordpress.com/ [Accessed 4 November 2015].

FitzSimons, P., 2003. *The rugby war*. Sydney: HarperSports.

Georgakis, S., 2015. Four reasons rugby union in Australia is struggling: Despite the Wallabies' success. *The Conversation*, 30 October. Available from: https://theconversation.com/four-reasons-rugby-union-in-australia-is-struggling-despite-the-wallabies-success-49741 [Accessed 4 August 2017].

Goldblatt, D., 2007. *The ball is round: A global history of football*. London: Penguin Books.

Goldlust, J., 1987. *Playing for keeps: Sport, the media and society*. Melbourne: Longman Cheshire.

Grenfell, M., 2015. Pierre Bourdieu on sport. *In*: R. Giulianotti, ed. *Routledge handbook of the sociology of sport*. London and New York: Routledge, 61–71.

Haigh, G., 2007. *The cricket war: The inside story of Kerry Packer's World Series Cricket*. Melbourne: Melbourne University Press.

Hargreaves, J., 1986. *Sport, power and culture*. Cambridge: Polity.

Invictus, 2009. Film. Directed by Clint Eastwood. USA: Warner Brothers.

Jackson, S. J., ed., 2014. *The other sport mega-event: Rugby World Cup 2011*. London: Routledge.

Massoud, J., 2011. League and union heavyweights watch two games collide in hybrid clash between St Augustine's and Keebra Park. *The Daily Telegraph*, 12 May. Available from: www.dailytelegraph.com.au/sport/nrl/league-and-union-heavyweights-watch-two-games-collide-in-hybrid-clash-between-st-augustines-and-keebra-high/story-e6frexnr-1226054535930 [Accessed 10 November 2015].

McKay, J., Hughson, J., Lawrence, G. and Rowe, D., 2000. Sport and Australian society. *In*: J. Najman and J. Western, eds. *Sociology of Australian society: Introductory readings* (3rd ed.). Melbourne: Macmillan, 275–300.

McKay, J. and Miller, T. 1991. From old boys to men and women of the corporation: The Americanization and commodification of Australian sport. *Sociology of Sport Journal*, 8(1), 86–94.

Meddows, D., 2014. Jarryd Hayne quits NRL for NFL: Fans react with shock. *The Daily Telegraph*, 15 October. Available from: www.dailytelegraph.com.au/sport/nrl/teams/eels/jarryd-hayne-quits-nrl-for-nfl-fans-react-with-shock/news-story/fb8a9919949c-b45a4cb353ed51ec90c5 [Accessed 20 November 2017].

Miller, T., Lawrence, G., McKay, J. and Rowe, D., 2001. *Globalization and sport: Playing the world*. London: Sage Publications.

Parliament of Australia, 2017. Broadcasting legislation amendment (broadcasting reform) bill 2017. Available from: www.aph.gov.au/Parliamentary_Business/Bills_Legislation/Bills_Search_Results/Result?bId=r5907 [Accessed 20 November 2017].

Perry, J., 2017. Andrew Forrest still positive about prospects for proposed Indo Pacific Rugby Championship. Available from: www.abc.net.au/news/2017-10-27/forrest-reveals-new-details-indo-pacific-rugby-championship/9094110 [Accessed 20 November 2017].

Richards, H., 2006. A game for hooligans: The history of rugby union: Edinburgh and London: Mainstream. *ABC News*, 27 October. www.abc.net.au/news/2017-10-27/forrest-reveals-new-details-indo-pacific-rugby-championship/9094110

Rowe, D., 1995. *Popular cultures: Rock music, sport and the politics of pleasure*. London: Sage Publications.

Rowe, D., 2011. *Global media sport: Flows, forms and futures*. London and New York: Bloomsbury Academic.

Rowe, D., 2016. 'Great markers of culture': The Australian sport field. *Media International Australia*, 158(1), 26–36.

Smith, W., 2017. Rugby's humiliating crisis deepens. *The Weekend Australian*, 7 August. Available from: www.theaustralian.com.au/sport/opinion/wayne-smith/something-good-has-to-come-out-of-rugbys-unholy-mess/news-story/7e4347857ffdc656bfdd07b66 4cc5311 [Accessed 20 November 2017].

Steen, R., 2014. *Floodlights and touchlines: A history of spectator sport*. London: Bloomsbury.

Stensholt, J., 2013. Lions tour a winner for tourism industry. *Australian Financial Review*, 25 February. Available from: www.afr.com/lifestyle/lions-tour-a-winner-for-tourism-industry-20130224-je8pn [Accessed 10 November 2015].

Ward, S., 2015. Healthy TV audiences for final as 2015 Rugby World Cup hailed as 'biggest and best' yet. *Sportcal*, 2 November. Available from: www.sportcal.com/News/news_free_article.aspx?articleID=108037&source=e&cid=99860 [Accessed 10 November 2015].

Wenner, L. A., ed., 1998. *MediaSport*. London: Routledge.

Part 2
Across cultural fields

8 'Crossing the technical rubicon'
Marketizing culture and fields of the digital[1]

Brett Hutchins

Introduction

> Information technology, and all that it now offers, has crossed the technical rubicon into the realm of consciousness, to the realm of culture. Multi-media today gives us instruments which allow us to shape information in so many forms that they can become an integral part of our life's experience.
>
> (Commonwealth of Australia 1994, n.p.)

Presented under the heading of 'Multi-media: Cultural Production in an Information Age', the above statement in the 1994 national cultural policy, *Creative Nation*, combines insight into the likely impacts of digital media and communications on the cultural industries with a dash of technophilia. The timing and tone of this policy are important markers of a period in which the Internet was popularly narrated as a revolutionary catalyst for self-expression, consciousness and personal freedom. For instance, the ground-breaking Mosaic graphical web browser had been launched just a year earlier, making the experience of surfing the World Wide Web both more pleasurable and widely available. The mid-1990s also signalled the 'moment of *Wired*', a magazine and brand that popularized digital technologies through a heady mix of hyperbole, romanticism and faux counter-cultural sentiments (Streeter 2011). *Wired's* stories and headlines promoted a quixotic worldview in which networked computing somehow made it possible simultaneously to 'change the world, overthrow hierarchy, express yourself, *and* get rich' (Streeter 2011, p. 133; emphasis in the original).

Despite a shared focus on the 'information superhighway', the differences between the futures envisioned by *Creative Nation* and *Wired* are unmistakable. *Creative Nation* articulated a necessary and ongoing role for the state and policy in the production, circulation and promotion of Australian national culture, both at home and abroad, encompassing the broadcasting, telecommunications, film, television and information technology sectors, amongst others. Digital media and communications are forms, networks and infrastructures to be leveraged in support of this goal. In contrast, the consumer technology boosters at *Wired*, and their fellow travellers on the NASDAQ stock exchange, promulgated a future in which governments are rendered obsolete by a utopian form of 'good capitalism' (Streeter

2015, p. 3108). This mode of capitalism promised to unleash the transformative power of an aggressively individualist, free market, hi-tech entrepreneurial ethos on a global scale (Marwick 2013; Streeter 2011). Digital innovation – or, more accurately, 'novelty in technology' (Arthur cited in Banks 2012, p. 159) – *is* culture in this formulation, as entrepreneurs collude with venture capital to 'change the world' and to disrupt existing social, cultural and political systems.

The problem with this position is that the individualist model of hi-tech capitalism prevailed, capturing the cultural and political imagination and giving rise to a powerful 'Silicon Valley ethos' (Levina and Hasinoff 2017). Fine words about the importance of the cultural and creative industries, as broadly conceived, have been expressed by political leaders in Australia and elsewhere over the years. But, with varying levels of enthusiasm, successive governments have subscribed to a formula in which the circulation and expression of national culture through digital media is the *de facto* result of the state 'getting out of the way' of market actors. Under this formula, benign neglect somehow releases the energies of networked digital communications, democratizing online expression and fostering user-generated content (a stance that ultimately benefitted US-based global corporate behemoths such as Facebook, Apple, Amazon, Netflix and Alphabet [Google's parent company]). Nation-state intervention is, from this perspective, limited to commercial incentives to stimulate investment and market activity in the cultural industries, thereby encouraging digital innovation and the export of products, platforms and services to the region and world. It is an approach that has delivered uneven outcomes at best, as the spluttering performance of the video games development industry indicates (Commonwealth of Australia 2016; Keogh 2017). Indeed, the current Australian Prime Minister, Malcolm Turnbull, embodies both this trajectory and the 'animal spirits' of the early web. Turnbull invested in the Internet Service Provider, OzEmail, in 1994 and became its Chairman. He was AU$60 million wealthier after the company's sale in 1999 to the ill-fated WorldCom, watching on as the 'dot com bubble' burst in 2000 and 2001 (Head 2002). Turnbull, at the time of writing (December 2017), leads an embattled federal government devoid of an articulated national cultural policy, let alone one that considers the role of digital media in maintaining a distinctive national culture.

This chapter approaches *Creative Nation* as a 'symbolic text' that is 'a marker of social, technological and economic shifts' (Homan 2016, p. 39), particularly given the historical intersection between its release and the popular excitement that surrounded the World Wide Web in the 1990s. This landmark policy is used to analyse why a clear vision of the interdependence between digital and online media and the explicit development of national culture through policy has fallen by the wayside. This capacity was central to government thinking in 1994, built on a foundational assumption:

> If, as a nation, we can create a vibrant multi-media industry, we will go a long way to ensuring that we have a stake in the new world order yet retain a distinctly Australian culture.
>
> (Commonwealth of Australia 1994, n.p.)

Given the social and cultural foundations of technology (MacKenzie and Wajcman 1999), digital media and communications promised significant rewards for the nation and its cultural industries if supported in a sustained and strategically coherent fashion. However, culture has been ignored as a key policy priority in the years that have followed, as digital media and communications became overdetermined by an interlocking corporate investment, trade and market agenda (O'Connor 2016). The neglect commenced in earnest after the election of the John Howard-led Coalition national government in 1996, followed by a series of Labor and Coalition governments in the ensuing decades.[2]

The case presented in this chapter begins by outlining why 'fields of the digital' is a useful concept in thinking through the relationship between cultural production and digital media. In its support for a nationally focused set of cultural industries, *Creative Nation* is positioned as an example of why an evolving sense of national culture and identity needs to be maintained in the face of globalizing media and commercial forces and the effects of failing to do so. Actively supported and/or encouraged by government, these effects have resulted in the subjugation of culture to economic interests under a market framework, resulting in a wholesale capture of digital innovation by the logic of capital. The chapter concludes by suggesting that, in terms of federal government policy settings around digital media and communications, culture is now little more than a by-product of Science, Technology, Engineering, and Mathematics (STEM)-dominated national innovation agenda and economic productivity concerns.

In an effort to comprehend this lamentable state of affairs, attention now turns to French sociologist, Pierre Bourdieu, and his concept of field. Bourdieu, it should be noted, did not analyse technology in a systematic fashion, meaning that the following discussion draws on applications, adaptations and critiques of field theory in the context of media-related industries, practices and communications (Benson and Neveu 2005a, 2005b; Bourdieu 2005; Couldry 2012; Hesmondhalgh 2006; Homan 2016; Ignatow and Robinson 2017; Marlière 1998; Thompson 1995).

Fields of the digital

Presented as part of a theoretical tripartite framework alongside capital and habitus, Bourdieu's (1993) concept of field is helpful in identifying why a limited conception of the relationship between digital media, culture and policy persists. 'The digital' exists at multiple scales, across intersecting sites, and possesses variable features. The field is necessarily transformed into dynamically interlaced and multiplying fields, drawing in an array of technological infrastructures, cultural and economic activities and communications and media practices. These elements vary in scale, encompassing cultural production and consumption, national network construction and policy-making, and trade policies and intellectual property frameworks. A substantive and consistent vision of the public good and of cultural value is, therefore, essential in articulating the role and function of national culture in relation to transnational digital information flows and the multinational private interests that channel and commodify them. The need for an active state and policy sector is underlined by economic asymmetries between the resources available to global technology corporations and to many national governments. For instance, the combined cash reserves of Apple, Microsoft, Alphabet/Google, Cisco and Oracle are estimated to be over US$500 billion (AU$650 billion), compared with the AU$66 billion (US$47 billion) held in Australia's foreign reserves at the end of 2015 (McDonald 2016).[3]

'Fields of the digital' signals a rethinking of how fields interact, intimating the existence of countless intermeshed fields that are, to differing degrees, structured by and/or embedded in digital communications networks (cf. Ignatow and Robinson 2017). By way of contrast, Bourdieu's theory is based on an account of modernity in which the social world is subject to identifiable differentiation into specialized spheres of action – politics, economics, journalism, religion, education etc. – that exhibit degrees of autonomy, semi-autonomy and interdependence vis-à-vis other fields over time (Couldry 2012; Hallin 2005). Bourdieu's account adheres to the 'heavy' institutional logics of the nation-state as expressed under the conditions of industrialism. However, the rise of informationalism and transnational digital communications introduces a more fluid or 'liquid' set of social relations, as expressed through the logics and morphology of the network (Bauman 2000; Castells 2000). In a mediatized age, the problem is to understand how fields interact dynamically given the role of media and networked communications in and across almost every field. As media theorist Stig Hjarvard (2013) states:

> we find that the media occupy a prominent place in a growing number of fields' heteronomous poles, thereby challenging those fields' autonomous poles. Thus, the degree of mediatization may be measured according to how much the respective field's [sic] autonomous pole has weakened. The media, too, have autonomous and heteronomous poles.
>
> (p. 40)

Fields now operate in parallel and interdependently at different scales depending on the users and purposes of the communication networks in question. There were once 'fields inside fields inside fields (like a series of Russian dolls) parallel to each other in their internal organisation' (Benson and Neveu 2005b, p. 4). The effects of digitalization and datafication mean that fields acquire relatively porous membranes that change shape and move in and out of each other, as well as expand and contract depending on the activities occurring in and around the network.

The challenge of digital media and communications is to make sense of increasingly extended chains of interdependence within and between fields (Elias 1978). The difficulty for the cultural industries is that governments and policy-makers have frequently ignored this challenge, opting instead to diminish the 'public good' by assessing it primarily in terms of wealth creation and commercial success (Turner 2012, p. 113). A similar story can also be told in the US, UK, many countries in Europe and parts of Asia and Latin America. The consolidation of 'neoliberalism as *doxa*' (Chopra 2003) was (and is) a simultaneously economic, political and cultural phenomenon. The ascendancy of the information technology, digital media and telecommunications sectors globally, combined with the ideological dominance of neo-liberal economic policies and governments, naturalized a new set of political arrangements and policies. These policy settings legitimated a 'grand contradiction' – 'a passion for [state] intervention in the name of non-intervention [in markets]' (Grantham and Miller 2010, p. 174). This process established a seemingly unassailable affinity between the policies thought necessary for technological innovation and high levels of privatization, deregulation of markets, the free flow of capital, falling levels of taxation and reduced wage costs (Couldry 2010, 2012; Dwyer 2010; Harvey 2005; Levina and Hasinoff 2017; Miller 2007; Rushkoff 2016).

Mark Andrejevic (2013) contends that the market now acts as 'the master algorithm' in an 'Internet-facilitated information society' (p. 64). Profit maximization equates with cultural authority, with this authority then reaching into 'the realms of the political and social' (pp. 64–65). A troubling self-legitimating logic is evident in this equation. From the viewpoint of the major tech-firms, it is self-evident that 'the market knows best' because the popularity of their hardware, software, networks, user-generated content, user-bases and advertising shows this to be the case.[4] But sitting beneath their quarterly reporting statements is the fact that companies and services such as Facebook, Snapchat and Apple are feeding voraciously on the raw material of mediatized cultures – communication, symbols, representations, stories, information, images, audio, individual and collective expression and creative communities of variable geography and durability. Few industries highlight this development more starkly than news media and journalism, in which powerful social media intermediaries cannibalize content and reorder the distribution of news by 'sharing analytics' and algorithmic processes (Dwyer and Martin 2017, p. 1095).

The term 'fields of the digital' highlights an apparent contradiction. At one level, the complexity of interactions within and between fields increases exponentially in relation to the growing size, density and use of digital media and communication networks, which are further complicated by newer sociotechnical assemblages such as mobile Internet and sensor-based networks (Andrejevic and Burdon 2015; Herman et al. 2015). This pattern, on the surface at least, makes it difficult for any single field to exercise a determining power over other fields. Yet, at another level, in the eyes of national policy-makers, the economic field exerts primary definitional force in the assessment and manifestation of cultural value across a vast range of activities, including broadcasting, publishing, film, news and games. This situation highlights why the role of governments and policy-makers continues to matter – they perform a major role in deciding how digital technologies are distributed and operate through funding and subsidies, research priorities, education systems, community-based media programs, regulation of media and telecommunications markets and the provision and allocation of network infrastructures. The consistent failure of governments to update and connect cultural policy agenda like *Creative Nation* to these mechanisms is not because of digital technologies *per se* or the complexity of mediatized cultural fields. It is, rather, about a lack of political will to harness the operation of digital media, and the intermeshed fields that flow through them, for anything other than marketized outcomes. The result is a prioritization of economistic categories such as efficiency, competitiveness, productivity and price signals that overwhelm attempts to promote distinctive forms of national cultural expression through policy development and implementation. This situation has continued even as loud voices have been raised from within the cultural, creative and arts sectors about the destructive effects of these categories on the priorities and resources required to enlarge 'the greater public good' (Eltham 2016, p. 2; see also Keep 2015; Schultz 2016).

Viewed through the lens of Bourdieu's sociological project, 'fields of the digital' speaks to how longer-term historical currents travel within emergent contemporary conditions. The communication dynamics made possible by digital media forms and practices since the 1990s are new and require sensitization to mediatization processes and specific forms of network power (Castells 2009; Couldry and Hepp 2017). But these dynamics are also subject to the institutional effects of a longstanding ideological compact between the state, corporations, financial institutions and markets, which exerts considerable force in privileging the economic above all else. In a lecture addressing the condition of the journalistic field delivered in Lyon in 1995, Bourdieu stated that 'all microcosms are constructed against the commercial', a development with threatening consequences not only for journalism but 'in every field' (Bourdieu 2005, p. 43). 'The commercial' presents this threat because:

> As Einsteinian physics tells us, the more energy a body has, the more it distorts the space around it, and a very powerful agent within a field can distort the whole space, cause the whole space to be organized in relation to itself.
>
> (p. 43)

The state of cultural policy in relation to digital media is, I argue, a manifestation of this threat and distortion in the network society. There is nothing 'natural' about the 'advertising-saturated, audience-ratings-driven media culture' that Bourdieu critiqued over two decades ago (Benson and Neveu 2005b, p. 2), nor about today's analytics driven – data mining – algorithmically governed – privacy-eroding digital media culture that perpetuates the systematic commodification of culture and everyday life (cf. Andrejevic 2013; Fuchs 2015; Morozov 2015; Mosco 2014).

An Australian Internet?

The significance of *Creative Nation* as Australia's first comprehensive national cultural policy cannot be underestimated. Its release represented a much-needed 'governmental framing of culture' that moved cultural policy out of the 'backwater' in which it had previously been trapped in many industrialized democracies (Cunningham 1992, p. 22). Nonetheless, *Creative Nation* has also been subject to fair criticism. It displays an occasionally defensive and ahistorical posture about the assault of 'homogenised international mass culture' (Rowe et al. 2016, p. 9). In the matter of accessing state funding schemes, it confirms an unhelpful 'majors-indie divide' that is biased towards the 'institutional heft' of major performing arts companies (Meyrick cited in Eltham 2016, p. 19).[5] It is also noticeably short on detail regarding copyright regulation given that it deals with 'multi-media' and the 'information superhighway' (Homan 2016, p. 39).[6]

Despite these and other weaknesses, *Creative Nation* confronts a difficult question in the early history of the World Wide Web, especially as the mid-1990s was a time when the swift diffusion of online communications fuelled teleological assumptions about the imminent hegemony of global media. Is it possible for government to support the construction or 'making' of national identity through digital and online media (cf. Turner 1994)? *Creative Nation*, in its treatment of multi-media, answers this question in the affirmative, declaring that 'it is what we put onto the [information] highway that really matters' (Commonwealth of Australia 1994, n.p.). This statement is accompanied by perceptive observations about the need to encourage 'dialogue and interaction between the creative and software communities' and a series of targeted measures. Areas identified include film (the Australian Film Commission), national cultural institutions (museums and galleries), broadcasting (the Australian Children's Television Foundation), telecommunications (the Telecommunications Policy Review), education (schools, tertiary institutions and the Australian Film, Television and Radio School) and industry (the Australian Multi-Media Enterprise).

The position advanced in *Creative Nation* is that government can and should support the continuing (re-)creation of national culture through digital media and communications. It is a prescient claim in light of social and political events in the years since, including the reinvigoration of assorted ethno- and religiously based nationalisms around the world and the prominence of political movements based on populist appeals to nationalism (e.g., France's National Front, the Bharatiya Janata Party in India, the Chavistas in Venezula, the Tea Party in the US, the UK Independence Party and Australia's One Nation). In consumer and tourism markets, national identities are now subject to appropriation and mobilization for branding purposes in an effort to 'sell' the nation for international consumption (Volcic and Andrejevic 2016; see also Chris Gibson's discussion of tourism in Chapter 9 of this volume). National factors also continue to display resilience in television industries and systems, informed by a range of cultural, linguistic, market and technological variables (Turner 2009; Turner and Tay 2009).

Digital and mobile scholar Gerard Goggin recognized fourteen years ago that there is, in fact, an 'Australian Internet' shaped by local, national, regional and global interactions and relations (2004, p. 5; see also Miller and Slater 2000). Discourses and experiences of the nation and the national are embedded in the way that people located in specific national and cultural contexts experience, use and understand the Internet and its manifold applications. These phenomena are fundamental to how users of the Australian Internet connect to 'international networks and media flows' and the ways in which contested national identities fit within these 'larger frames of reference' (Goggin 2004, pp. 6–8). The announcement of the *National* Broadband Network (NBN; my emphasis) in 2009 – 'the single largest nation building infrastructure project in Australian history' (Swan 2009) – offers symbolic and material endorsement of Goggin's argument. The network has since served as a site of sharply conflicting political visions about the role of the state, regulatory arrangements and private investment in nation-building efforts.[7] The controversy surrounding the NBN also connects to a recently rediscovered focus on the role of national media systems (e.g., in Australia, Brazil and China) in structuring media cultures and practices. Even in the midst of globalization processes, nation-states and national spaces remain central to how media businesses, markets and cultures operate because there is 'no inevitable, straightforward shift from the local and national to the global' (Flew and Waisbord 2015, p. 632).

It is a problematic time for national governments to neglect cultural policy given the threat and actuality of so-called digital disruption, which has imploded many reliable assessments of cost, labour inputs and commercial returns in relation to intellectual property in particular (e.g., book and magazine publishing, journalism, popular music, broadcasting; Mason 2016). A progressive and adaptable sense of national history and identity, and their associated forms of cultural expression, are arguably more important than ever under these conditions. A compelling example of advocacy for the value of government investment in national culture is offered by Australian writer, editor and academic Julianne Schultz in her 2016 Brian Johns Lecture. She displays an appreciation of how 'fields of the digital' trigger a high level of complexity in the flow of content and culture, as well as revealing a much older story about the exercise of market power in and across national territories.

Schultz explains that the largest and best-resourced technology corporations are able to leverage economies of scale in digitally networked media and markets. She uses the shorthand term and acronym 'the Age of F-A-A-N-G' (Facebook, Apple, Amazon, Netflix and Google) to emphasize the reach and influence of these companies. Their rapacious appetite for cultural content of all types means that national cultural institutions and industries are caught in a pincer movement. Pressing on one side are FAANG and their many competitors. In conjunction with highly mobile venture and private equity capital, these companies accumulate revenue and content by capturing and commodifying the media practices and experiences of millions of users:

> we are seeing a massive redistribution of wealth from the cultural sector, where meaning is created, to the technology sector, which has figured out how to market, distribute, reach and make money out of it in ways the cultural industries never imagined possible....
>
> What makes this different to say, the rise of the multinational firm of the middle years of the 20th century – the great corporations that sold energy, transport and consumer goods – is that culture and the art and craft of making meaning are at the heart of the new corporations....

The new mega profitable firms make their billions by capturing and creating meaning and belonging: personal information, news, video, copyright, education, music, and information that is the sinew of everyday life.

(Schultz 2016, n.p.)

The routine experience of shared culture is channelled towards commercial objectives by digital media services that, by design, eliminate the connective tissue of non-commodified civic and public spaces (Couldry and Turow 2014; Couldry and van Dijck 2015). Pressing on the other side are governments and politicians which, in their valorization of economic agenda, find it easier to attack or reduce the budgets of national cultural institutions such as the Australia Council and the Australian Broadcasting Corporation (ABC) than to intervene in markets. This mindset makes it more likely that an expanding set of cultural expressions, activities and identities will be captured and curated by FAANG and their ilk.

There is an irony in the situation outlined by Schultz. The intangible values of creativity, belonging and sharing long perpetuated by national cultural industries and institutions are the very same as those fetishized and commodified by connective media services such as Facebook, YouTube and Twitter (van Dijck 2013). The conclusion of Schultz's analysis recalls Bourdieu's critique of the distorting effects of 'the commercial' on every field, meaning that the purpose of cultural policy and funding by government needs to be defended and maintained or 'we will be reduced as citizens to passive consumers in a digital marketplace that values us only for our ability to pay' (Schultz 2016, n.p.).

Conclusion: the ideas boom (and bust)

The continuing absence of a national cultural policy leaves open the question of whether or how culture features in other government policies dealing with digital innovation and the technology sector. This is a subject deserving of a separate essay-length critique. The Department of Industry, Innovation and Science's *Australia's Digital Economy Update* (Australian Government 2016) and the *National Innovation and Science Agenda* (Australian Government 2015) both call for examination in this regard. These documents ignore the cultural industries as sites of meaningful innovation or implicitly reduce them to the status of by-products of an 'exciting' and 'agile' digital economy. The latter, in particular, is one of Prime Minister Turnbull's signature policies, featuring the dubious slogan 'Welcome to the Ideas Boom' on its cover (Australian Government 2015). It presents a vision of Silicon Valley-style entrepreneurialism taking root in Australia in which culture *is* venture capital, start-ups and a commercial 'innovation ecosystem' (p. 8). It is also a model based on a limited understanding of history, underestimating both the duration and scale of public sector involvement, investment and research in the founding and growth of the information technology and digital media industries in the US (Castells 2001; Lander and Schmidt 2017).

Taken from *Creative Nation*, the quotation presented at the outset of this chapter alludes to the crossing of the Rubicon River in Northern Italy by Julius Caesar and his army in 49 BC, which set off a chain of events that helped form the Roman Empire. By way of analogy, the Internet and the digital 'revolution' it unleashed represent the passing of a technical threshold. Media and communications and the 'realm of culture' are now mutually constituted to an unprecedented degree. Such ideas are reflected in the adaptation of Bourdieusian theory, or 'fields of the digital', in an effort to deal with the operation and social structuring effects of digital networks and media use. From a policy perspective, however, the Rubicon crossed in the mid-1990s was one in which culture became synonymous with marketization and economistic categories, fuelled by rapid expansions in information technology, digital media and telecommunications. For all its significance and good intentions, the seeds of this development are even embedded in the Introduction of *Creative Nation*: 'This cultural policy is also an economic policy. Culture creates wealth' (Commonwealth of Australia 1994, n.p.). The trouble is that, in the subsequent absence of a detailed and evolving national cultural policy, private wealth creation is the governing logic of culture in the digital age.

Notes

1 An Australian Research Council (ARC) Future Fellowship (FT130100506) supported the research presented in this chapter.
2 Although a serious effort was made to redress this state of affairs in March 2013 with the launch of the national cultural policy *Creative Australia* (Commonwealth of Australia 2013) by the then Federal Minister for the Arts, Simon Crean. Unfortunately, Crean was sacked from his ministerial post just 12 days after the launch of *Creative Australia* following a botched Labor Party leadership spill. His government was voted out of office six months later. *Creative Australia* was disregarded by the incoming Coalition government and, especially, its new Arts Minister, George Brandis, and then scrapped altogether in the 2014–15 budget.
3 Apple's cash reserves alone were estimated to be US$215.7 billion (AU$279 billion) in 2015.
4 Conveniently ignoring the political, civic, legal, environmental, market competition, privacy and security issues that flow from this situation.
5 This ongoing divide arguably helped set the scene for the actions of the then Arts Minister, George Brandis, in 2016. Funded by cuts to the Australia Council, Brandis set up a (now partially defunct) National Program for Excellence in the Arts that favoured the large companies. Ben Eltham (2016, p. 1) offers a vivid account of the 'bloodbath' that occurred on 13 May 2016 because of this policy preference. Referred to as 'Black Friday' within the arts sector, 65 organizations were defunded and over 100 others were informed that their four-year funding applications had been unsuccessful.
6 In 2013, the issue of copyright was revisited in the aforementioned then Labor government's *Creative Australia* policy (Homan 2016; Commonwealth of Australia 2013).
7 A theme satirized by the Australian television comedy series *Utopia* (www.abc.net.au/tv/programs/utopia/).

References

Andrejevic, M., 2013. *Infoglut: How too much information is changing the way we think and know*. New York: Routledge.
Andrejevic, M. and Burdon, M., 2015. Defining the sensor society. *Television and New Media*, 16(1), 19–36.

Australian Government, 2015. *National innovation and science agenda report.* Canberra, ACT: Australian Government.

Australian Government, 2016. *Australia's digital economy update.* Canberra, ACT: Department of Industry, Innovation and Science.

Banks, J., 2012. The iPhone as innovation platform: Reimagining the videogames developer. *In*: L. Hjorth, J. Burgess and I. Richardson, eds. *Studying mobile media: Cultural technologies, mobile communication, and the iPhone.* New York: Routledge, 155–172.

Bauman, Z., 2000. *Liquid modernity.* Cambridge, UK: Polity Press.

Benson, R. and Neveu, E., eds., 2005a. *Bourdieu and the journalistic field.* Cambridge, UK: Polity Press.

Benson, R. and Neveu, E., 2005b. Introduction: Field theory as a work in progress. *In*: R. Benson and E. Neveu, eds. *Bourdieu and the journalistic field.* Cambridge, UK: Polity Press, 2–25.

Bourdieu, P., 1993. *The field of cultural production: Essays on art and literature.* Cambridge, UK: Polity Press.

Bourdieu, P., 2005. The political field, the social science field, and the journalistic field. *In*: R. Benson and E. Neveu, eds. *Bourdieu and the journalistic field.* Cambridge, UK: Polity Press, 29–47.

Castells, M., 2000. *The rise of the network society* (2nd ed.). Oxford, UK: Blackwell Publishers.

Castells, M., 2001. *The internet galaxy: Reflections on the internet, business, and society.* Oxford, UK: Oxford University Press.

Castells, M., 2009. *Communication power.* Oxford, UK: Oxford University Press.

Chopra, R., 2003. Neoliberalism as *doxa*: Bourdieu's theory of the state and the contemporary Indian discourse on globalization and liberalization. *Cultural Studies*, 17(3–4), 419–444.

Commonwealth of Australia, 1994. *Creative nation: Commonwealth cultural policy* (revised ed.). Canberra, ACT, Australia: Department of Communications and the Arts.

Commonwealth of Australia, 2013. *Creative Australia: National cultural policy.* Canberra, ACT, Australia: Office for the Arts.

Commonwealth of Australia, 2016. *Game on: More than playing around: The future of the Australia's video game development industry.* The Senate Environment and Communications References Committee, April.

Couldry, N., 2010. *Why voice matters: Culture and politics after neoliberalism.* London: Sage Publications.

Couldry, N., 2012. *Media, society, world.* Cambridge, UK: Polity Press.

Couldry, N. and Hepp, A., 2017. *The mediated construction of reality.* Cambridge, UK: Polity Press.

Couldry, N. and Turow, J., 2014. Advertising, big data, and the clearance of the public realm: Marketers' new approaches to the content subsidy. *International Journal of Communication*, 8, 1710–1726.

Couldry, N. and van Dijck, J., 2015. Researching social media as if the social mattered. *Social Media and Society*, 1(2), 1–7.

Cunningham, S., 1992. *Framing culture: Criticism and policy in Australia.* North Sydney, NSW: Allen and Unwin.

Dwyer, T., 2010. *Media convergence.* Maidenhead, Berkshire, UK: McGraw-Hill.

Dwyer, T. and Martin, F., 2017. Sharing news online: Social media news analytics and their implications for media pluralism policies. *Digital Journalism*, 5(8), 1080–1100.

Elias, N., 1978. *What is sociology?* London: Hutchinson.

Eltham, B., 2016. *When the goal posts move: Patronage, power and resistance in Australian cultural policy 2013–2016*, Platform Paper 48. Melbourne: Currency House.

Flew, T. and Waisbord, S., 2015. The ongoing significance of national media systems in the context of media globalization. *Media, Culture and Society*, 37(4), 620–636.

Fuchs, C., 2015. *Culture and economy in the age of social media*. New York: Routledge.

Goggin, G., 2004. Antipodean internet: Placing Australian networks. *In*: G. Goggin, ed. *Virtual nation: The internet in Australia*. Sydney: University of New South Wales Press, 2–12.

Grantham, B. and Miller, T., 2010. The end of neoliberalism. *Popular Communication*, 8(3), 174–177.

Hallin, D., 2005. Field theory, differentiation theory, and comparative media research. *In*: R. Benson and E. Neveu, eds. *Bourdieu and the journalistic field*. Cambridge, UK: Polity Press, 224–247.

Harvey, D., 2005. *A brief history of neoliberalism*. Oxford, UK: Oxford University Press.

Head, B., 2002. A decade of life with OzEmail. *Sydney Morning Herald*, 14 October. Available from: www.smh.com.au/articles/2002/10/14/1034561094085.html[Accessed 3 March 2017].

Herman, A., Hadlaw, J. and Swiss, T., 2015. Introduction: Theories of the mobile internet: Mobilities, assemblages, materialities and imaginaries. *In*: A. Herman, J. Hadlaw and T. Swiss, eds. *Theories of the mobile internet: Materialities and imaginaries*. New York: Routledge, 1–11.

Hesmondhalgh, D., 2006. Bourdieu, the media and cultural production. *Media, Culture and Society*, 28(2), 211–232.

Hjarvard, S., 2013. *The mediatization of culture and society*. London: Routledge.

Homan, S., 2016. A contemporary cultural policy for contemporary music? *Media International Australia*, 158, 37–47.

Ignatow, G. and Robinson, L., 2017. Pierre Bourdieu: Theorizing the digital. *Information, Communication and Society*, 20(7), 950–966.

Keep, E., 2015. Tech crunch: How the new corporation crushed the culture industries. *In*: P. McGuiness, ed. *Copyfight*. Sydney: New South Publishing, 54–67.

Keogh, B., 2017. Australia's videogames are inventive, acclaimed and world-class, so where's the government support? *The Conversation*, 30 May. Available from: https://theconversation.com/australias-videogames-are-inventive-acclaimed-and-world-class-so-wheres-the-government-support-78465 [Accessed 11 June 2017].

Lander, E. S. and Schmidt, E. E., 2017. America's 'miracle machine' is in desperate need of, well, a miracle. *The Washington Post*, 5 May. Available from: www.washingtonpost.com/opinions/americas-miracle-machine-is-in-desperate-need-of-well-a-miracle/2017/05/05/daafbe6a-30e7-11e7-9534-00e4656c22aa_story.html?utm_term=.edfd4ee688bf [Accessed 6 May 2017].

Levina, M. and Hasinoff, A. A., 2017. The Silicon Valley ethos: Tech industry products, discourses, and practices. *Television and New Media*, 18(6), 489–495.

MacKenzie, D. and Wajcman, J., 1999. Introductory essay: The social shaping of technology. *In*: D. MacKenzie and J. Wajcman, eds. *The social shaping of technology* (2nd ed.). Buckingham, UK: Open University Press, 3–27.

Marlière, P., 1998. The rules of the journalistic field: Pierre Bourdieu's contribution to the sociology of media. *European Journal of Communication*, 13(2), 219–234.

Marwick, A. E., 2013. *Status update: Celebrity, publicity, and branding in the social media age*. New Haven, CT: Yale University Press.

Mason, P., 2016. *Postcapitalism: A guide to our future*. London: Penguin Books.

McDonald, H., 2016. Taxing times as tech giants shift profits. *The Saturday Paper*, 28 May. Available from: www.thesaturdaypaper.com.au/world/north-america/2016/05/28/taxing-times-tech-giants-shift-profits/14643576003297 [Accessed 28 May 2016].

Miller, D. and Slater, D., 2000. *The internet: An ethnographic approach*. London: Routledge.
Miller, T., 2007. *Cultural citizenship: Cosmopolitanism, consumerism, and television in a neoliberal age*. Philadelphia, PA: Temple University Press.
Morozov, E., 2015. Socialize the data centres! *New Left Review*, 91, 45–66.
Mosco, V., 2014. *To the cloud: Big data in a turbulent world*. Boulder, CO: Paradigm Publishers.
O'Connor, J., 2016. *After the creative industries: Rhetoric and reality in twenty-first century Australian culture*, Platform Paper 47. Melbourne: Currency House.
Rowe, D., Noble, G., Bennett, T. and Kelly, M., 2016. Transforming cultures? From *Creative Nation* to *Creative Australia*. *Media International Australia*, 158, 6–16.
Rushkoff, D., 2016. *Throwing rocks at the google bus: How growth became the enemy of prosperity*. London: Portfolio Penguin.
Schultz, J., 2016. Australia must act now to preserve its culture in the face of global tech giants. 2016 Brian Johns Lecture. Republished by *The Conversation*, 2 May. Available from: https://theconversation.com/australia-must-act-now-to-preserve-its-culture-in-the-face-of-global-tech-giants-58724 [Accessed 2 May 2016].
Streeter, T., 2011. *The net effect: Romanticism, capitalism, and the internet*. New York: New York University Press.
Streeter, T., 2015. Steve Jobs, romantic individualism, and the desire for good capitalism. *International Journal of Communication*, 9, 3106–3124.
Swan, W., 2009. New national broadband network. Joint media release with Prime Minister, Minister for Finance, Minister for Broadband. *Australian government: The treasury*, 7 April. Available from: http://ministers.treasury.gov.au/DisplayDocs.aspx?doc=pressreleases/2009/036.htm&pageID=003&min=wms&Year=&DocType [Accessed 1 February 2017].
Thompson, J. B., 1995. *The media and modernity*. Cambridge, UK: Polity Press.
Turner, G., 1994. *Making it national: Nationalism and Australian popular culture*. St Leonards, NSW: Allen & Unwin.
Turner, G., 2009. Television and the nation: Does this matter anymore? *In*: G. Turner and J. Tay, eds. *Television studies after TV: Understanding television in the post-broadcast era*. London: Routledge, 54–64.
Turner, G., 2012. *What's become of cultural studies?* Thousand Oaks, CA: Sage Publications.
Turner, G. and Tay, J., eds., 2009. *Television studies after TV: Understanding television in the post-broadcast era*. London: Routledge.
van Dijck, J., 2013. *The culture of connectivity: A critical history of social media*. Oxford, UK: Oxford University Press.
Volcic, Z. and Andrejevic, M., eds., 2016. *Commercial nationalism: Selling the nation and nationalizing the sell*. Basingstoke, Hampshire, UK: Palgrave Macmillan.

9 Touring nation

The changing meanings of cultural tourism

Chris Gibson

Introduction

In this chapter, I revisit *Creative Nation* (Commonwealth of Australia 1994), with tourism at the forefront. When *Creative Nation* dealt with tourism, it was within the prism of a slightly naïve and nationalist version of the attractions of Australian life. Rather than merely promoting the location, however, *Creative Nation* was also about promoting a distinctive and confident Australian culture. Rural legacies lingered, with traditional Australian cultural touchstones such as the outback and Uluru, but it was moving, cautiously, towards other registers as well – typified by the use of Indigenous rock band Yothu Yindi in international promotions.

Two decades later, the nature of tourism has transformed considerably – as has the demography and cultural diversity of tourists themselves. In the context of globalization and transnationalism, boundaries between forms of mobility have blurred (Hannam et al. 2006), along with diverging degrees of political contestation and scrutiny. Millions of people are fleeing national borders in search of safety and hopeful futures, at the same time that many millions more are boarding planes or trains on gap years and exchanges, working holidays, cruises, conference trips and family reunions. To Australia, more than eight million visitors now arrive annually (ABS 2017). Ours is an age in which mobilities are both increasingly surveilled and made easier by cheap flights, tablets and apps.

So much have such boundaries between forms of mobility blurred that the singular term 'tourism industry' now appears redundant. In Leiper's (2008, p. 237) words, 'the contention that tourism is supported by one giant industry has no robust theoretical foundation'. Tourism is a 'polyglot' economic formation (Ioannides and Debbage 1997, p. 229), aggregating industries, mobilities and activities. Some overlapping industries are wholly dedicated to serving tourists, and others less so. For *Creative Nation*, it was this cross-sectoral potential in tourism that appealed most. And while there have been many successes since, with notable opportunities for the Australian cultural sector, limited thinking and ingrained assumptions have persisted, to the detriment of Australian arts and creative industries.

As I discuss below, Australian tourism now finds itself in a more ambivalent position than when *Creative Nation* was released. The global cultural tourism market is increasingly complex and competitive. Gourmet, luxury and cruise ship tourism are on the rise as part of the 'experience economy', as travellers become more concerned with visceral encounters than mere sightseeing. Likewise, eco-tourism and experiences 'off the beaten track' are increasingly popular, motivated by the quest for 'authenticity' beyond busy urban lives. New social media platforms, Airbnb, and TripAdvisor ratings services have all altered the tourism experience, in turn underpinning new urban tourism campaigns that link place promotion to industrial heritage, craft production and local cultural 'scenes'. Indigenous tourism meanwhile has struggled. Nonetheless, emboldened by past successes and notwithstanding such movements, contemporary Australian tourism promoters persist with singular marketing campaigns promoting a shared national culture. After briefly returning to the *Creative Nation* document itself, I explore and expand on such themes.

Revisiting *Creative Nation* – was tourism an afterthought?

Creative Nation sought to place Australian culture – understood as organically generated from within communities and via artistic pursuits – firmly on the political agenda. It emerged within a context of globalization that saw 'what is distinctly Australian about our culture ... under assault from homogenised international mass culture' (1994, p. iv). What made our culture distinctly Australian were our inheritances and our geography: Indigenous, British and multicultural legacies, overlaid with changing diasporic and migrant networks. A strong sense of place loomed in *Creative Nation* as both a condition and characteristic of Australian culture and as an asset for future commercial cultural industries growth.

That same sense of place invited connections between the cultural sector and tourism. For the latter, a sense of place is an underpinning and essential asset (Gibson 2009). Tourism capitalism seeks to commodify entire places and all that they contain; to spill outwards from the edges of hotel, travel and transport industries to saturate all other elements of place (Crouch 2000). A sense of place provides cues for the construction of marketing texts and visual frames – the tourist gaze (Urry 1990) – while infusing the everyday sites and encounters that distinguish tourist destinations.

Tourism was certainly in vogue at the time of *Creative Nation*. In just the year prior, Sydney had been announced as the host of the 2000 Summer Olympics. Visitor numbers had already tripled since the 1980s (to three million annually) and export earnings had grown from AU$1.9 billion to AU$10.7 billion. Within a month of *Creative Nation*'s release, Sydney's controversial third airport runway had opened, angering local residents with noise pollution, but expanding massively the airport's capacity in anticipation of unlimited international visitor growth.

From this heady mix of tourism growth and travel infrastructure investment emerged growing recognition of the potential for cultural tourism. In the words of *Creative Nation*, cultural tourism 'embraces the full range of experiences visitors can undertake to learn what makes a destination distinctive – its lifestyle, its heritage, its arts, its people – and the business of providing and interpreting that culture to visitors' (1994, p. 82; see also chapters by Bennett [art], Stevenson [art fairs] and Waterton [heritage], this volume). From their responses to the National Visitor Bureau's annual surveys, tourists made it clear that, beyond sunbathing and photographing the Opera House, they wanted deeper cultural experiences as part of their holidays and especially with regard to Indigenous culture.

It was strange, then, that tourism appeared as something of an afterthought within *Creative Nation*. Tucked away into a couple of pages at the end of the document, there were broad statements acknowledging the tourism sector's economic importance, but few details other than a token announcement of a relatively small amount of funding towards 'further develop[ing] links between the Dept of Tourism, the Australia Council and the Department for Communication and the Arts to initiate programs to provide further opportunities for cultural tourism'. Only AU$250,000 would be made available annually for initiatives to enhance business skills of the cultural industries as they applied to tourism, to improve access by the cultural industries to tourist markets or to identify new tourist markets for cultural products. While *Creative Nation* arguably had quite outward- and forward-looking things to say about culture, there was scant detail, or action, on tourism.

This was doubly puzzling given that so many of *Creative Nation*'s other portfolios linked strongly with tourism, which ought to have provided a clear answer to the perennial problem of audience development already identified across the performing and visual arts. The Commonwealth government had a real stake in tourism, too: it provided direct support for flagship institutions that were also tourist attractions – the National Library, National Gallery and National Museum in Canberra and the National Maritime Museum in Sydney – as well as indirect support for tourist-friendly arts companies such as the Australian Opera and Ballet. Federal film subsidies also indirectly contributed to tourism through depictions of Australian culture and landscapes, as in the case of *Priscilla: Queen of the Desert*.

Where *Creative Nation* was arguably strongest on tourism was in the area of festivals, and questions of culture and the arts in regional Australia. It oversaw the creation of Festivals Australia to 'assist in bringing high quality arts activities to Australian regional festivals' and pinned cultural activity to rural and regional regeneration strategies. Its recognition that festivals are 'an important way of bringing the arts, audiences and whole communities together', giving communities 'a creative focus, help[ing] celebrate achievements and for community identity' pre-empted the proliferation and dispersed success of rural and regional festivals in the following decade (Gibson et al. 2010, p. 281).

Beyond festivals, however, *Creative Nation* had remarkably little detail on where and how tourism could more deeply intersect with the cultural sector. There was much promise, but which mechanisms might encourage deeper integration between the cultural sector and tourism were, in *Creative Nation*, left tantalizingly underexplored.

Cultural tourism: from the fringes to a diverse mainstream

What has transpired since *Creative Nation*? Most obvious is that cultural tourism has become decidedly mainstream. In the 1990s, cultural tourists were an exception to the holiday 'masses' – a novel and lucrative, but elite, niche. Now practically all forms of tourism incorporate cultural elements. In *Creative Australia*, which was published in 2013, the Federal Government acknowledged that cultural and heritage visitors to Australia made 'substantial contribution to the local economies' (Commonwealth of Australia 2013, p. 91). They cited 2010 figures that some 23.2 million cultural and heritage visitors 'contributed approximately $28 billion in tourism expenditure to the Australian economy' (Commonwealth of Australia 2013 p. 91). More than eight million people now visit the Sydney Opera House annually, 1.4 million of whom are tourists who attend over 1,200 paid performances, generating three-quarters of a billion dollars in tourism income to Sydney (Deloitte Access Economics 2013). Cultural tourism is, undoubtedly, big business.

But cultural tourism is now also much more globally competitive. Driving cultural tourism patterns internationally is a host of factors, from the rise of social media, travel blogs and selfie culture, to the influence of television, film and popular culture. Peter Jackson's *Lord of the Rings* films not only injected investment into New Zealand's film production and animation industries but spawned massive visitor numbers to the South Island. Japan grew as a destination, considered safe, with great food, 'authentic' local craft traditions, and shopping. Meanwhile, Portugal and Croatia emerged as 'cool' cultural tourism destinations because, in the words of one travel writer, they had 'the cultural attractions that visitors look for . . . bustling cities, unique architecture, a great culinary scene and excellent local wine, as well as some extremely friendly people' (Groundwater 2017, p. 17). The latter has also had enormous exposure via the television show, *Game of Thrones*. So much so, that Dubrovnik is struggling to cope with the influx of seasonal tourists, especially from visiting cruise ships, forcing city authorities to impose stricter limits on numbers entering its medieval centre (Morris 2017).

Such competition and trends can also be fickle. *Game of Thrones* led Iceland's tourism visitor numbers to triple between 2011 and 2016 (566,000 to 1.7 million) (Groundwater 2017). Colombia, Sri Lanka and Iran all witnessed their tourism industries collapse amidst political strife, but since have become more stable and are now 'hot' cultural tourism destinations. In 2016, President Obama announced relaxation on scheduled flight bans from the U.S. to Cuba, changing entirely the fortunes of that country's cultural tourism sector. Meanwhile, after Donald Trump's election, his infamous travel ban announcement led to a 30 per cent drop in international tourist bookings to the US, while those to neighbouring Canada boomed. Responsiveness and adaptiveness increasingly characterize what is necessary to compete internationally for cultural tourism.

From a shrimp on the barbie to luxury local oysters

Back in 1993, Australian tourism could seemingly do no wrong. Visitor numbers grew impressively each year. The Australian Tourism Commission's 'Shrimp on the barbie' advertisements featuring Paul Hogan had captured American audiences, in just three months turning Australia from number 78 on the U.S. 'most desired' vacation destination list to number 7 (Upe 2014). The Australian dollar was at its lowest in a decade (trading at 66c to the U.S. dollar), making it a cheap place to visit for Americans as well as growing numbers of Japanese tourists and European backpackers. The latter steadily established trails of longer-term visitation throughout coastal, rural and outback towns, directing tourist dollars away from the Sydney Opera House and Harbour Bridge and deepening the trickle-down effect into places such as Byron Bay, Kakadu and beyond (Gibson and Connell 2003). New cultural tourism markets for musicians, Indigenous cultural experiences and craft production emerged along the backpacker trail.

By the 2010s, in a much more competitive market globally, the dollar had nearly doubled in value. Australia had become a prohibitively expensive destination. Backpacker and cheap package holiday markets had stalled. American and Japanese tourists sought cheaper options, gripped by the global financial crisis. Overseas visitor numbers went backwards for the first time in two decades.

The nature of cultural tourism had shifted, too. With a strong dollar, Australia needed to provide higher quality cultural experiences aimed at higher disposable income tourists, a new segment known as 'aspirational travel' (Oates 2015a), seeking luxury and indulgence – out of the ordinary experiences above one's humdrum life. No longer was the prospect of gazing upon scenic landscapes enough to attract tourists, the 'experience economy' involved more active corporeal participation: eating, drinking, cycling and soaking up an atmosphere. The popularity of 'foodie' culture and cooking reality television shows spilled over into cultural tourism. Infusing aspirational travel was a burgeoning set of elite expectations: luxury, quality, gourmet and exceptional. According to Penny Rafferty, Executive Officer of Luxury Lodges of Australia: 'Among our customers, there's definitely a sense of "I deserve it", and they're prepared to spend their money on experiences over things. I think that represents the sophistication and the maturity cycle of luxury travel today' (quoted in Oates 2015a, p. 1). In the 1990s, international visitors ranked a visit to a zoo to see Australian native animals as the most appealing event to attend; by 2015, it had become a food and wine festival (Tourism Australia 2015).

Not only did Australian tourism have to contend with the problem of the high dollar. It also had an image problem. Beyond wine, international visitors didn't equate Australia with luxury. The 'beachy', laid-back, egalitarian, 'shrimp on the barbie' vibe that underpinned 1990s tourism and that saw the Sydney Olympics celebrated as friendly and unpretentious was antithetical to a new international visitor market focused on premium and exclusive experiences.

Market demographics had also shifted. Australian families were taking advantage of the strong dollar by having their annual summer holiday overseas rather than in local beachside towns. Among international arrivals, older, single travellers were more prevalent; less common were the traditional European backpackers, whose capacities to undertake working holidays were also made more complicated by legislative change around visas. Entire travel companies emerged dedicated to bespoke overseas tours of gardens, galleries and food culture for solo travellers in the 50+ age bracket. Numbers of Japanese tourists fell away, jeopardizing previously booming regions, such as the Gold Coast and Cairns, and newly affluent middle-class Chinese tourists became a major market.

Such demographic shifts altered the market conditions for cultural tourism. Chinese tourists, for example, were said to hold different expectations around cultural activities. When Deloitte Access Economics was commissioned to produce a major report on the viability and economic strategy for the Sydney Opera House, it found that Chinese visitors were twice as likely to cite it as a reason to visit Sydney compared with British tourists. They not only photographed the Opera House, but attended its events much more frequently than other nationalities because, in Deloitte Access Economics' (2013, p. 38) words, the Opera House is 'readily associated among a cadre of highly prestigious brands such as Aston Martin, Christian Dior, Giorgio Armani, Chanel, Ferrari and Moet & Chandon'. Other than the exceptional Opera House, Deloitte argued, Australia lacked 'high status' cultural offerings to appeal to this growing market.

After the constraints of the high-dollar period, visitor numbers again grew in 2015, with the dollar falling to helpful new lows. Australian tourism providers had to some degree caught up with international trends. New luxury lodges and boutique hotels came on line. Successes eventuated from marketing luxury experiences to 'foodies', who wanted fresh local produce, seafood, wine and 'spectacular outdoor dining' (Tourism Australia 2015). Tourism Australia's 'There's nothing like Australia' campaign focused on upscale dining experiences, with a 2014 sub-campaign, Restaurant Australia, featuring celebrity chefs. Visitors were encouraged to post selfies, sightseeing pictures and photos of their meals on Instagram with the hashtag #seeaustralia. At the time of writing, Tourism Australia's @Australia Instagram account is the world's largest and most tagged tourism and travel brand account, with over 2.7 million followers and 2.4 million photos tagged with #seeaustralia. Behind the scenes, greater cooperation ensued between specific actors within this nexus: new luxury accommodation facilities established tacit relationships with high-end dining establishments and wineries, and with networked social media a key platform. Even the Minister for Tourism helped out, 'pushing out his own media releases and tweeting' (Oates 2015b, p. 1). A far cry from a shrimp on the barbie, in 2016, Tourism Australia released its Aquatic and Coastal campaign: its banner image was instead a photograph of affluent guests at a luxury Tasmanian lodge 'at a table in the water eating oysters harvested from a few feet away'. The egalitarian ethos of a mythic shared Australian culture that had underpinned earlier tourist appeal had been usurped by new bourgeois values.

From national to urban and regional cultures

The other shift in cultural tourism globally has been geographical, as promotional agencies and campaigns moved from marketing national cultures to local, city and regional attractions. Australian television audiences saw advertisements for California rather than for the United States, or for Wellington rather than New Zealand. Domestically, Victoria began the trend, marketing urban culture through its memorable 'Lose Yourself in Melbourne' campaign (Publicis Mojo 2006).

Evoking the Parisian *flâneur*, advertisements in sepia tones followed a young couple exploring Melbourne's architectural heritage and famed laneways, accompanied by giant balls of red and blue thread. That campaign not only shifted the geographic focus from state to city, but appealed to couples rather than families with children, to an emergent market of domestic weekend getaway-shopping tourists, as well as to a younger demographic interested in heritage, small bars and cafes. Clever tourism marketing buttressed the city's already burgeoning (and, it must be said, very self-conscious) reputation as Australia's cultural capital.

Other campaigns produced by the same advertising agency, Publicis Mojo, followed for rural Victorian destinations, including Daylesford; and other states followed suit with campaigns focused on cities and regions. The South Australia Tourism Commission dedicated individual advertisements to Adelaide and Kangaroo Island and then won the prestigious Grand Prix award at the Cannes Corporate Media and TV Awards for its 'The Barossa: Be Consumed' advertisement (2013; see: https://youtu.be/vtFqMMjMSMc). Set to the ominous tones of Nick Cave & the Bad Seeds' 'Red Right Hand', the earthy advertisements stole and then trumped Melbourne's hipster zeitgeist: they followed a bearded man and pale-skinned woman, in Victorian-era garb, foraging and hunting for rustic local ingredients; baking loaves of bread in antique ovens and plucking feathers from game birds; walking the region's grassy paddocks and vineyards along drystone walls, with close-ups of dusty boots, insects and the region's famed soils. Linking bodily pleasures, food and sense of place, the visceral pleasures of the 'tactile life' (Causey 2014) had finally triumphed over the scenic gaze.

Accompanying this shift was a growing global awareness of the importance of urban cultural 'scenes' and economies of 'taste' to metropolitan-scale tourism promotion. In an age of social media, Instagram profiles and endless acts of self-curation, distinctive forms of urban cultural tourism emerged that *Creative Nation* could not have pre-empted: good food, cafes and bars, galleries, events, locally made crafted goods and fashion, markets and live music. Tourism became more than mere sightseeing: it was about tastes, smells and sounds (Waitt and Duffy 2010). A new generation of digitally connected urban explorers emerged, sceptical of traditional marketing, more interested in staying in Airbnb apartments in lived local neighbourhoods than luxury chains in business districts. Cities needed an edgy feel, an urbane outlook and distinctive cultural legacies linked to local histories of creativity, manufacturing and craft that brought a preference for a gentrified industrial aesthetic. The new generation of digitally connected tourists were more likely to stay and spend money in funky Brooklyn than bland Manhattan; in Shimokitazawa rather than Shinjuku in Tokyo, in Fitzroy rather than the Melbourne CBD, 'bringing an authentic, bespoke travel experience to life', in the words of Tourism Australia General Manager Katherine Droga (quoted in Oates 2015a, p. 1).

Exactly how the cultural sector interacted with such new forms of tourism – and tourists – evolved in complex ways. The rise of Airbnb saw local hosts 'curate' accommodation experiences that were much closer to the local action, recommending local cafes or live music venues, although Airbnb also brought its own tensions and criticisms (Gurran and Phibbs 2017). TripAdvisor reviews led to more scrutiny among tourists regarding restaurants, galleries, breweries and hip streets.

The challenges of gentrification were also brought to the surface: cities that had converted port facilities into leisure zones or that busily promoted office and apartment tower developments on previously industrial lands ended up with slick but placeless business districts and harbourside precincts. Sydney's George Street might as well have been Midtown Manhattan; Melbourne's Docklands and Sydney's Darling Harbour were more or less the same as Baltimore's Inner Harbor or Singapore's Clark Quay. And, for the new generation of urban explorers, such obviously packaged precincts had little appeal: no organic nightlife, less diversity, too many chain stores and tourist 'tat' (Hae 2012). Accompanying real estate pressures affected affordability and left fewer vacant, low-rent warehouse spaces – all of which worked against the cultural sector (Curran 2010) and, in turn, made overly 'packaged' tourist precincts less appealing to millennial tourists.

Cities could ameliorate this problem somewhat by building designated cultural quarters that were hosts to flagship galleries, libraries, entertainment centres and theatres. Melbourne forged ahead with Federation Square and Brisbane with its Southbank Precinct. Such areas mobilized *Creative Nation*'s concern to maximize the convergence and commercial potential of the arts sector and tourism. They also reflected a growing sense of inter-city competition and shifting priorities among collecting and exhibiting institutions, home to flagship touring exhibitions linked to domestic tourism campaigns. In this context, the NSW Art Gallery's plans to expand facilities dramatically with its 'Sydney Modern' wing were driven less by goals to facilitate cultural exchange or education, and more by building larger spaces to enable it to compete with the National Gallery of Victoria for the premier touring blockbuster exhibitions (Nicholls and Power 2017). In sync with *Creative Nation*'s aspirations, such spaces, institutions and exhibitions furthered the arts sector's drift from the patronage model towards concerns with commercial viability and stimulating tourist audiences.

From cultural production to consumption … and back again?

Notwithstanding more sophisticated commercial strategies, the emergence of cultural precincts dominated by flagship institutions and blockbuster events was, at its core, about the spectacular and about cultural consumption rather than cultural *production* (Mercer and Mayfield 2015). Beyond cultivating commercial dispositions, *Creative Nation* had also sought to foster grassroots cultural production and the craft economy.

Nevertheless, cultural policy advocates grew deeply concerned about the growing chasm between spectacular and consumption-orientated urban spaces, and struggling local, organically derived forms of arts and creative industries development (Grodach et al. 2017). Rather than working with the disorder and contradictions found in most city spaces (the unpredictable and spontaneous 'frisson' that contributes 'buzz' to urban life), the very idea of the cultural precinct relied upon ordered categories, classifications and cartographies. Urban policy had focused primarily on consumption, amenities and real estate development, resulting in few attempts to address property speculation and conversion of low-rent space, despite research that showed an association between such spaces and craft and cultural industries development (Chapple 2014). Promoting spaces of consumption led to the loss of dilapidated but low-rent industrial spaces, contributing to the displacement of small, independent, and artistic businesses (Shaw 2014). Moreover, spaces of spectacular culture reinforced passive modes of artistic engagement, seemingly oblivious to 'newer, performative, emotional and sensual forms of cultural taste' (Franklin and Papastegiadis 2017, p. 1). The Museum of Old and New Art (MONA) in Hobart, Tasmania, was arguably the exception to the rule; its success in challenging audiences *and* enlivening an entire state's cultural scene demonstrating what could have been done elsewhere, too.

Indigenous cultural tourism

A final theme retrospectively discussed here is Indigenous cultural tourism. *Creative Nation* made much of the potential for tourism to support enterprise growth and employment for Aboriginal and Torres Strait Islander peoples, accompanied by greater protection of Aboriginal cultural heritage, principally around visual designs, amidst growing copyright breaches and theft of rock art depictions.

Since then, there have been successes along with tensions, frustrations and exaggerated policy claims. In Cairns, the Tjapukai Cultural Centre packaged Aboriginal culture for mass tourists (becoming one of Australia's only Indigenous cultural tourism offerings available to cruise ship passengers disembarking on day trips). Indigenous co-management of national parks at Uluru, Kakadu and Katherine Gorge facilitated enterprises that engaged visitors emotionally and viscerally with Indigenous ontologies (Waitt et al. 2007). Indigenous micro-enterprises such as those at Lombadina, Western Australia, brought small numbers of tourists to be immersed in local culture, bush food and craft. Indigenous-owned and -controlled art centres (such as the Buku-Larrnggay Mulka Centre in Yirrkala, Northern Territory) emerged as 'hybrid economic institutions' (Altman 2005, p. 11), blending customary and commercial imperatives. They ensured a degree of control over cultural representation, and returns from commercial sales.

Elsewhere, questionable relationships and commercial exploitation prevailed among private sector, non-Indigenous-owned art retailers (Wright and Morphy 2000). Mainstream tour operators' desires for pre-packaged and repeatable products clashed with seasonal and ceremonial duties, while training and material welfare benefits for local Indigenous people were found lacking (Dyer et al. 2003). The perennial risks of intruding on tribal life and essentializing Aboriginal culture persisted, reinforcing tourism marketing of Indigenous people as 'primeval' (Waitt 1999, 142). As Sophie Grigi from NGO Survival International succinctly put it, 'a way of life isn't a commodity' (quoted in Junker 2017, p. 16). Nevertheless, Aboriginal artists and tourism enterprises continue to navigate customary and commercial worlds, 'adept in acting in different arenas in which the same objects can have very different meanings and values' (Morphy 2000, p. 130). Successful Indigenous tourism products emerged, with craft and cultural production at the core, aimed at bringing in much needed cash revenue to remote communities, generating employment and training pathways and educating non-Indigenous people (Burarrwanga et al. 2008; Koenig et al. 2011).

Meanwhile, schisms continued to widen between the microscale politics of Indigenous art and craft enterprises and both national policy-making and international tourism market trends. Government policies continue to position cultural tourism as an instrument for sustaining Indigenous communities, a panacea for socioeconomic disadvantage in remote communities. Yet, they invariably rest on rhetoric rather than substance – policies 'that lack the rigour and depth to realise any legitimate moves towards achieving sustainable tourism development for indigenous peoples' (Whitford and Ruhanen 2010, p. 475). And, while the Sydney Olympics cultural programming brought renewed legitimacy to Aboriginal cultural expressions, interest in Aboriginal culture among international visitors has since faded, from over half of international visitors surveyed in the 1990s to a third in the 2010s (Tourism Australia 2015). Large-scale studies of international tourist demand for Indigenous tourism reported declining numbers, low awareness, preference and intentions to participate (Ruhanen et al. 2015). Only 14 per cent had actually participated in an experience incorporating Indigenous culture.

Not helping matters, Australian tourism industry marketing strategies have lapsed back into clichés. In 2006, the AU$180 million 'Where the bloody hell are you?' campaign featuring bikini model Lara Bingle was a monumental flop; the advertisements were banned in the UK because of the swear word and had to be re-written for Asia (Upe 2014). Subsequent efforts – in 2008, Tourism Australia piggybacked on Baz Luhrmann's film *Australia*; in 2010, Oprah Winfrey was lured to Australian shores to film two episodes in front of icons such as the Sydney Opera House and Uluru – remained dominated by a sightseeing/scenic model of travel based on the tourist gaze. It took until 2015 before Tourism Australia, the peak national tourism agency, finally developed a campaign for international tourism promoting Indigenous culture (Oates 2015b). Even then it was only a three-minute online film – admittedly with very high production values, but still a far cry from its more expensive television advertisements and launches.

At around the same time, another much larger, more lavish campaign to market Australia was launched by Tourism Australia, at a gala event in New York City, with an advertisement starring Australian heart-throb actor Chris Hemsworth. As one critic described at length:

> One wealthy-looking 40-something couple after another looks longingly out to sea from helicopters, beaches, boats, and hillsides with kangaroos hopping by. There are a few shots of casual dining experiences but nothing that really grabs you ... The tourism bureaus for Vancouver, Cape Town, and Carmel made this same video in the 1990s ... it appears the tourism board is turning to some easy clichés without embracing what the clichés meant to tourism there in the first place. At least Hogan was uniquely Australian and selling something bigger than eating oysters on a pretty beach.
>
> (Oates 2016, p. 1)

While tourism itself had been transformed – evolving a diverse array of mobilities encompassing corporeal pleasures, urban cultural scenes and Indigenous micro-enterprises – national tourism marketing appeared stuck in a rut, relying on a simplistic version of, rather than re-making, Australian culture.

Conclusion

Like so many other areas covered in this volume, and indeed, traversing a large number of them as a cross-field influence, tourism has reoriented itself around the commercial opportunities available through commodifying culture. As is so often the case elsewhere, there is a continued mismatch between lived experiences of Australian culture, tourists' perceptions and how tourism marketing and products respond to it. Australia remains, in the eyes of international tourism marketing, a land of kangaroos, beaches and beer – perhaps increasingly a wine and seafood destination, but hardly urbane or multicultural, with Indigenous cultural hybridity conspicuously absent.

Shortly after *Creative Nation*'s release, cultural geographer Gordon Waitt analysed the then national tourism advertisements for Australia, concluding that their narrow range of appeals to 'paradise' and 'adventure' via imagery of beaches, reefs, outback and bush landscapes 'maintain a myth of Australian national identity originating from oppressive colonial and patriarchal relations' (1997, p. 46). Over two decades later, it seems that little has changed. As Julian Lee (2009, n.p.), Media and Marketing Editor of the *Sydney Morning Herald*, contends, 'do we really need to have a one-size-fits-all ad for Australia? Unlike a Mars Bar or McDonald's, which delivers the same experience the world over, people come to Australia for different reasons'. Critiquing tourism marketing's essentializing of Australian culture was no longer only an academic exercise but something done by tourism and marketing industry people themselves. A growing number of tourists now want more than just a gaze and more than sanitized urban cultural precincts. They desire diverse corporeal and visceral engagements, to meet local people and to have real interactions in lived neighbourhoods. To eat, smell or hear a place. To be immersed in it. There are innate opportunities here for the cultural sector, but much of the promotion of Australian tourism is still fixated on clichés, the scenic and on the premise of a shared national culture.

According to Tourism Australia's own research, some 28 per cent of visitors desire experiences with local culture and art. While they may not figure as prominently as beaches and wildlife in such surveys, creative expressions are still nevertheless a major defining facet of Australian culture, as *Creative Nation* itself acknowledged. Australian cultural fields now encompass lively urban scenes, maker communities and Aboriginal art, dance and musical expressions. No doubt there are continued challenges for such fields to connect more deeply with tourism, from urban explorers posting selfies on Instagram, to visitors with half a day disembarking from cruise ships. Changing our national tourism promoters' ingrained assumptions and ways of doing things may ultimately prove the more significant hurdle. In the tourism domain, at least, arts and creativity remain underappreciated, largely disconnected from national policy-making and off the grid of travel circuits.

References

Altman, J., 2005. *Brokering Aboriginal art*. Kenneth Myer Lecture in Arts & Entertainment Management, Deakin University.
Australian Bureau of Statistics, 2017. *Overseas arrivals and departures*, Australia, Dec 2016. Canberra: ABS, Cat. No. 3401.0.
Burarrwanga, L. L., Maymuru, D., Ganambarr, B., Wright, S., Suchet-Pearson, S., Lloyd, K. and Ganambarr, R., 2008. *Weaving lives together at Bawaka, North East Arnhem Land*. Newcastle: University of Newcastle.
Causey, J., 2014. Brooklyn Makers: Food, Design, Craft, and Other Scenes from the Tactile Life. San Francisco: Chronicle.
Chapple, K., 2014. The highest and best use? Urban industrial land and job creation. *Economic Development Quarterly*, 28(4), 300–313.
Commonwealth of Australia, 1994. *Creative nation*. Canberra: AGPS.
Commonwealth of Australia, 2013. *Creative Australia*. Canberra: AGPS.
Crouch, D., 2000. Places around us: Embodied lay geographies in leisure and tourism. *Leisure Studies*, 19, 63–76.
Curran, W., 2010. In defense of old industrial spaces: Manufacturing, creativity and innovation in Williamsburg, Brooklyn. *International Journal of Urban and Regional Research*, 34(4), 871–885.
Deloitte Access Economics, 2013. *How do you value an icon? The Sydney Opera House: Economic, cultural and digital value*. Sydney: Deloitte. Available from: www.deloitteaccesseconomics.com.au/uploads/File/Sydney%20Opera%20House.pdf [Accessed 19 June 2017].
Dyer, P., Aberdeen, L. and Schuler, S., 2003. Tourism impacts on an Australian indigenous community: A Djabugay case study. *Tourism Management*, 24(1), 83–95.
Franklin, A. and Papastegiadis, N., 2017. Engaging with the anti-museum? Visitors to the Museum of Old and New Art. *Journal of Sociology*. Available from: http://journals.sagepub.com/doi/abs/10.1177/1440783317712866
Gibson, C., 2009. Geographies of tourism: Critical research on capitalism and local livelihoods. *Progress in Human Geography*, 33(4), 527–534.
Gibson, C. and Connell, J., 2003. Bongo Fury: Tourism, music and cultural economy at Byron Bay, Australia. *Tijdschrift voor Economische en Sociale Geografie*, 94(2), 164–187.
Gibson, C., Waitt, G., Walmsley, J. and Connell, J., 2010. Cultural festivals and economic development in regional Australia. *Journal of Planning Education and Research*, 29(3), 280–293.
Grodach, C., O'Connor, J. and Gibson, C., 2017. Manufacturing and cultural production: Towards a progressive policy agenda for the cultural economy. *City, Culture and Society*. Available from: www.sciencedirect.com/science/article/pii/S187791661730084X
Groundwater, B., 2017. After a fashion. *Sydney Morning Herald*, 27–28 May, 16–21.
Gurran, N. and Phibbs, P., 2017. When tourists move in: How should urban planners respond to Airbnb? *Journal of the American Planning Association*, 83, 80–92.
Hae, L., 2012. *The gentrification of nightlife and the right to the city*. New York: Routledge.
Hannam, K., Sheller, M. and Urry, J., 2006. Mobilities, immobilities and moorings. *Mobilities*, 1, 1–22.
Ioannides, D. and Debbage, K., 1997. Post-Fordism and flexibility: The travel industry polyglot. *Tourism Management*, 18, 229–241.
Junker, U., 2017. It's power to the peoples. *Sydney Morning Herald*, 5–6 August, 16–17.
Koenig, J., Altman, J. and Griffiths, A. D., 2011. Indigenous livelihoods and art income: Participation, production and returns from woodcarvings in Arnhem Land, north Australia. *Australian Geographer*, 42, 351–369.

Lee, J., 2009. Tourism body needs to get lost. *Sydney Morning Herald*, 19 February. Available from: www.smh.com.au/business/tourism-body-needs-to-get-lost-20090218-8bii.html [Accessed 19 June 2017].

Leiper, N., 2008. Why 'the tourism industry' is misleading as a generic expression: The case for the plural variation, 'tourism industries'. *Tourism Management*, 29, 237–251.

Mercer, D. and Mayfield, P., 2015. City of the spectacle: White Night Melbourne and the politics of public space. *Australian Geographer*, 46, 507–534.

Morphy, H., 2000. Elite art for cultural elites: Adding value to Indigenous arts. *In*: C. Smith and G. Ward, eds. *Indigenous cultures in an interconnected world*. Sydney: Allen & Unwin, 129–144.

Morris, H., 2017. Tourists and cruise ships could be turned away under new plans to protect Dubrovnik. *The Telegraph* (London), 11 August, 13.

Nicholls, S. and Power, J., 2017. Art gallery of NSW gets $244m for Sydney Modern 'global museum of the future'. *Sydney Morning Herald*, 13 June, 3.

Oates, G., 2015a. Tourism Australia uses food to drive luxury travel spending. *Skift*. Available from: https://skift.com/2015/12/07/tourism-australias-food-marketing-is-helping-drive-luxury-travel-spending/ [Accessed 19 June 2017].

Oates, G., 2015b. Tourism Australia loads up on content for aboriginal travel campaign. *Skift*. Available from: https://skift.com/2015/07/30/tourism-australia-loads-up-on-content-for-aboriginal-travel-campaign/ [Accessed 19 June 2017].

Oates, G., 2016. Tourism Australia introduces Chris Hemsworth as its new Crocodile Dundee. *Skift*. Available from: https://skift.com/2016/01/25/tourism-australia-introduces-chris-hemsworth-as-its-new-crocodile-dundee/ [Accessed 19 June 2017].

Publicis Mojo, 2006. Lose yourself in Melbourne. *Advertising campaign for Visit Victoria*. Available from: www.youtube.com/watch?v=jENsTGWzC3g [Accessed 6 August 2017].

Ruhanen, L., Whitford, M. and McLennan, C., 2015. Indigenous tourism in Australia: Time for a reality check. *Tourism Management*, 48, 73–83.

Shaw, K., 2014. Melbourne's Creative Spaces program: Reclaiming the 'creative city' (if not quite the rest of it). *City, Culture and Society*, 5(3), 139–147.

Tourism Australia, 2015. *Food and wine*. Available from: www.tourism.australia.com/documents/TASI10033_TA_Snapsho_of_Food_and_Wine_in_Australia_v07.pdf [Accessed 19 June 2017].

Upe, R., 2014. Hogan hero: Why this is our best tourism ad ever. *Traveller*, 20 January. Available from: www.traveller.com.au/hogan-hero-why-this-is-our-best-tourism-ad-ever-31leg [Accessed 19 June 2017].

Urry, J., 1990. *The tourist gaze*. London: Sage Publications.

Waitt, G., 1997. Selling paradise and adventure: Representations of landscape in tourist advertising. *Australian Geographical Studies*, 35, 47–60.

Waitt, G., 1999. Naturalizing the 'primitive': A critique of marketing Australia's indigenous peoples as 'hunter-gatherers'. *Tourism Geographies*, 1, 142–163.

Waitt, G. and Duffy, M., 2010. Listening and tourism studies. *Annals of Tourism Research*, 37, 457–477.

Waitt, G., Figueroa, R. and McGee, L., 2007. Fissures in the rock: Rethinking price and shame in the moral terrains of Uluru. *Transactions of the Institute of British Geographers*, 32, 248–263.

Whitford, M. M. and Ruhanen, L. M. 2010. Australian Indigenous tourism policy: Practical and sustainable policies? *Journal of Sustainable Tourism*, 18, 475–496.

Wright, F. and Morphy, H., 2000. *The art and craft centre story*. Alice Springs: Desart & ATSIC.

10 Indigeneity, cosmopolitanism and the nation
The project of NITV

Ben Dibley and Graeme Turner

Introduction

The establishment of a National Indigenous Television Network (NITV) in Australia has been an important step in recognizing, sharing and mediating Indigenous cultures on broadcast television. The product of many years of lobbying, negotiation and contestation, NITV now broadcasts 24 hours a day into Australian homes from its base in the Special Broadcasting Service (SBS) network. NITV's location within one of the two publicly funded broadcasting channels constituted a sharp break from Indigenous television's prior history in community media, and debates about the implications of that rupture surrounded NITV's initial establishment. While developing as a separate free-to-air digital channel, NITV has had to deal with more far-reaching and perhaps intractable issues as it builds its identity and its audience – while remaining committed to the progressive cultural remit behind its institutionalization. That remit is one of the relatively small number of examples in recent times where cultural policy in Australia has taken on a straightforwardly progressive task and where an intervention in cultural development has the objective of delivering social benefit to the community. In this chapter, we suggest that NITV has adopted what is effectively a nationing role for the Indigenous media field in Australia, setting out to naturalize and embed the formations of Indigenous culture within mainstream or non-Indigenous conceptions of national identity.

However, there are several obstacles to this project. The modest scale of the NITV commissioning budget, the current capacities of the local Indigenous production industry and the requirement that NITV broadcast for 24 hours, seven days a week, all combine to make it impossible to fill the schedule with local content. NITV's adoption of material from Indigenous channels from around the world is its means of addressing this problem. While this is an appropriate strategy, it carries with it a range of contingent effects, some of which might be counter-productive. It is possible that the viewer looking for Australian Indigenous content, for instance, will often be disappointed, as they contend with a schedule that curates a mix of global cultures – some Indigenous, some not. If that were the case, and there is some evidence to support that possibility, then this form of cosmopolitanism would seem to be an unhelpful discursive frame for a project that is focused upon a progressive redefinition of Indigeneity within the Australian mediascape.

For it to have the political and cultural purchase that it seeks, it is important that NITV goes beyond the embrace of multiple versions of cultural identities that are implied within liberal conceptions of the cosmopolitan or, indeed, within liberal conceptions of multicultural nationhood. However, in defence of this strategy, it is important to acknowledge that NITV's use of international content also reflects the importance of its partnerships with global Indigenous channels, which not only supply content for the Australian network, but also enable the circulation of the stories of Australian Indigenous peoples outside Australia – something that is entirely consistent with NITV's objectives. Furthermore, there is merit in NITV demonstrating the existence of something like an Indigenous cosmopolitanism which gathers around global expressions of Indigeneity and benefits from the establishment of an 'Indigenous public sphere' that is on more than a national scale (Hartley and McKee 2000). In what follows, then, we examine what is unfolding as a complex cultural and political positioning for NITV as it works to centre itself within the Australian public service broadcasting (PSB) mainstream.

The origins of NITV

The federal policy commitment to develop an Indigenous media production industry in Australia dates back to *Creative Nation* in 1994, when SBS Independent was established. SBS Independent commissioned a number of key Indigenous productions over the next decade or so, most notably the justifiably celebrated documentary series, *First Australians*, which was produced by Blackfella Films. However, it is important to recognize that Indigenous communities had been producing their own television programs and services for their own communities on a 'pro-am' basis since the mid-1980s (Michaels 1986):

> Over two decades, remote [Indigenous] groups developed a complex broadcasting system based on local control, regional networking and cross-platform production. By 2005, around 300 hours a year of original content were being transmitted on Imparja's second satellite channel, produced and collated by remote media organizations. The service was called Indigenous Community Television.
>
> (Rennie and Featherstone 2008, p. 52)

The success of Indigenous Community Television (ICTV) for its communities, and its capacity to generate successful programming notwithstanding what Rennie (2008, p. 104) describes as its 'clapped out' technological infrastructure, were among the factors cited by those lobbying to attract government interest in establishing some kind of national television service for Indigenous content. They had significant traction, at least in putting Indigenous broadcasting onto the policy agenda. There were government reviews of Indigenous Broadcasting in 2005, 2009 and 2010, and they emanated from several portfolios: the Departments of Communication, Information Technology and the Arts (2006), of the Prime Minister and Cabinet (2010), and of Environment, Water, Heritage and the Arts (2009) (see Meadows 2012).

The outcome of the first of these reviews was the establishment of NITV in 2007 as a narrowcast free-to-air satellite and pay television service. This was a significant step into the mainstream, but it was taken by transferring funding from ICTV to SBS, with whom NITV was to be formally affiliated. The government provided AU$50 million over four years in support, and SBS was required to take on greater responsibility for Indigenous programming. This decision to replace ICTV with NITV registered as the 'key policy moment in Indigenous media policy' (McCallum et al. 2012, p. 25), but it was not universally welcomed. Some argued that this arrangement fundamentally changed the character and function of what had been most valuable about ICTV – displacing the screening of almost entirely Indigenous content 'produced mostly by small bush communities and mostly in local or regional languages' (Meadows 2009, p. 123). NITV represented a shift towards a broader national audience, and it was argued that it came at the cost of those who had most benefited from ICTV – Indigenous communities and, in particular, remote communities. Before ICTV's satellite access was effectively switched off so that NITV could be given sole access to Imparja's Channel 31 carrier, Channel 31 had been used to 'deliver ICTV free-to-air in more than 150 remote Aboriginal communities and uncounted homes with satellite receivers' (Rijavec 2007, n.p.). For many of those who had worked within Indigenous community media, this was a disaster, a policy intervention that was, according to Frank Rijavec, 'careless, crude and unnecessary':

> The proposal to install a one-size-fits-all Indigenous Television Service at the expense of ICTV is looming as the biggest policy failure in Indigenous media since the invention of Aboriginal television in the Pitjantjatjara and Warlpiri lands over 20 years ago. It is a clumsy shotgun wedding between disparate Indigenous media interests that will set community media back a decade.
> (2007, p. 1)

While there was a complex political history underlying this position, at the policy level the battleground reflected competing models for the future of a national Indigenous media sector: a pro-am but publicly funded nationally networked community media model on the one hand, and a much more industry-oriented and commercial national broadcasting model on the other (not an unfamiliar set of oppositions within the cultural policy space). For the former, the service to Indigenous communities at the local level was the priority, while, for the latter, that service was to take its place as one component within a larger national strategy of developing a sustainable Indigenous media production industry. The debates at the time are well covered by Ellie Rennie and Daniel Featherstone (2008), and by Therese Davis's recent account of the development of the Indigenous screen production industries (2018 forthcoming), and we do not go further into them here. However, it does seem as if the conflicting models in play, in a context where, as Rennie puts it, 'the words "nation", "community" and "commerce" carr[ied] different meanings and political imperatives than they do for mainstream Australia' (2008, p. 104), meant that some argued that the initial establishment of

NITV fell between two stools. Rennie suggests that it effectively wiped out the community media network which had established the need for a more substantial investment in Indigenous television, but without allocating the nation-wide, free-to-air television channel needed for its political and cultural objectives and for the further development of the production industry (2008, p. 104). This situation changed significantly with the establishment of the NITV channel as the third national free-to-air digital broadcasting channel within SBS in 2012, and with ICTV, late in the same year, recommencing its own digital television channel, broadcasting to those communities with access to the remote television satellite network (Meadows 2012).

The NITV project

On their website, NITV describes its Reithian remit: to 'inform, educate and entertain its Indigenous and non-Indigenous audiences about the issues that matter, through providing a rich diversity of culture, languages and talent' (*About NITV* 2015). NITV allocates 75 per cent of its budget to the acquisition and commissioning of programs from the Australian Indigenous production sector. The channel reaches an average of two million Australians each month and presents the only nightly television news service that covers Aboriginal and Torres Strait Island stories from across the country. The program schedule has included NITV's most popular sports program, the long-running *Marngrook Footy Show* (devoted to Australian rules football), current affairs programs such as *Living Black, Awaken* and *The Point*, and documentary and factual content, such as *First Australians, Songlines on Screen* and *Our Stories*. It is significant that, in contrast to all the other commercial networks, the dominant genre of NITV's primetime locally produced programming is factual (41 per cent in 2015–16), with news and current affairs the second largest genre (22 per cent in 2015–16). More than 50 per cent of the content screened during primetime is locally produced.

The move into the mainstream that NITV represents for Indigenous media has occurred in concert with the broader development of the commercial Indigenous film and television production industries in Australia. In recent years, we have seen films with Indigenous themes such as *Samson and Delilah* (2009) and *Ten Canoes* (2006) achieve major critical recognition internationally; Indigenous director, Wayne Blair's, debut feature, the musical comedy-drama, *The Sapphires*, proved a box office hit in 2012; and Indigenous actors such as Deborah Mailman and Miranda Tapsell have achieved popular recognition from television viewers, as evidenced by their nominations for Australian television's Logie Awards. As Davis argues, the commercial and critical success of Indigenous film and television productions 'overturns the long held view within the industry that Australian feature films with Indigenous themes are box-office poison' (2018 forthcoming, n.p.). Davis quotes Sandra Levy, former Chief Executive of the Australian Film, Television and Radio School, who claimed that we can now 'confidently say that Australian Indigenous [screen creatives] have become a force to be reckoned with'. They are, she said, 'firmly at the heart of contemporary screen practice' as they use 'film and television to document their cultures, promote social change and entertain. These productions are now "mainstream"' (Davis 2018 forthcoming, n.p.).

Of course, a move into the mainstream for Indigenous cultural production was never going to be uncontested. In something of a replay of debates about the commercial promotion of Indigenous art here and overseas, there are accusations of financial exploitation and of cultural incorporation (that is, the surrendering of key aspects of cultural difference as the price of inclusion) in relation to some of the projects that have been promoted as Indigenous productions (cf., Davis 2016). In response to the broader accusations of 'incorporation', however, Davis argues that the embrace of the mainstream Indigenous production industry is 'a long term strategic objective to ensure the sustainability of Indigenous cultural production and hence Indigenous culture' (2018 forthcoming, n.p.). There is both an economic and a cultural objective here, and they are tightly intertwined. However, the cultural objective is one that would benefit from clarification. That objective is not one of simply 'teaching' non-Indigenous audiences about Indigenous cultures – indeed, Davis says, such an approach 'burdens Indigenous people with the role of having to explain themselves and their culture', so rendering Indigeniety as 'a problem' (2018 forthcoming, n.p.). Rather, she takes up Marcus Lacey's point that film and television productions provide Indigenous people with a means of 'sharing knowledge' about Indigenous cultures. This arrangement, she goes on, 'assumes a reciprocal relationship between Indigenous screen creatives/ Indigenous on-screen subjects and their mainstream audiences, opening out possibilities for greater respect and understanding of Indigenous knowledges of this country' (2018 forthcoming, n.p.).

In the surveys and follow-up interviews conducted for the empirical arm of the larger research project[1] from which this book emerges, we found evidence that audiences understood that strategy. In what is probably an exemplary articulation of what NITV is trying to achieve, one of our non-Indigenous respondents had this to say in a household interview:

> [NITV factual programs] are trying to tell you about what the Aborigines are trying to do and pretty much there's a lot of positive aspect[s] about the Aborigines presented in those reports which I like…. Because general perception is not always accurate, but what you see out in the city is a really bad image of Aborigines, right, and most of the time on the news it comes they are fighting about land rights, they are fighting about this, fighting about that, and it's presented more as if they just want more money out of somebody to abuse, which is not the truth…. [NITV] brings a positive picture of the community.

Overwhelmingly, those we interviewed who had watched NITV expressed their understanding of the cultural contribution made by the channel, and were very positive about its existence and the kinds of content that it screened.

Nonetheless, another of our non-Indigenous interviewees did express their disappointment at the amount of imported content, and indicated that was their reason for not watching the channel as much as I thought I would've when it first started: I thought this is great and we'll really be into that but there's lots of shows on there that aren't Indigenous that I think it surprised me and – yeah, so that was a shock really – not a shock, it just – I don't know. Every time you turned it on it was something that wasn't Indigenous.

It is notable that 22 per cent of the Aboriginal and Torres Strait Islander sample in our survey, when asked if they had watched any programs broadcast on NITV, said that they had not. That missing 22 per cent is a concern for NITV,[2] and it is not unreasonable to suppose that it might relate to the difficulty that we noted at the beginning of this discussion: how to fill as much of the NITV 24-hour viewing schedule as possible with content from local Indigenous producers.

Given the size of its commissioning budget and the fact that it has not been increased since it was established, NITV's capacity to generate enough local material is limited. Nonetheless, an early description of NITV, cited in Rennie (2008, p. 104), as a 'content aggregator', is no longer appropriate. There is a much stronger strategic direction in its commissioning and selection of content. That said, and even though it delivers an extraordinary volume of content with that budget, NITV is still forced to fill the schedule with imported content and repeats. To be clear, at present it screens a much greater proportion of locally produced than imported content. According to the 2016 SBS Annual Report, NITV screened a total of 381.42 hours of first-run locally produced content in prime time, compared with 259.23 hours of imported first-run content. Its dependence on repeated screenings, though, is high, even in prime time. In 2016, NITV screened a total of 713.49 hours of locally produced repeated content in prime time, and a total of 648.45 hours of repeated imported content in prime time. It is notable that, in relation to repeat screenings, the gap in volume between local and imported content considerably closes. If we look at the total volume of repeat versus first-run across both categories and all genres, the network's reliance on repeated screenings is very clear. Again, in prime time, and across all genres, the total hours of repeat programming were 1,361.94 out of a total of 2,003.90 hours screened. The figures are even more dramatic when we look at the 24-hour schedule. While the ratio of local to imported first-run programming is roughly similar to that in prime time (779.7 hours for local content to 365.52 hours of imported content), the total hours of repeat programming is 7,244.65 against a total of 8,390.34 screened.

There are many problems that this programming raises for the broadcaster. Among the most obvious is that the high level of repeats risks turning away viewers who have encountered this content before; as a result, one cannot imagine NITV operating as a channel on which audiences would stay through the schedule. Indeed, in our interview with Tanya Orman, NITV's channel manager, she indicated that its problem was not so much attracting an audience to individual programs, but keeping them around for the next one, or perhaps even building some old-fashioned channel loyalty. Our survey results also suggested that there was still a problem in attracting non-Indigenous audiences in the first place; over 50 per cent of the respondents in the general sample said that they had not watched any programs broadcast by NITV. The schedule looks slightly unconventional: with its tendency to strip content across the week in the same time slots as well as its comparatively high reliance on repeats, it works differently to its free-to-air competitors. In some ways, the scheduling strategy is a hybrid of pay-TV and free-to-air (FTA); a legacy of NITV's original location on the pay-TV network Foxtel. Consequently, the schedule requires a more deliberate and selective mode of consumption than is necessarily the case for the other FTA channels. While NITV doesn't employ the kind of looping and replaying that characterizes much of pay-TV scheduling, where we would have, for instance, individual episodes of *Law and Order* screened consecutively over three or four hours, neither does it have the volume of content that would enable it to provide the degree of choice enjoyed by viewers of the commercial channels or its PSB partners. Given the expansion of choice in the sector generally since the arrival of the digital channels and streaming services such as Netflix, departures from practices that have become conventional on other services probably disadvantage NITV.

The problem that interests us most, though, is related to what we are suggesting is NITV's nationing remit: the way in which it sets out to use NITV as a means of sharing the culture of Australia's Indigenous people with non-Indigenous Australians. As Tanya Denning-Orman puts it, 'Indigenous voices telling Indigenous stories for all Australians to embrace' (2016, n.p.). It is important to stress that we are not suggesting that this remit operates as means of 'integrating' Indigenous culture into the Australian mainstream; rather, it seems to us that it might actually work in almost the reverse manner – by integrating non-Indigenous Australians into Indigenous Australia. This strategy turns conventional arguments about inclusion on their head. If this is the case, then, it is important that the concept of Indigeneity that is embedded in the manner in which the channel operates, a concept of Indigeneity that is both within and beyond the national, maintains the clarity of its articulation if it is to achieve this objective. Imported programming is selected, clearly, for its consonance with this mission: there is a strong presence of Maori TV among other Indigenous television initiatives, and an implicit affiliation with the struggle for visibility, equality and justice that continues to occupy Indigenous communities world-wide as well as African-Americans in the United States.

There are further strategic considerations that play into the selection of imported programming for NITV.[3] First of all, NITV is a partner with a number of Indigenous channels from around the world through its membership of the *World Indigenous Television Broadcasters Network*. This affiliation not only provides NITV with access to programming content from these channels, but also involves reciprocal opportunities to have its programming broadcast on those channels. It enables NITV to disseminate its own stories about Indigenous Australia globally, doing the work of correcting stereotypes and misinformation in the way that our interview respondent quoted earlier suggested was being accomplished in Australia. This element of internationalization is a valuable contribution to NITV's broader mission. Also, the thematic principles implicit in the selection of material are motivated by the need to ensure that the content broadcast is focused on issues or experiences that will seem relevant to Australian Indigenous audiences while also informing Australian non-Indigenous audiences about the cultures and experiences of Indigenous peoples globally. Should these meanings be opaque to viewers, the channel's promotions aired in connection with NITV's ten-year anniversary have made its editorial principles explicit.

Cosmopolitanism, the nation and Indigeneity

Despite the previous discussion, there is still the question of whether these strategic imperatives impact in the desired way on the experiences of actual NITV viewers: is it likely that their expectations of Australian Indigenous content would be disappointed at times by even the most astute selection of thematically focused global content? While the value of the international partnerships managed through content exchanges is fundamentally important to the channel, their value is not necessarily visible to the viewer in search of local Indigenous content. There is, of course, the underpinning problem of the current levels of funding and the extent to which they have hamstrung NITV's role in developing the Australian Indigenous production industry. We are aware that the layers of ambivalence accompanying the NITV project are actually about failures at the policy level rather than within the institution itself. But there remain questions about the implementation of the channel's cultural project: its capacity to properly pursue its nationing project for Australian Indigenous cultures. We do understand the value of, and the rationale for, the imported content used and can see how that makes sense at an institutional level. However, at the level of consumption – for both Indigenous and non-Indigenous viewers – we think there remains a danger that this strategy for building the schedule risks implying a relatively casual equivalence between diverse global Indigenous cultures and the specificities of their political and cultural conditions. This is a flattening out that seems implied in the industry's term, 'world Indigenous content'. Here, NITV could be regarded as offering opportunities for the consumption of representations of Indigeneity as just another domain of cosmopolitanism.

There are other ways of framing this dilemma. The promotion of a schedule that serves as a linking of Indigenous Australian stories of survival, resistance and resilience with those of Indigenous peoples around the world does work towards establishing transnational networks and alliances supporting the recognition and development of Indigenous communities and their claims for land and cultural rights (Ginsburg 2011). This outcome could be seen as troubling any easy project of mainstreaming by drawing on transnational comparisons of forms of cultural revival and resistance to colonialism and racism. Such a view would also generate a sense of the varied ways in which the channel might work differently for its two primary audiences: for Indigenous Australians and for non-Indigenous Australians. For the non-Indigenous, at its best, the channel does weave Indigenous stories deep into the national fabric, celebrating Indigenous contributions and achievements that have been previously erased or ignored, while articulating forceful counter-narratives of the nation's history from Indigenous perspectives. For Indigenous audiences, at its best, the channel builds connections and forms of solidarity both within and beyond the boundaries of the nation-state, between Indigenous communities within Australia, and between First Nation peoples around the world. So, the project of nationing in play here has multiple levels, carrying with it potential conflicts and contradictions as well as possible coalitions and collaborations.

Of course, introducing the notion of cosmopolitanism here reveals just what kinds of potential contradiction are involved. While there is a serious body of work which promotes the notion of cosmopolitanism as a progressive formation, it is usually in the context of a critique of the value of the concept of the nation or of ideologies of nationalism (Held 2010). Our view of the NITV project as a form of nationing places it in opposition to such formulations. NITV's political and cultural objective is to reshape a particular aspect of the nation – the ways in which non-Indigenous Australians know about, experience and understand Indigenous cultures and histories. It is not simply about embracing the multicultural nor merely seeking to promote the tolerance of difference in the service of opening up new opportunities for cultural consumption – what Hage (1998, 2003) has described as 'cosmo-multiculturalism'. It is about changing how Australians conceptualize their national identities by providing the cultural and political conditions for a properly informed inclusion of Indigenous Australians and their cultures within the 'imagined community' and the shared culture of the nation (Anderson 1991). There is also, however, the particular role that NITV plays for Indigenous audiences: telling their stories, replaying their own versions of their cultures and identities back to them. So, for this audience, too, it is an even more direct and explicit form of nationing. This is, of course, a contentious process. Concerns persist that elements of the channel's constituency remain underrepresented, contending that it 'features little content which reflects remote Indigenous Australia' (Meadows 2016, p. 36). However, this criticism emphasizes how this project of nationing must also be performed in ways that are sensitive to the internal differences within and between Australia's Indigenous communities. And it must always be alive to Australian Indigenous communities' relation to the nation-state, which is itself deeply ambivalent. Although it is both a source of violence and exclusion, it is also the primary social and political context in which their identities and freedoms must be negotiated and secured for the foreseeable future.

These ambivalences and contradictions are embedded in what NITV has been set up to do and in the role that it has been required to play in defining how both Indigenous and non-Indigenous Australians know and think about Indigeneity as fundamental components of their imagined community. Even with these complicating factors, however, as a relatively isolated instance in recent times of the Australian government's investment in a cultural policy strategy that is explicitly nationing and implicitly progressive, NITV stands in some relief to the withdrawal from the use of cultural policy as a means of nation formation, and of cultural intervention, that so many of the contributions to this book document. However, if NITV is a nationing project, it does not share in a conventional 'nationing' logic in the sense of promoting policy and institutional arrangements in which participants come to subsume their identities, values and belonging under the 'national sign'. As we have noted,

NITV does not straightforwardly share in a logic of inclusion in the sense of folding those who were once marginal or disavowed into the national narrative. Rather, NITV proceeds, it seems, with the purpose of integrating non-Indigenous Australians into Indigenous Australia. This is a process informed not by a logic of inclusion but one of accountability, in which to be integrated is to recognize land rights, the importance of Indigenous self-determination, of issues of justice, the protocols of country and so on. Similarly, if transnationalism is conventionally posed as a countervailing or at least moderating force to that of nationing, NITV might serve as a counter example. We have suggested that NITV's embrace of a transnational Indigeneity expressed through the channel's commitment to global Indigenous programming is ambivalent with regard to its nationing agenda. However, there can be little doubt that NITV's strategic Indigenous cosmopolitanism has played a crucial role in meeting institutional objectives in less than ideal policy conditions and in mediating the cultural politics of a complex constituency. In this sense, we might say that the success of NITV's nationing has been contingent, in part, on a particular form of transnationalism – an Indigenous cosmopolitanism.

Notes

1 The 'Australian Cultural Fields' project was supported by the Australian Government through the Australian Research Council (DP140101970). The project was awarded to Tony Bennett (Project Director, Western Sydney University), to Chief Investigators Greg Noble, David Rowe, Tim Rowse, Deborah Stevenson and Emma Waterton (Western Sydney University), David Carter and Graeme Turner (University of Queensland), and to Partner Investigators Modesto Gayo (Universidad Diego Portales) and Fred Myers (New York University). Michelle Kelly (Western Sydney University) was appointed as Project Manager/Senior Research Officer. The project has additionally benefited from inputs from Ien Ang, Ben Dibley, Liam Magee, Anna Pertierra and Megan Watkins (Western Sydney University)
2 This opinion was expressed in a personal interview with Tanya Orman, the Director of NITV, in the SBS offices in Sydney on 24 July 2017.
3 Some of the material in this paragraph, and from time to time throughout the chapter, is drawn from the interview with Tanya Orman. While we have not quoted directly from this interview, it has served as important background to the account that we provide in this chapter, and we are grateful to Tanya for giving us some of her valuable time.

References

About NITV, 2015. Available from: www.sbs.com.au/nitv/article/2015/06/25/about-nitv

Anderson, B., 1991. *Imagined communities: Reflections on the origin and spread of nationalism.* London: Verso.

Davis, T., 2016. *Australian Indigenous film and television in a transnational frame.* Unpublished paper presented to the Crossroads in Cultural Studies Conference, Sydney, December.

Davis, T., 2018 forthcoming. Australian Indigenous screen in the 2000s: Crossing into the mainstream. *In*: B. Goldsmith and M. Ryan, eds. *Australian screen in the 2000s.* London: Palgrave Macmillan.

Denning-Orman, T., 2016. #OscarsSoWhite need not mean #LogiesSoWhite but we need more diversity on our screens. *The Guardian.* Available from: www.theguardian.com/commentisfree/2016/feb/29/oscarssowhite-need-not-mean-logiessowhite-but-we-need-more-diversity-on-our-screens

Department of Communications, Information Technology and the Arts, 2006. *Indigenous television report: Report of the review into the viability of establishing an Indigenous television service and the regulatory arrangements that should apply to the digital transmission of such a service*. Canberra: Ausinfo.

Department of the Environment, Water, Heritage and the Arts, 2009. *Summary report on the findings of the review of National Indigenous Television (NITV)*. Canberra.

Department of Prime Minister and Cabinet, 2010. *Review of Australian government investment in the Indigenous broadcasting and media sector*. Canberra. Available from: http://arts.gov.au/sites/default/files/broadcasting-review-pdf

Ginsburg, F., 2011. Native intelligence: A short history of debates on indigenous media and ethnographic film. *In*: M. Banks and J. Ruby, eds. *Made to be seen: Perspectives on the history of visual anthropology*. Chicago: University of Chicago Press, 234–254.

Hage, G., 1998. *White nation: Fantasies of white supremacy in a multicultural society*. Sydney: Pluto Press.

Hage, G., 2003. *Against paranoid nationalism: Searching for hope in a shrinking society*. Sydney: Pluto Press.

Hartley, J. and McKee, A., 2000. *The Indigenous public sphere: The reporting and reception of indigenous issues in the Australian media*. Oxford: Oxford University Press.

Held, D., 2010. *Cosmopolitanism: Ideals and realities*. Cambridge and Malden, MA: Polity Press.

McCallum, K., Meadows, M., Waller, L., Dunne Breen, M. and Reid, H., 2012. *The media and Indigenous policy how news media reporting and mediatized practice impact on Indigenous policy: A preliminary report*. Canberra: Faculty of Arts and Design, University of Canberra.

Meadows, M., 2009. Walking the talk: Reflections on Indigenous media audience research methods. *Participations: Journal of Audience Studies*, 6(1), 118–136.

Meadows, M., 2012. When the stars align: Indigenous media policy formation 1988–2008. *In*: K. McCallum, M. Meadows, L. Waller, M. Dunne Breen and H. Reid. *The media and Indigenous policy how news media reporting and mediatized practice impact on Indigenous policy: A preliminary report*. Canberra: Faculty of Arts and Design, University of Canberra, 23–32.

Meadows, M., 2016. Dangerous dancing: A commentary on australian Indigenous communication futures. *Media and Communication*, 4(2), 33–37.

Michaels. E., 1986. *The Aboriginal invention of television in Central Australia 1982–1986*. Canberra: Australian Institute of Aboriginal Studies.

Rennie, E., 2008. Making it on your own: Australian Indigenous television. *Metro Magazine*, 158, 92–103.

Rennie, E. and Featherstone, D., 2008. The potential diversity of things we call TV: Indigenous community television, self-determination and NITV. *Media International Australia*, 129, 52–66.

Rijavec, F., 2007. Careless, crude and unnecessary. *Online Opinion*, 19 July, 1–4. Available from: www.onlineopinion.con.au/view.aspt?article=6127&page=0

Special Broadcasting Service, 2016. *SBS 2016 annual report*. Available from: http://media.sbs.com.au/aboutus/SBS_Annual_Report_2016.pdf

11 Making multiculture

Australia and the ambivalent politics of diversity

Ien Ang and Greg Noble

Introduction

Creative Nation was launched in 1994 at a time of heightened public awareness of the changes brought about by mass immigration to the make-up of Australian society. These changes can be succinctly understood under the banner of 'multiculturalism'. A problematic and contested term, multiculturalism broadly refers to the recognition that demographic changes, as a consequence of the influx of migrants from all corners of the world, have led to the development of a nation that is increasingly ethnically and linguistically diverse, and that governments have a role to play in managing this diversity. This task includes involving ethnic minorities in the cultural life of the nation. Australia's first national cultural policy was explicit about this governmental responsibility. A central concern of *Creative Nation* was with the role of culture in the articulation of national identity. So, if 'culture' is 'that which gives a sense of ourselves' (p. xx), then it stands to reason that national policy should assume 'ourselves' as an intrinsically diverse and plural people. In this regard, the project of 'making culture' is, or should be, conceived as one of 'making multiculture', where 'difference' is both valued and nurtured in the endeavour of 'nationing' (see Rowe, Turner and Waterton, this volume). *Creative Nation* certainly presents its credentials in this respect, stating that '[m]ulticultural Australia – a society which is both diverse and tolerant of diversity, which actively *encourages* diversity – is one of our great national achievements' (p. xxx). It is this encouragement of diversity – in both cultural production and cultural consumption – that is at stake in the insertion of multiculturalism into cultural policy. This chapter will describe some of the ways in which it has occurred in Australia from the 1980s to today.

Drawing on data from the Australian Cultural Fields project, including interviews with key figures in the sector, we argue that the intersection of multiculturalism and national cultural policy is a difficult one, troubled by ambiguous definitions, competing goals and contradictory logics (Khan et al. 2015). This is even more so in the twenty-first century, when the term 'multiculturalism' itself has lost much of its political purchase. Significantly, the word is hardly deployed in *Creative Australia*, the Labor government's short-lived cultural policy of 2013, even though there is copious talk of 'diversity'. It doesn't appear at all in the Coalition government's *Multicultural Australia* 'statement' of 2017 (Australian

Government 2017). Moreover, as Rowe, Turner and Waterton point out in the Introduction to this book, today, cultural policy is less a matter of national identity construction and more about positioning national culture as an object of industry policy in the context of increased globalization and commercialization. At the same time, the social phenomena which discourses of multiculturalism sought to address have only become more evident since the beginning of this century, as global migration flows have massively intensified in terms of volume, frequency and directional patterns. This is particularly so in Australia, a country which, since the end of the Second World War, has proportionally taken in very high numbers of migrants, and where, to all intents and purposes, everyday multiculturalism (Wise and Velayutham 2009) has become a routine part of social experience, especially in cities. Twenty-first-century Australia is characterized by a dynamic diversification of diversity (Vertovec 2007; Noble 2011), a reality which is difficult to capture and address in cultural policy. In this context, as we will argue, the evolution of Australia's multiculture is as much an organic result of the increasingly pervasive cultural diversity on the ground as it is the outcome of deliberate policy settings.

Making multiculture in the arts

Creative Nation did not introduce a multicultural agenda in Australian cultural policy, nor was it the first official document to celebrate cultural diversity. The Australian Bicentenary of 1988, which commemorated the arrival of the First Fleet of British ships in Sydney Harbour two centuries earlier and marked the founding of modern Australia, was a grand 'Celebration of a Nation' with a strong emphasis on inclusiveness and multiculturalism, recognizing Australia's undeniable diversity due to decades of mass immigration (Kleist 2017, pp. 136–139). It was in the early 1970s that the Whitlam Labor government officially declared Australia a 'multicultural society', although it took some time to give some concrete meaning to the term (Jupp 2001). As a public policy, Australian multiculturalism has always been linked with the issue of immigrant settlement and integration policies. Engagement with cultural issues, particularly the arts, was peripheral to multicultural policy, and any engagement was shaped by questions of migrant welfare which framed the way in which multiculturalism entered the realm of cultural policy.

The Whitlam government introduced the social democratic themes of 'access', 'participation' and 'community' into the discourse of public policy. This commitment to access and participation opened up new possibilities for cultural policy, especially in the realm of arts funding (Hawkins 1993). It took the form of advocacy and support for 'community arts' within the then newly established Australia Council of the Arts. Unlike the artform-specific Boards of the Australia Council (music, visual arts, performing arts, literature, etc.), whose work turned on promoting aesthetic excellence in those artforms, community arts did not refer to any specific form of cultural production but, rather, focused on enhancing access and participation in the arts for those who were considered culturally disadvantaged, either in physical or geographical terms or as a consequence of their age, ethnicity or socio-economic status. However, the space created for community arts within the Australia Council remained on the periphery. Its legitimacy as a distinct category of artistic endeavour was consistently questioned precisely because it did not commit to conventional – that is, culturally dominant – notions of artistic excellence, but operated 'outside of aesthetic discourses of value' (Hawkins 1993, p. 45). The benefits of cultural activity for communities were considered to be social rather than aesthetic; at the same time, it was emphasized that communities had the right to cultural self-determination.

It was within this framework of community arts and community cultural development that multiculturalism entered the policy terrain at the Australia Council. Initially, talk was about 'ethnic arts' and the focus was almost exclusively on cultural maintenance through support for the folk or traditional arts activities of non-English-speaking migrant groups. Links were set up with ethnic community organizations to get them interested in cultural policy issues, and a national network of multicultural arts officers was established. However, a limiting effect of this approach was the cultural ghettoization of multicultural arts within the narrow confines of migrant or ethnic constituencies. Although, by 1990, a much broader vision of multiculturalism as relevant for *all* Australians, not just migrants of non-English speaking background, had become current – articulated within the Australia Council in a new policy called Arts for a Multicultural Australia (AMA) – attempts to make multiculturalism a Council-wide responsibility have persistently met with resistance from certain sections outside the circle of community arts/cultural development advocates. According to Hawkins (1993, p. 88), this hostility was 'a result not only of racism but also of the desire to keep the "difficult" issues contained within community arts'. These 'difficult issues' pertained strongly to the neglect of aesthetic criteria and notions of artistic excellence in the idea of community arts, which meant for its critics a devaluing of Art. By association, 'multicultural arts' was tarred with the same brush, consolidating the perception that it was a marginal cultural activity producing marginal art conducted by marginal (Non-English-Speaking Background (NESB)) artists for cultural communities on the margins of society. The implication was that 'multicultural artists' (whoever they might be) were perceived not as creative contributors to the nation, but as subjects whose disadvantage needed to be addressed through forms of affirmative action.

The insertion of multiculturalism into arts policy through the category of 'community arts' has thus impeded its integration into the mainstream national understanding of Australian art. This is despite repeated exhortations – of which *Creative Nation* was an important marker – that Australia is a multicultural nation and that, therefore, Australian art should be inclusive of all the different cultural strands within it, thereby reimagining Australian national identity as decidedly open, diverse and hybrid. Such hybridity is increasingly a feature of artistic practices but is rarely captured in arts policy (Khan et al. 2015). Khan et al. (2013, p. 232) characterize two key approaches to 'multicultural arts' adopted in Australian cultural policy:

> a 'targeted' approach which understands 'multicultural arts' as a distinct artistic and administrative category requiring its own resources and support;

and a broader 'mainstreaming' approach which characterises 'multicultural arts' as relevant to 'all Australians'.

It is fair to say, however, that the second, more cosmopolitan approach has never managed to displace the first, more welfarist approach. Instead, 'multicultural arts' has remained positioned on the margins of the art world, occupying the ambiguous space between contrasting discourses of 'access' and 'excellence', anthropological and artistic meanings of 'culture', and social and aesthetic understandings of art. Efforts by leading multicultural advocates to critique dominant notions of 'excellence' in a bid to reposition cultural diversity in the arts as the leading edge of national cultural innovation (e.g., Castles and Kalantzis 1994; Gunew and Rizvi 1994; Papastergiadis 2003) have never gained much traction.

This marginalization continues to this day, and operates at both the 'community' and 'arts' ends of the spectrum. As writer, playwright, director and consultant, Paula Abood (interview, 2017) says, speaking about her work with migrant and refugee groups, 'some people might call it the multicultural arts sector … but [for her] the field is the community cultural development field'. 'Cultural work' has become a focus for engaging communities, often funded by local councils rather than the Australia Council, because, in her experience:

> the self-absorbed arts world is very unreflexive. They think they are the arts end of the universe and they produce fabulous art and get the lion's share of funding, but they are [a] very monocultural, very white, very heritage world.

Edmund Capon (interview, 2017), the high-profile former director of the Art Gallery of New South Wales (AGNSW), may disagree with Abood's view of the art world, but he told a parallel story of marginalization in the realm of 'high art'. Appointed to the AGNSW in 1978 in part because of his expertise in Asian art – 'it was China that brought me here' – he initiated a series of major exhibitions with this regional focus, alongside the conventional exhibitions of Western art. As he observes, 'this was really new stuff at the time, because the Australian public had never really seen Chinese paintings'. He established an Asian art department in the Gallery and appointed people sympathetic to his agenda. But, although Asian art, especially contemporary, has acquired greater visibility, he concedes that it is still not part of the 'mainstream' Australian art field: 'to my mind it still doesn't have the presence in the institutional psyche [of the Gallery] that it should have … it's still slightly on the periphery'. Indeed, he suggests that the sector has become more 'Eurocentric' in recent years, despite the changing nature of Australia's cultural diversity and the increasing number of Australians of Asian background.

In 2000, the Australia Council updated its *Arts for a Multicultural Australia* policy (introduced in 1993, the year before Creative Nation), subtly renaming it *Arts in a Multicultural Australia* (emphasis added). Just a few years later, however, this policy was abolished, signalling the end of a targeted and explicit endeavour to embrace multiculturalism within the Council's ambit. Instead it has had, since 2008, a *Cultural*

Engagement Framework (CEF), which adopts a more multidimensional understanding of diversity. While it is emphasized that diversity is 'at the heart of the Australia Council's Strategic Plan', cultural diversity (in the restricted sense of immigration-induced ethnic diversity) now sits next to First Nations peoples, children and young people, older people, people with disability, and regional and remote Australia as the diversity priority areas of the CEF (Australia Council n.d.) (see Figure 11.1).

This broadening of 'diversity' is in line with the pronouncements in *Creative Australia* (2013), where the use of the term to describe contemporary Australia is pervasive, and with governmental uses of diversity in demonstrating the 'cultural wealth' of the nation (Gibson 2001). Yet the implications of this move from multiculturalism to diversity in cultural policy are not straightforward. One could argue that it signifies a waning of commitment to a multicultural Australia at a time when levels of immigration are higher than ever. But, it may also represent the exhaustion of particular forms of multicultural policy-making and the language associated with it. For better or worse, the discourse of multiculturalism

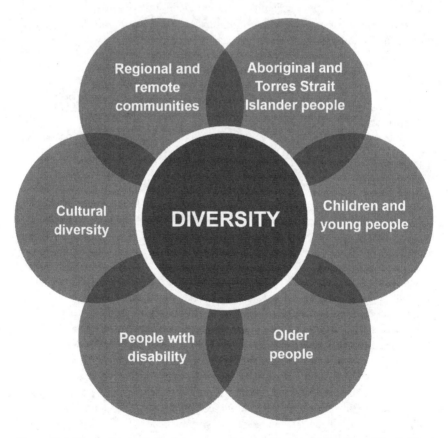

Figure 11.1 Dimensions of diversity according to the Australia Council's *Cultural Engagement Framework.* Used by permission.

has always been predicated on the existence of 'ethnic communities', which are presumed to be static, bounded and homogeneous entities. However, this rigid, compartmentalized understanding of multicultural society is increasingly at odds with the dynamic, heterogeneous and inescapably intercultural realities of migrant life and culture. According to Frank Panucci (interview 2017), the Australia Council's Executive Director of Grants and Engagement, a multiculturalist policy tends to be too schematic to capture such a complex and dynamic diversity. He refers to the need to develop policy frameworks based on the idea of intersectionality, which stresses that social identities are not one-dimensional (that is, constituted exclusively by class, gender or ethnicity), but shaped by multiple, overlapping and intersecting relations of power and hierarchy.[1] Panucci asserts that the new *Cultural Engagement Framework* would, in principle, be more agile and open to the different, multi-dimensional diversities to which cultural policy might respond. In theory, the *Cultural Engagement Framework* seems to offer a more robust, nation-wide attempt to grapple with these competing scales and foci. In practice, however, the absorption of cultural diversity into the broader template of many kinds of diversity can lead to a diversion of attention from multicultural arts. For example, since the introduction of the CEF the concentrated focus has been on 'disability'. Meanwhile, it is clear that the politics of diversity is symbolically central to the desire of making Australia 'a culturally ambitious nation', as the Australian Council's 2014–2019 Strategic Plan has it, even if it remains marginal to actual policy implementation.

Making multiculture in the media

A parallel but different story can be told about the intersection of multiculturalism and cultural policy in the realm of the media. A uniquely important role in the project of making multiculture in Australian media is played by the Special Broadcasting Service (SBS), a government-funded media organization whose charter is 'to provide multilingual and multicultural radio and television services that inform, educate and entertain all Australians, and in doing so, reflect Australia's multicultural society' (Special Broadcasting Service Act 1991). SBS's origins can also be traced back to the early 1970s. Established as a social democratic response to the perceived social disadvantage experienced by migrants, many of whom spoke little or no English, SBS began modestly as an 'ethnic radio' service broadcasting in several languages other than English. By 1980, 'multicultural television' was added to the SBS remit, and by 1991 the organization's institutional status was secured with its official incorporation as Australia's second public broadcaster. The adjective 'special' in its name betrays a kind of junior relationship to the country's premier public broadcaster, the Australian Broadcasting Corporation (ABC), which is presumed to cater to the general national audience. Yet, it is fair to say that SBS has contributed to a greater level of mainstreaming of multiculture in the media than has been the case in the arts, even if in this realm, too, associations with 'ethnic communities' have tended to act as a barrier to SBS's national popularity. Throughout its history, SBS has harboured conflicting interpretations of the services that a multicultural broadcaster should provide, which has meant a persistent need to bridge the continuing tensions between the 'special' and the 'general', the ethno-specific and the cultural mainstream, and minorities and the dominant majority in a context shaped by tensions between the demands of public and commercial broadcasting (Ang et al. 2008, p. 19).

If 'reflecting Australia's multicultural society' is SBS's brief, as its Charter says, translating it into concrete policies of media production and programming is far from straightforward. Here, differences between radio and television as media platforms are worth stressing, as they entail quite different affordances and requirements *vis-à-vis* their real and imagined audiences. SBS Radio has over the years remained true to its original purpose of catering to the special needs and interests of ethnic communities through language-specific programming. Reflecting the increasingly wide range of originating countries of migrants, the number of languages in which SBS Radio broadcasts has risen sharply from eight in the 1970s to 74 today, which is indicative of how complexly diverse multicultural Australia has become. The purpose of SBS Radio programming is not simply that of community cultural maintenance, but the creation of an inclusive, multilingual public sphere which is national in scope. The organization's relative autonomy from ethnic communities has enabled it to pursue a more innovative agenda, going beyond the welfarist logic of traditional multiculturalist policy and catering for ethno-specific interests, towards a more ambitious cosmopolitan multiculturalism where the focus is on promoting cultural worldliness rather than parochial, cultural self-interest. This cosmopolitan philosophy of multicultural broadcasting was developed within SBS in the 1990s, when then Managing Director Malcolm Long, inspired by Robert Hughes' (1993) *Culture of Complaint*, coined the credo of 'navigating difference' as the unifying approach to SBS programming across media platforms (Ang et al. 2008, p. 22).

On television, a cosmopolitan approach to programming was forced on the organization almost by default due to its tight budget, compelling it to rely on purchased international programs rather than producing its own programs. SBS made a virtue out of this requirement by selecting programs – movies, documentaries and TV series – from around the world, mostly in languages other than English. Such programs would meet SBS's Charter obligations and respond to the linguistic and cultural needs of particular ethno-specific segments of multicultural Australia, but they also provided an opportunity for general audiences ('all Australians') to familiarize themselves with other, less well-known cultures. In other words, such programs would not only be 'bringing the world back home', but also show audiences that 'the world is an amazing place' (as two early SBS slogans would have it).

This cosmopolitan, multilingual television culture was underpinned by the highly innovative use of subtitling, which became a central cultural technology to enable cross-cultural communication and the navigation of difference. Internationally, the practice of subtitling was deployed in some countries, usually to translate English-language programs (particularly, the dominant American shows) into different national languages. But, at SBS the opposite took place:

foreign-language films and TV programs were provided with subtitles in English. Subtitling was preferred over dubbing, not just because it was cheaper but, more importantly, because it was truer to SBS's multicultural mission. While dubbing erases the traces of the original language in favour of English monolingualism, subtitling shows respect for linguistic diversity. In this way, SBS has contributed to a greater presence of other languages in Australian public culture.

However, the pressure to maximize audiences ensured that the hegemony of English was never challenged. Even though SBS has contributed to greater public acceptance of subtitled world cinema, for example, this kind of cosmopolitan programming could attract only relatively small – some would say elite – audiences, which was considered unsustainable for an organization with a national remit and which, despite being a public broadcaster, had to compete for audience share in a field dominated by the commercial networks. As a consequence, even within SBS, English-language programming has gradually come to dominate in a bid to increase accessibility and audiences. For example, the nightly SBS World News bulletin, which has provided a cosmopolitan alternative to the more insular news programs of other television broadcasters (including the ABC), now regularly skips the use of subtitles for international news items, using voiceovers instead to communicate the words of important, non-English speaking global figures. Critics have argued, as a result, that SBS has diluted its multilingual, multicultural commitments in pursuit of becoming more mainstream (Carey 2010).

At the same time, the extent to which SBS has contributed to a diversification or cosmopolitanization of mainstream culture itself is considerable. Here, it is interesting to look at SBS's own commissioned productions, which have become a larger slice of the television schedule in more recent times. These programs have included efforts to insert multicultural content into popular genres (such as the cop show *East West 101*, featuring a Muslim police officer; the drama *Sunshine*, focusing on the lives of young African migrants, and sitcoms such as *The Family Law*, featuring a Chinese-Australian family), as well as the award-winning documentary series *Go Back To Where You Came From*, which followed six Australians with differing opinions on asylum seekers being taken on a 'reverse' journey to that taken by refugees to reach Australia. First broadcast in 2011, this show intervened in the highly emotive debate about asylum seekers which, by adopting a reality TV format, attracted huge audiences, becoming the highest-rated program for SBS in that year. These examples suggest that SBS has become more adept at promoting a more *popular* multiculturalism, where cultural difference and diversity is presented as a normalized reality, intrinsic to mainstream society (Ang et al. 2008, p. 20).

One area where SBS has had particular success in this regard is sport. It can pride itself on having popularized soccer (association football), a sport which was not mainstream and was popular mainly with migrant communities until well into the 1980s. Showing football – dubbed 'the world game' – was a major priority for SBS Television from the start, when it began to bring football coverage from most major football countries. In doing so, it contributed much to the growth of football audiences in Australia. Football on SBS is a unique example of a cultural production strategy that is simultaneously ethnic, cosmopolitan and popular: it satisfied migrant interests, opened Australians up to the world, and managed to attract increasingly large audiences. In this way, SBS became a catalyst for making Australian culture more 'worldly'. When SBS's chief champion of football Les Murray – whose original name was Laszlo Urge, having come to Australia as a refugee from Hungary as a 12-year-old in 1957 – died in August 2017, he was given a State funeral, which was symbolic of the importance of his role in promoting that more worldly culture.

Another example is the way in which Australia has come to participate in the Eurovision Song Contest. For years, SBS TV had broadcast the annual contest and helped develop a passionate following for this musical extravaganza among Australian audiences, not least those with European migrant backgrounds. Due to SBS's longstanding commitment to the event, Australia has been allowed to participate in the competition since 2015. Interestingly, the three performers selected to date to represent Australia were all accomplished singers of non-Anglo minority backgrounds: Guy Sebastian in 2015, who is of mixed-race descent born in Malaysia; Korea-born Dami Im in 2016; and Isaiah Firebrace in 2017, who is of Aboriginal descent. This strategic selection of artists demonstrates SBS's ingenuity in 'reflecting Australia's multicultural society' at one of the world's biggest live entertainment events (Carniel 2017). At the same time, it has adroitly inserted multiculturalism into the heart of mainstream Australian popular culture, making it commercially viable.

Beyond policy: commercialization, fragmentation or productive proliferation?

The cases of the arts and broadcast media described above suggest that making multiculture is a challenging process. Although official discourse (such as that of *Creative Nation* and *Creative Australia*) has always emphasized that multiculturalism is relevant 'for all Australians', indicating that cultural diversity is significant to the nation as a whole, in practice the focus of multicultural policies has tended to be confined to the minority space of 'ethnic communities', warranting affirmative action to cater to their special interests. In the arts field, 'multicultural arts' has been associated predominantly with a deficit model of arts funding, where the main goal is increasing access and participation, rather than excellence and innovation. In the media field, as represented by SBS, 'multicultural radio' has always maintained its philosophical and operational definition as broadcasting in many 'ethnic' languages, while there has been a more varied range of interpretations of 'multicultural television' across the spectrum of ethnic, cosmopolitan and popular orientations. Television's status as the most widely used medium in the second half of the twentieth century made it necessary for SBS, as a national public broadcaster, to find creative compromises to reconcile these three potentially conflicting orientations. As we have shown above, there are some examples of great success in this regard (McClean 2013).

However, SBS's popular success has also attracted criticism from advocates of multiculturalism, accusing it not only of betraying its multicultural mandate, but of pandering to commercialism (Nolan and Radywyl 2004). Indeed, it is no secret that SBS's embrace of more popular programming – including its huge investments in sport (also including live broadcasts of the Tour de France, for example) – is motivated to a large extent by a desire to maximize ratings, a key indicator of commercialization. There has also been increasing pressure to increase revenue from advertising and sponsorship (which is permitted for SBS but not the ABC), which can have negative implications for multicultural representation on television. For example, showing programs from migrants' countries of origin was initially an important objective for SBS Television. However, it soon became clear that programs from countries with less-developed television industries (such as Greece or Turkey) were seen as 'too ethnic' to attract broad, cross-cultural audiences – that is, as not commercial enough. As a result, priority was given to importing 'quality' programs from countries with more established and less culturally 'foreign' screen cultures such as France, Italy and, more recently, Scandinavia. Consequently, whole areas of world culture, including those with large diasporic populations in Australia, such as the Arab-speaking countries or China, tend to remain invisible on SBS Television.[2]

The dilemma of commercialization points to some of the limitations of what national cultural policy can achieve in the making of multiculture. The aim of cultural policy, by formulating directives or incentives, is to shape the cultural field according to some stated desirable goals and objectives. In other words, it is an attempt to effect cultural change 'from above'. However, cultural change also happens 'on the ground', as a consequence of organic developments in society at large, and which may well be ahead of any policy framework. Panucci (2017) admits as much, observing, with regard to the Australia Council's work, that past policies have tended to have been 'done *to* people not *with* people'. Thus, rather than working with a predetermined set of targets directed at a fixed range of ascribed community identities, as a multiculturalist policy tends to do, he says:

> I'm more interested in what happens to the young Algerian who arrived as a refugee to Australia 10 years ago who may have been a playwright in Algeria. Is that person applying to the Australia Council? Does that person even think that they have a place to continue to practise and develop their arts practice and their cultural endeavours in Australia, and that an agency like the Australia Council is a place where they could come to and have a conversation about what that might look like, and how they could achieve success through the Australia Council?

Panucci's perspective gestures to the inevitable limits to the reach and relevance of a national arts body. Whether or not the Algerian playwright would engage with the Australia Council to pursue their artistic practice, it is clear that a huge diversity of cultural activity is being unleashed throughout Australia as part of a spontaneous cultural development without any involvement of the Australia Council or other national cultural institutions, such as SBS, and sometimes even without any reference to Australia, and aided strongly by commercial initiatives. This development includes the dozens of commercially run satellite TV channels that connect diasporic populations to home country cultures, or the passionate engagement of migrant youth with transnational pop forms such as K-pop and J-pop. As Panucci (2017) points out, 'there are performers who arrive in this country from certain countries, 10,000 tickets are sold to a venue, that artist comes in, does three performances, flies out of Australia and you would not know it from any mainstream newspaper'. Such popular events point to the increasing commercial viability of multicultural entrepreneurialism beyond the realm of the cultural mainstream.

Randa Kattan (interview 2017), CEO of the Arab Council Australia, cites the example of the proliferation of Arab film and cultural festivals as evidence of a shifting dynamic in Australia's multiculture. Where there was once a single Arab Film Festival, there are now Lebanese, Palestinian, Egyptian and Iraqi film or cultural festivals. This proliferation of multicultural film festivals is sustained partly by government grants, and partly by commercially 'savvy' organizers catering to diasporic and mainstream cosmopolitan audiences (Dolgopolov 2013). For those favouring a politics of pan-Arab identity, the multiplication of Arabic-language festivals may be problematic but, as Kattan argues, we now function in a 'market-place' of culture. Multiculturalism has shifted from being a space where ethnic community organizations led the way in delivering to their 'community', to a more dispersed set of networks, organizations and events in which commercial interests play a significant role. As Abood (2017) observes, the community cultural development sector is at the forefront of this cultural proliferation, augmenting older, 'ethnic community' models of multiculturalism: 'there's cross-cultural work happening, ethno-specific work promoted *across* communities and it engages lots of different people'. She also talked about the role of commercial activity in the sector, echoing Panucci's observation about highly localized but vibrant multicultural events, especially in Western Sydney, Australia's most culturally and linguistically region:

> in every community there are entrepreneurs ... In the Arabic community, there's an ecology of newspapers, and radio stations, and promoters, and entrepreneurs ... if you drive down Parramatta Road in Granville sometimes there's a big poster of a singer coming from Lebanon, or somewhere, and everyone will go and see that singer.

For her, that's why the sector is 'thriving' and why 'the cultural field is really interesting'. While government grants continue to be central, many practitioners are now pragmatic about where they get funding. Mohammed Ahmed, director of the Sweatshop Western Sydney Literacy Movement (interview 2017), admitted that 'money is so important because there's a kind of romanticization of how we make art' and that he was prepared to seek it anywhere: from philanthropic bodies, corporate sponsorships, local businesses and councils, Foreign Affairs cultural diplomacy grants, crowdfunding as well as commercial initiatives. Indeed, this promiscuous entrepreneurialism suggests that, while in dominant understandings of cultural policy making commercialization is often considered a force to argue against and be resisted, in the multicultural realm it has been an *enabling* driver of cultural development in response to burgeoning grassroots community desires and marginalized consumer demands generally ignored by mainstream cultural institutions.

Conclusion

Reports over many years have identified ethnicity as a problem regarding arts participation (Australia Council 2010, 2014), as an absence of involvement in the mainstream cultural life of the nation. But the picture is much more complex. While diversity remains a 'predicament' for the sector (Ang 2005), there is much more going on in terms of cultural participation than attending mainstream cultural institutions. There are, as Abood (2017) has described it, 'many worlds' in the arts and cultural sectors in Australia. Beyond the recognized field of national culture, there is both fragmentation and productive proliferation, propelled by diversifying cultural initiatives which are often transnational in focus and increasingly commercially viable. This trend is suggestive of ongoing tensions between policy as government rhetoric and the everyday lives of Australians, between perceptions of ethnically-defined communities and the cultural complexities which frame those lives, between 'cosmopolitan' and 'welfarist' conceptions of multiculturalism, and between public and commercial imperatives in cultural production (such as in the media). Multiculture is thus being made on a day-to-day basis in ways that both exceed and undercut the national policies of making multiculture. But, it is also a domain where much remains to be done, both in terms of national policy and institutional practices, to address gaps unfilled by the inevitable biases of commercialism.

Notes

1 The concept of intersectionality was coined in the 1980s by U.S. black feminist legal scholar Kimberlé Crenshaw to address the compound impact of race and gender on the lives of minority populations, specifically black women. The term has seen a renewed interest in recent times as a way of recognizing intersecting dimensions of identity and power relations and is slowly being taken up in public policy analysis – for example, in the area of health (e.g., Hankivsky and Cormier 2011).
2 The one Chinese show that made it to prime time on SBS TV was dating show *If You Are the One*, the popularity of which extended beyond diasporic Chinese audiences to reach broader Australian constituencies.

References

Ang, I., 2005. The predicament of diversity: Multiculturalism in practice at the art museum. *Ethnicities*, 5(3), 305–320.
Ang, I., Hawkins, G. and Dabboussy, L., 2008. *The SBS story: The challenge of cultural diversity*. Sydney: UNSW Press.

Australia Council, 1993. *Arts for a multicultural Australia*. Surry Hills: Australia Council.
Australia Council, 2000. *Arts in a multicultural Australia*. Surry Hills: Australia Council.
Australia Council, 2010. *More than bums on seats*. Canberra: Australian Government.
Australia Council, 2014. *Arts in daily life: Australian participation in the arts*. Canberra: Australian Government.
Australia Council, n.d. *Cultural engagement framework* [online]. Available from: www.australiacouncil.gov.au/programs-and-resources/cultural-engagement-framework/ [Accessed 9 November 2017].
Australian Government, 2017. *Multicultural Australia: United, strong, successful (Australia's multicultural statement)*. Canberra: Australian Government.
Carey, C., 2010. Lost in translation, subtitlers get the chop. *Sydney Morning Herald*, 9 June. Available from: www.smh.com.au/entertainment/tv-and-radio/lost-in-translation-subtitlers-get-the-chop-20100609-xvdm.html [Accessed 29 November 2017].
Carniel, J., 2017. Welcome to Eurostralia: The strategic diversity of Australia at the Eurovision Song Contest. *Continuum*, 31(1), 1–11.
Castles, S. and Kalantzis, M., 1994. *Access to excellence: A review of issues affecting artists and arts from non-English speaking backgrounds (Volume 1: Overview report)*. Canberra: Office of Multicultural Affairs, Department of the Prime Minister and Cabinet.
Dolgopolov, G., 2013. Ethnic, diasporic, multicultural? The film festival as policy and Practice. *In*: A. Jakubowicz and C. Ho, eds. *'For those who've come across the seas ... ': Australian multiculturalism: Theory, policy and practice*. North Melbourne: Australian Scholarly Publishing, 68–82.
Gibson, L., 2001. *The uses of art: Constructing Australian identities*. St Lucia: University of Queensland Press.
Gunew, S. and Rizvi, F., eds., 1994. *Culture, difference and the arts*. St. Leonards: Allen & Unwin.
Hankivsky, O. and Cormier, R., 2011. Intersectionality and public policy: Some lessons from existing models. *Political Research Quarterly*, 64(1), 217–229.
Hawkins, G., 1993. *From Nimbin to Mardi Gras: Constructing community arts*. St. Leonards: Allen & Unwin.
Hughes, R., 1993. *Culture of complaint: The fraying of America*. Oxford: Oxford University Press.
Jupp, J., 2001. The institutions of culture: Multiculturalism. *In*: T. Bennett and D. Carter, eds. *Culture in Australia: Policies, publics and programs*. Cambridge: Cambridge University Press, 259–277.
Khan, R., Wyatt, D. and Yue, A., 2015. Making and remaking multicultural arts: Policy, cultural difference and the discourse of decline. *International Journal of Cultural Policy*, 21(2), 219–234.
Khan, R., Wyatt, D., Yue, A. and Papastergiadis, N., 2013. Creative Australia and the dispersal of multiculturalism. *Asia Pacific Journal of Arts and Cultural Management*, 10(1), 25–34.
Kleist, O., 2017. *Political memories and migration: Belonging, society and Australia Day*. London: Palgrave Macmillan.
McClean, G., 2013. National communication and diversity: The story of SBS. *In*: A. Jakubowicz and C. Ho, eds. *'For those who've come across the seas ... ': Australian multiculturalism: Theory, policy and practice*. North Melbourne: Australian Scholarly Publishing, 45–56.
Noble, G., 2011. 'Bumping into alterity': Transacting cultural complexities. *Continuum*, 25(6), 827–840.

Nolan, D. and Radywyl, N., 2004. Pluralising identity, mainstreaming identities: SBS as a technology of citizenship. *Southern Review*, 37(2), 40–65.

Papastergiadis, N., ed., 2003. *Complex entanglements: Art, globalisation and cultural difference*. London: Rivers Oram Press.

Vertovec, S., 2007. Super-diversity and its implications. *Ethnic and Racial Studies*, 30(6), 1024–1054.

Wise, A. and Velayutham, R., eds., 2009. *Everyday multiculturalism*. London: Palgrave Macmillan.

Interviews

Abood, P., 2017. 3 April.
Ahmed, M., 2017. 20 April.
Capon, E., 2017. 22 February.
Kattan, R., 2017. 17 March.
Panucci, F., 2017. 26 July.

Afterword
Undoing the bonds of nation/
rediscovering dead souls[1]

Toby Miller

David Rowe, Graeme Turner, Emma Waterton and their contributors have done us a profound service by tracing the commodification of Australian cultural policy over the last quarter of a century. Their point of departure, the Federal Government's *Creative Nation* document, appeared in 1994. It forwarded a vision of the good life that was connected to commerce, but not limited to or by it – mammon was just one influence.

Nevertheless, the abiding lesson from this collection is that the policy's advocates birthed a commodified lifeworld, one that subsequently coursed through multicultural television, electronic games and pretty much everything in-between. Cultural nationalism was trumped by capitalism. In what follows, I'll engage with that position in the context of my understanding of prior Australian history before considering nationalism and cosmopolitanism from an international perspective (usefully done in this volume's chapter (10) on Indigenous television by Ben Dibley and Graeme Turner).

The Australian situation[2]

Our editors discern 'a pervasive tendency towards the commercialization of national culture' and 'the increasing influence of globalism and/or transnationalism'. They argue that over the past two decades, a 'cultural nationalist model … has been reconfigured and its discourses and principles, on the whole, devalued'. The evidence lies in 'a wave of deregulation and disinvestment across a range of cultural industries'. This transformation has reached the point where 'culture now tends to be located in those portfolios most directly responsible for national economic and industrial development'.[3]

Australia's associated scholarly slippage from critical cultural policy studies to creative industries advocacy has been well-covered (see, for example, Turner 2011) and needs no further rehearsal in this context. Suffice it to say that my teeth started to gnash at the familiarity of this story, and to appreciate our editors' and authors' insights. The post-industrial futurism of the New York intellectuals of the 1960s has claimed its latest victims. The key 'sluggers' – Daniel Bell (1977), Zbigniew Brzezinski (1969), and Alvin Toffler (1983) – saw their predictions for a ternary U.S. economy redisposed to remake Australia, as per the warping vision of their latter-day legatee, Richard Florida (2008), and his pride of obedient antipodean acolytes (who, for example, helped him do 'a couple of very special things in, in Noosa').[4]

In some ways, the transformation traced in this volume is unsurprising. Sooner or later, attempts by artists, the third sector and progressive critics to put monetary value on cultural production in terms cognizable by reactionary econocrats, led to the dominance of the latter's neoclassical sorcery. As Bogart tells Bergman in *Casablanca* (1943), 'Maybe not today. Maybe not tomorrow, but soon, and for the rest of your life'. Merton's (1936) rule of unintended consequences eagerly steps up to bat when conjunctures change, and formerly dominant discourses legitimize emergent forces or are transformed by them. The notion of art-for-art's sake (remember that '*l'art pour l'art*' was always something of a joke – after all, MGM Latinized it as a corporate motto, above that leonine roar) is always compromised by the overdetermining overlap of social and aesthetic norms and expectations. In Diego Rivera's (1932, p. 51) famous words, '[A]rt is a social creation'.

But there has been some kind of change. Always-already utilitarian uses of culture were once undertaken in the service of religion, the monarchy, or revolution. Now they seek to convert 'at-risk' youth in the global North to carefully calibrated, moderate conduct or to stimulate the services sector of the economy. George Yúdice (2009) uses the term 'culture as resource' to describe this mixture of identity politics, welfarism and secondary accumulation. The constitutive connection of cultural nationalism to corporate norms and state desires has been a defining problem for Australian historiography and the Left around the world (Pascoe 1979; Anderson 2016). The Enlightenment teleologies of liberal and Marxist histories have never known how to manage the petty thuggishness and state violence of nationalism and its persistent capacity to overcome supposed world-historical agents of magical change, be they *bourgeois* individuals or social classes. In the Australian case, encounters between race and class have provided crucial faultlines for understanding the past. Along with the dispossession of native peoples, the pre-Federation Australian Labor Party's (ALP's) strident anti-Asian rhetoric in the name of high wages helped to birth the country's constitutive racism (McQueen 2004). The Liberal Party's belated discovery of nationalism as a vote-winner in the 1970s was, in turn, an answer to the ALP's similarly belated discovery of working-class migrants as an industrial and psephological bloc, despite hopes that it bespoke a shift from nationalism to multiculturalism (Castles et al. 1988). The history is outlined in this book's chapter (11) on multiculturalism by Ien Ang and Greg Noble.

Australia has dependent cultural relations with the U.S. and the UK and economic ones with those nations, plus China and Japan. The economy has always been an intimate issue for this semi-peripheral, semi-metropolitan nation – wealthy but weak, worried yet weary, arrogant and anxious, vexed while vested. Born from post-imperial protectionism, and dependent for its development on being a farm and a quarry, Australia embodies the Dutch Disease (Ebrahim-zadeh 2003) so fully that it has generated its very own Gregory Thesis (1976).

Capital investment in natural resources has largely precluded the development of industries that add value through local labour, ever since neoliberal warlocks flexed their muscles via the first Whitlam government's assault on manufacturing through tariff cuts and the weasel-words 'Industries Assistance Commission' (Warhurst 1982). Twenty years later, just prior to *Creative Nation*'s release, the task of building neoliberalism was declared by some to have overtaken that of nation-building (Pusey 1991).

Unsurprisingly, cultural policy in Australia indexes that story. It has routinely 'double-declutched' between artistic and industrial norms, from representing the nation to funding capitalists, from *avant-garde* short cinema to tax breaks for indolent local and Yanqui producers (Dermody and Jacka 1987; Burns and Eltham 2010) on the prowl for what they call free money (i.e., neither loans nor equity). Today's museums, with their neoliberal talk of visitor experiences and diverse publics, inherit the legacy of early Australian anthropology's British heritage in its museum-based dedication to racial difference (i.e., hierarchy – see, for example, Barrett and McManus 2007). And the Australian Broadcasting Corporation (formerly, Commission) has always been required to be popular in order not to appear elitist, while simultaneously being damned for taking away opportunities from the commercial sector by attracting mass audiences (Inglis 2006a, 2006b). I defer to *Making Culture's* authors' profound knowledge of Australia's slippery shift from cultural policy to creative industries and its oleaginous embrace of contemporary capitalism as part of that manoeuvre. But it is worth noting just how pragmatic and discriminatory local nationalism has often been. And that takes me to nationalism on a different *palette*.

Nationalism elsewhere

For conservative ethno-nationalists, the nation is a constant across history, albeit changing with time and circumstance (Herder 2002, p. 297). It is sustained through supposedly indelible ties: origin myths, languages, customs, physiques and religions (Smith 2000). But, for those more in thrall to modernity, such claims are always already historical fictions carved from invented traditions (for example, Hindutva today; Nandy 1998). Far from being the outcome of abiding mythologies, the materiality and idea of the nation derived from the Industrial Revolution, which brought places together that had not previously deemed themselves linked in any way. Relatively isolated, subsistence villages were transformed by the interdependence engendered by capitalist organizations, the commodification of everyday relations and the sense of unity generated from nation-binding technologies and institutions, most notably print and the public school (Gellner 1988). By the time of 1919's Treaty of Versailles, the victorious powers regarded national self-determination (apart from freedom for their own 'possessions') as the best route to peace, along with a return to open markets and a state system of governance that would control the warlike tendencies of the losers and others. But imperialism was not dismantled, and when the Depression hit, the immediate response was restrictive trade practices, such as tariffs and other barriers. Alongside the emergence of fascist nationalism, it produced the conditions of possibility for the Second World War. Similar responses followed the oil shocks of the 1970s (Strange 1979).

So, the idea of nations as guarantors of peace was compromised by the victors protecting their own empires, then distorting the trading system because of an enormous economic crisis. Meanwhile, the ideology of nationalism, always close to doctrines of autochthony, autarky and autarchy, was used by the emergent great powers (the USSR, Japan, Germany and Italy) to justify political or racial superiority in much the way as the established U.S., French and British imperialists did. Although the claims and efforts of ethno-nationalists frequently fail to override more universal ideas promulgated through religion, democracy and human rights (Horkheimer 2013), where the *bourgeoisie* failed to adopt comprehensively liberal ideas, and technological connections across borders were countered by local demagoguery, collective ideas of superiority and destiny found fecund fields. A refusal to identify with humanity as a whole was at the core of this kind of nationalism (Adorno 1997, 2007; Adorno et al. 1950). Labour was conceived of as a national entity, along with ethnicity, ideology, and language, and new communications technologies were harnessed in the name of the sovereign-state. Ethno-nationalist and modern theories blended.

Consider the right-wing use of Gramsci's idea of the national popular by authoritarian and dictatorial regimes across Latin America from the 1940s to the 1990s. They harnessed class interests secreted as national ones, which became common sense for both Left and Right (Galeano 1997). The same applies to South Asia and segments of the Arab and African worlds (Halliday 2005). The breakup of formal empires has seen an explosion of sovereign states and their attendant national myths. The number of countries across the globe has gone from a few dozen in 1945 to over 200 today, and most major conflicts since World War II have been over attempts to create new nations. At the same time, people keep leaving their places of birth in rapidly increasing numbers and mostly voluntarily, to make better lives for themselves, but also as desperate refugees. The United Nations (UN) estimates that 258 million people were international migrants in 2017, up from 220 million in 2010 and 173 million in 2000. The vast majority live in Asia, Europe and North America (United Nations 2017). That mobility correlates with global warming in a reordering of the old climate-determinism argument that intense aridity or humidity lead to centralized control of water and oversized irrigation public works, thereby breeding despotism (Missirian and Schlenker 2017; Wittfogel 1967). The corollary is a tension between what is left behind, taken with, encountered, rejected and adopted (Banks 2014). The globe is full of people who feel as though they do not belong, either where they have left or where they have landed, as they flee the agonies of origin and experience the refusals of arrival. The essential hybridity of humanity is challenged by ethno-nationalism encountering global mobility, with each shaping the other.

Nationalism is routinely and rightly damned for its maleness, brutality, war-mongering, and other failings: Rosa Luxemburg (1986, p. 331) spoke for many when she denounced 'the empty wordiness of nationalism as an instrument of bourgeois domination'. The absurdity of nationalism is not confined to the Right: the spectre of Stalin is never far behind, lurking in off-screen space to jump us as if we were the second-last girl in an '80s horror movie. '[T]he whole, disastrous experience of "state socialism" which came to so abrupt and dramatic an end in 1989' has meant that 'the entire historical basis and trajectory of "the left" in serious politics has had to be rethought' (Hall 1995, pp. 25–26). And the desire of China to exercise 'sharp power' around the world takes culture as a core component of its desired hegemony (National Endowment for Democracy 2017).

That said, C.L.R. James (with Dunayevskaya and Lee 1986) always recognised the importance of nationalism versus internationalism as a litmus test of anti-colonial credentials – that a cosmopolitan worldview relied on appreciating local circumstances and working within them. The real enemy was bureaucratization, not nationalism. For Althusser (1971), it was essential that revolutionary forces recognize their specific conditions of existence, in workplaces and countries, but also that they identify with others, far away, speaking other languages, yet oppressed by similar forms of labouring life. The nation was, therefore, crucial, but its chauvinistic incantation in culture worked to pervert the kinds of identification that it engendered unless they were played with and contested, as per critical Mexican cultural nationalism's wry, ironic, yet respectful stance towards the country's foundational mythology and its cynical use by élites (García Canclini 1982).

This is another history, of longing for self-determination and resisting imperialism. The nation has, of course, been a core resistive concept of decolonialization, providing a means of registering claims for inclusion in both narratives and institutions (Cabral 1973) – a veritable font of resistance to imperial suzerainty. Kwame Nkrumah (1969, p. 88) avowed that '[n]ationalism is the ideological channel of the anti-colonialist struggle' and Lyotard (1993, p. 238) viewed it as a key response to 'the profound *desocialization* produced by imperialism'. Du Bois (1942, p. 72) referred to the 'personal apostles of African nationalism, who wander across the vast distances of Africa and talk with the people'. And it is clear that peripheral and semi-peripheral nationalism can be democratizing and enabling as well as exclusionary and repressive. It successfully invokes theories and commitments that do not disappear, despite myths of anti-nationalism, globalization and technological determinism (Carey 2002).

Cosmopolitanism?

What of cosmopolitanism as an alternative, emerging from much older origins than those associated with contemporary neoliberalism and globalization? A core Enlightenment ideal, cosmopolitanism suffered with the ongoing triumph of the nation-state and nationalist ideology, but became *au courant* again due to the need for ways of living together in a globalizing economy with vast migration and cultural exchange. Its linguistic heritage blends universalism with particularism – an encounter between the cosmos and the citizen staged again and again since Aristotle and frequently leading to a profound suspiciousness and doubt about one's loyalty (Benhabib 2011). This dialectic takes many forms: Edmund Burke (1774) addressing the electors of Bristol, Angela Davis (2003) calling for a new emancipation via the destruction of prisons, Jesus Christ teaching about universal equality and Immanuel Kant (2006) theorizing world citizenship.

Negative responses to it can be powerful, such as British Prime Minister Teresa May's (2016) asinine insult, 'If you believe you're a citizen of the world, you're a citizen of nowhere. You don't understand what the very word "citizenship" means', and Stalin (1946) referring to Jewish people as 'rootless cosmopolitans' because he regarded international cultural consciousness and identification as inimical to Leninism. But, for H. G. Wells (1902, p. 317), Jewish mobility 'gives the lie to our yapping "nationalisms"'.

Global capital is often regarded as a sign of cosmopolitanism's eventual triumph: socialists of the inter-war period welcomed multinational corporations as signs that economic nationalism had been succeeded by coordinated planning (Mandel 1968, p. 434). In the decolonizing burst from 1947 to the late 1970s, while some new countries sought import-substitution industrialization, others moved more successfully towards an export-oriented model via the New International Division of Labour. East Asian states, in particular, mobilized their reserve armies of peasantry to manufacture goods for the global North (Fröbel et al. 1980). Meanwhile, older nations in Latin America sought to elude, by any means possible, the horrors of dictatorship in the name of left or right-wing nationalism and the financial punishment meted out to leftist governments by international markets (Cardoso 2005; Vargas Llosa 2017). A third group favoured a fuller-throated Marxist anti-imperialism (Amin 1997). All these formations brokered a middle ground between nationalism and cosmopolitanism.

And something else was going on, both rhetorically and institutionally, towards cosmopolitanism. The histories of the League of Nations and the UN stand for the failure of world government. But their less grandiose, more technical subgroups have managed with reasonable success the international relations of telecommunications, postage, health and immigration. Those entities arose from a notion that the anarchic world of states could be governed in much the same way as individual sovereign states managed their populations. Beyond the utopian rhetoric of global peace that was so derided by realists (Miller 1981), classical theorists have argued for the success of a relatively ordered and peaceful world system since 1945 thanks to the strength of large states, their desire to eschew direct conflict with one another and the emergence of a raft of international organizations operating beyond territories and armies (Bull 2002). The comparatively technical tasks in which the International Telecommunication Union, World Health Organization and so on specialize have remained relatively free of conflict, by contrast with peacekeeping or culture.

At the same time, the definition of what constitutes national identity is contested because of the necessary hybridity of humanity. Consider Colombia. Ethnic/racial difference is defined there in ways that are at variance with Anglo norms: the state counts people as mixed race who would be deemed Indigenous, black, Asian and so on in Anglo countries. The *mestizo* majority is mostly made up of citizens with mixed ethnicity, a blend of Indigenous, Afro-Colombian, Asian, European, Sephardim and Arabic heritage. The prevailing ideology of *mestizaje* assumes a norm in which Colombians are said to be a mosaic of Indigenous and Caucasian. As the popular saying goes, 'Aquí en Colombia somos muy mezclados' [Here in Colombia we are all mixed] (Restrepo et al. 2014). The latest census (2005) identifies three non-*mestizo* minorities: 87 national Indigenous groups, comprised of 1.4 million people who live communally and use their original languages (3.4 per cent of the overall population); 4.3 million Afro-Colombian descendants of slaves (10.6 per cent); and 5,000 Gitano [Roma] (0.01 per cent) (Departamento Administrativo Nacional de Estadística 2007, p. 33). These minorities suffer massive inequality, but part of their capacity to form themselves as blocs and argue for redress derives from cosmopolitan identifications with First Peoples and slave descendants elsewhere, and their deployment of Enlightenment ideals (Cabezas-Cortés 2016; Perazzi and Merli 2017). But how does one deal with claims to universalism versus particular calls on rights in such situations?

Will Kymlicka (1995) seeks a *rapprochement* in the white-settler colonies of Australia, the US, Canada, and Aotearoa/New Zealand between majority White settlement, 'immigrant multiculturalism' (newer voluntary migrants, who deserve few cultural rights) and 'minority nationalism' (First Peoples, the dispossessed and the enslaved, who deserve many) via the notion of culture as an aid to individual autonomy through engagement with collective as well as individual histories. Conversely, Amélie Oksenberg Rorty (1995, pp. 162, 164) argues that cultural maintenance and development should be by-products of universal access to education, a 'primary condition of free and equal citizen participation in public life'. She opposes public funding to sustain familial or religious cultural norms, calling instead for a curriculum that will generate flexible cosmopolitans who learn about their country and its 'global neighbors'. Rorty's argument is a culturalist restatement of human-capital *nostra* about individuals maximizing their utility through investment in skills. She rejects cross-cultural awareness as a necessary component of good citizenship and justice, but endorses it as good business sense; come on down the creative industries, and claim your prize.

Conclusion

I used to walk into cities pretty much anywhere and see monuments to socialism and national endeavour: the post office, railway station, telephone exchange, power station, clock tower and the public school – the great initiatives of socializing risk and equalizing access that made Western Europe, Australasia and North America modern. Today, their shady, shadowy equivalent is the data centre – our dirty, coal-powered euphemized cloud. It, too, relies on socialized risk – the corporation running it almost certainly receives public subsidies, no matter where the server farm is located in the world. But this is no public monument to the nation; rather, it is a clandestine testament to today's norm of capitalism for the poor and socialism for the wealthy, secreted behind an everyday office-block façade (a cybertarian shift is well explained here in by Brett Hutchins' chapter (8) on the digital).

November 2017, when I started drafting these words, found me in Catalunya, and a world where the centralizing force of capital seemed compromised by nationalist populism. Hundreds of thousands of people had marched the previous

Saturday for the right to a referendum on independence. They wanted to become their own nation – or not; but above all, they wished to vote on the proposition. Anarchists, greens and leftists jumped on the local nationalist bandwagon – or perhaps they helped form it. Meanwhile, the political descendants of Franco who ran the government in Madrid sent in the Guardia Civil (akin to the Federal Police in Australia) to confront and batter those who attempted to vote. The international Left rallied behind the Catalans. I think that they were right in terms of the anti-democratic police brutality of the national government, but they needed to consider such questions as widespread corruption, bigotry and a secondary labour market in Catalunya: two of the most powerless groups, working-class migrants from Málaga and Latin America who built the region's infrastructure and continue to characterize its proletariat. Catalans often refer to the two groups derisively as 'xarnega' (Niño-Murcia and Rothman 2008). Many of them refuse to learn Català, and they generally oppose independence. And, at the same moment as this bloc was celebrated on the Left elsewhere, 60,000 Poles were marching with banners that read: 'Europe will be white or deserted' and 'Clean blood'. As *The Economist* (2017) has observed of resurgent nationalism:

> The Alternative for Germany has won 94 seats in the Bundestag. Marine Le Pen of the National Front won a third of the vote in France's presidential election. In Hungary, Austria and the Czech Republic nationalists have taken power, just as they did in Poland.

The same article also cites Britain's referendum vote to leave the European Union, Turkey's increased militancy, moves away from constitutional pacifism in Japan, the power of Hindu supremacism in India, China's heavily mythologized expansionism and Russian belligerence as examples of a global nationalist drift.

Jean Baudrillard, annoying gadfly of the dialectic that he was, shared the following confession:

> I operate from a prejudiced position against nationalism, one which is anti-nationalist, or even anti-cultural. Somewhere within me there is a distancing away from what is closer to the bone, for that which is closer to one's own culture, one's country, family is that from which one cannot escape.
> (2015, p. 92)

Baudrillard is assuredly one of Samuel Huntington's (2004) evocations of the 'dead souls' lamented in Walter Scott's (1805) poem 'The Lay of the Last Minstrel,' guilty of denying the value of national affinity. But is Stuart Hall (2010, p. 185), whose recollection of Britain's birth of a New Left found him avowing that '[a]s a colonial, I certainly felt instinctively more at home in the more socially anonymous metropolitan culture'?

Scott's ode to nationalism, with its stirring lines 'Breathes there the man, with soul so dead, Who never to himself hath said, This is my own, my native land!' may resonate with Scotland's struggle and complicity with English empire. But its arrogant denial of identifications beyond the immediate, and fetishization of national unity, is no model for today, tomorrow or soon. Yet it seems ineradicable. The dilemma that divided dissidents of the post-war Russian empire continues: 'should Sovietization be resisted with cosmopolitanism or nationalism?' (Kristeva 1997, p. 8).

The key lesson to draw from these writings is that, wherever the creative industries operate, regardless of their incarnation in culture, policy or business formations, their principal mission is to animate and empower capital (Kleinhans 2011). Now that the nation's role in decolonization is formally over, it functions partly as an easy conduit for capital formation, and partly for its unfortunate diversion into ethnic identification. But that said, the cosmic ambivalence of my opening stanzas remains – as Perry Anderson (1989, p. 103) insists, nationalism is 'a mass phenomenon of elemental force in the last two centuries'. Consider the concept of a minor literature – 'the literature a minority makes in a major language … effected by a strong co-efficient of deterritorialization' (Deleuze and Guattari 1983, p. 16). And there is a lengthy leftist history of accepting and even promoting the nation 'as the primary mechanism of defense against the domination of foreign and/or global capital' (Hardt and Negri 2000, p. 44).

Neoliberalism has a poor record of economic growth next to the statist capitalism of China's 'powerful, centralized state authority firmly committed to a policy of techno-nationalism that has its origins, well before the reform era, in Mao's nation-building decades' (Ross 2009, p. 54). That provocation recalls a moment in Harry Watt's *The Overlanders* (1946), a British film set in Australia, when the laconically iconic Chips Rafferty rebukes John Fernside, who is playing a rather dubious English remittance man with plans for a 'Northern Territory Exploitation Company'. Chips says it's 'a national job, too big for little people like you'.[5] They'd been instructed to perform an impossible droving task to save the country from occupation, one recognizing that 'bullocks are more important than bullets'. The urgency and formality of the mission is that it is sent by telegram, that classic nation-binding technology of its day (a tendency examined in Graeme Turner's television chapter (5) here). So this volume stands testimony to the continued relevance of just such a gentle but assertive form of nationalism, brokered through the hybridity of multicultural policies, as a blend of the cosmopolitan with the local that engages in a mixture of conflictual and complicit relations with capital. 'Staging' that conflict is crucial if we are to make a difference.

Notes

1 This essay is dedicated to Julia Lesage and the late Chuck Kleinhans, with Julia's kind agreement. Their progressive, cosmopolitan, radical vision has long been an inspiration. See, for example, Kleinhans and Lesage (2016).
2 I last lived in Australia before *Creative Nation* was released, and have since spent a total of perhaps six months there, so my remarks are not those of an expert, though I hope they may be of some interest.
3 Others discern similar tendencies, but are much more sanguine about their effects (O'Regan and Potter 2013).

4 Florida's claim to own the 'creative class®' is asserted with the US Patent and Trademark Office via registration number 3298801. Bill Grantham alerted me to this wonder.
5 Thanks to Stuart Cunningham for confirming my understanding of this sequence.

References

Adorno, T. W., 1997. Opinion delusion society. Trans. H. W. Pickford. *Yale Journal of Criticism*, 10(2), 227–245.
Adorno, T. W., 2007. *Negative dialectics*. Trans. E. B. Ashton. New York: Continuum.
Adorno, T. W., Frenkel-Brunswick, E., Levinson, D. J. and Nevitt Sanford, R., 1950. *The authoritarian personality*. New York: Harper & Row.
Althusser, L., 1971. *Lenin and philosophy and other essays*. Trans. B. Brewster. New York: Monthly Review Press.
Amin, S., 1997. *Capitalism in the age of globalization*. London: Zed.
Anderson, B., 2016. Frameworks of comparison. *London Review of Books*, 21 January, 15–18.
Anderson, P., 1989. *Considerations on Western Marxism*. London: Verso.
Banks, J. A., 2014. Multicultural education and global citizens. *In*: V. Benet-Martínez and Y.-Y. Hong eds. *The Oxford handbook of multicultural identity*. Oxford: Oxford University Press, 379–395.
Barrett, J. and McManus, P., 2007. Civilising nature: Museums and the environment. *In*: G. Birch, ed. *Water wind art and debate: How environmental concerns impact on disciplinary research*. Sydney: University of Sydney Press, 319–344.
Baudrillard, J., 2015. *From hyperreality to disappearance: Uncollected interviews*. R. G. Smith and D. B. Clarke, eds. Edinburgh: Edinburgh University Press.
Bell, D., 1977. The future world disorder: The structural context of crises. *Foreign Policy*, 27, 109–135.
Benhabib, S., 2011. *Dignity in adversity: Human rights in troubled times*. Cambridge: Polity Press.
Brzezinski, Z., 1969. *Between two ages: America's role in the technotronic era*. New York: Viking.
Bull, H., 2002. *The anarchical society: A study of order in world politics* (3rd ed.). New York: Columbia University Press.
Burke, E., 1774. *Speech to the electors of Bristol*. Available from: http://press-pubs.uchicago.edu/founders/documents/v1ch13s7.html [Accessed 28 December 2017].
Burns, A. and Eltham, B., 2010. Boom and bust in Australian screen policy: 10BA, the Film Finance Corporation and Hollywood's 'race to the bottom'. *Media International Australia*, 136, 103–118.
Cabezas-Cortés, C. C., 2016. Consideraciones alrededor de regímenes de discriminación género/etnia sobre relaciones laborales en Colombia. *In*: L. A. Montenegro Mora, ed. *Retos de las relaciones de trabajo y de la seguridad social en el Siglo XXI*. San Juan de Pasto: Editorial UNIMAR, 71–81.
Cabral, A., 1973. *Return to the source: Selected speeches by Amilcar Cabral*. Africa Information Service, ed. New York: Monthly Review Press.
Cardoso, F. H., 2005. Scholarship and statesmanship. *Journal of Democracy*, 16(2), 5–12.
Carey, J. W., 2002. Globalization isn't new; anti-globalization isn't either: September 11 and the history of nations. *Prometheus*, 20(3), 289–293.
Casablanca, 1943. Dir: M. Curtiz.
Castles, S., Cope, B., Kalantzis, M. and Morrissey, M., 1988. *Mistaken identity: Multiculturalism and the demise of nationalism in Australia*. Sydney: Pluto Press.

Davis, A. Y., 2003. *Are prisons obsolete?* New York: Seven Stories Press.
Deleuze, G. and Guattari, F., 1983. What is a minor literature? Trans. R. Brinkley. *Mississippi Review*, 11(3), 13–33.
Departamento Administrativo Nacional de Estadística, 2007. *Colombia una nación multicultural: Su diversidad étnica*. Available from: www.dane.gov.co/files/censo2005/etnia/sys/colombia_nacion.pdf [Accessed 28 December 2017].
Dermody, S. and Jacka, E., 1987. *The screening of Australia volume 1: Anatomy of a film industry*. Sydney: Currency Press.
Du Bois, W. E. B., 1942. A chronicle of race relations. *Phylon*, 3(1), 66–86.
Ebrahim-zadeh, C., 2003. Back to basics: Dutch disease: Too much wealth managed unwisely. *Finance & Development*, 40(1). Available from: www.imf.org/external/pubs/ft/fandd/2003/03/ebra.htm [Accessed 28 December 2017].
The Economist, 2017. Vladimir's choice: Whither nationalism? 19 December. Available from: www.economist.com/news/christmas-specials/21732704-nationalism-not-fading-away-it-not-clear-where-it-heading-whither [Accessed 28 December 2017].
Florida, R., 2008. *Noosa talk* (part 1 of 9). Available from: www.youtube.com/watch?v=Qc40AtN9ok0 [Accessed 28 December 2017].
Fröbel, F., Heinrichs, J. and Kreye, O., 1980. *The new international division of labor: Structural unemployment in industrialised countries and industrialisation in developing countries*. Trans. P. Burgess. Cambridge: Cambridge University Press; Paris: Éditions de la Maison des Sciences de l'Homme.
Galeano, E., 1997. *Open veins of Latin America: Five centuries of the pillage of a continent*. New York: Monthly Review Press.
García Canclini, N., 1982. *Las culturas populares en el capitalismo*. Mexico City: Nueva Imagen.
Gellner, E., 1988. *Plough, sword and book: The structure of human history*. Chicago: University of Chicago Press.
Gregory, R. G., 1976. Some implications of the growth of the mineral sector. *Australian Journal of Agricultural Economics*, 20(2), 71–91.
Hall, S., 1995. Parties on the verge of a nervous breakdown. *Soundings*, 1, 19–33.
Hall, S., 2010. Life and times of the first New Left. *New Left Review*, 61, 177–196.
Halliday, F., 2005. *The Middle East in international relations: Power, politics and ideology*. Cambridge: Cambridge University Press.
Hardt, M. and Negri, A., 2000. *Empire*. Cambridge, MA: Harvard University Press.
Herder, J. G. von, 2002. *Philosophical writings*. Trans. and ed. M. N. Forster. Cambridge: Cambridge University Press.
Horkheimer, M., 2013. *Eclipse of reason*. London: Bloomsbury.
Huntington, S. P., 2004. Dead souls: The denationalization of the American elite. *The National Interest*, Spring, 5–18.
Inglis, K. S., 2006a. *This is the ABC: The Australian Broadcasting Commission, 1932–1983* (2nd ed.). Melbourne: Black Inc.
Inglis, K. S., 2006b. *Whose ABC? The Australian Broadcasting Corporation, 1983–2006*. Melbourne: Black Inc.
James, C. L. R., Dunayevskaya, R. and Lee, G., 1986. *State capitalism and world revolution*. Chicago: Charles H. Kerr.
Kant, I., 2006. *Toward perpetual peace and other writings on politics, peace, and history*. Trans. D. L. Colclasure. P. Kleingeld, ed. New Haven: Yale University Press.
Kleinhans, C., 2011. 'Creative industries', neoliberal fantasies, and the cold, hard facts of global recession: Some basic lessons. *Jump Cut: A Review of Contemporary Media*, 53.

Available from: www.ejumpcut.org/archive/jc53.2011/kleinhans-creatIndus/text.html [Accessed 28 December 2017].

Kleinhans, C. and Lesage, J., 2016. Mourning in America. *Jump Cut: A Review of Contemporary Media*, 57. Available from: www.ejumpcut.org/currentissue/-lastwordMourning/index.html [Accessed 28 December 2017].

Kristeva, J., 1997. *The portable Kristeva*. K. Oliver, ed. New York: Columbia University Press.

Kymlicka, W., 1995. *Multicultural citizenship: A liberal theory of minority rights*. Oxford: Oxford University Press.

Luxemburg, R., 1986. *Rosa Luxemburg speaks*. M.-A. Waters, ed. New York: Pathfinder Press.

Lyotard, J.-F., 1993. *Political writings*. Trans. B. Readings and K. P. Geiman. London: UCL Press.

Mandel, E., 1968. *Marxist economic theory volume two*. Trans. B. Pearce. New York: Monthly Review Press.

May, T., 2016. Theresa May attacks 'Freedom of Movement' culture. Accessed from: www.youtube.com/watch?v=pcbf6vMDlF0 [Accessed 28 December 2017].

McQueen, H., 2004. *A new Britannia: An argument concerning the social origins of Australian radicalism* (4th ed.). Melbourne: Penguin.

Merton, R. K., 1936. The unanticipated consequences of purposive social action. *American Sociological Review*, 1(6), 894–904.

Miller, J. D. B., 1981. *The world of states: Connected essays*. New York: St. Martin's Press.

Missirian, A. and Schlenker, W., 2017. Asylum applications respond to temperature fluctuations. *Science*, 358(6370), 1610–1614.

Nandy, A., 1998. The twilight of certitudes: Secularism, Hindu nationalism and other masks of deculturation. *Postcolonial Studies*, 1(3), 283–298.

National Endowment for Democracy, 2017. *Sharp power: Rising authoritarian influence*. Available from: www.ned.org/wp-content/uploads/2017/12/Sharp-Power-Rising-Authoritarian-Influence-Full-Report.pdf [Accessed 28 December 2017].

Niño-Murcia, M. and Rothman, J., eds., 2008. *Bilingualism and identity: Spanish at the crossroads with other languages*. Amsterdam: John Benjamins.

Nkrumah, K., 1969. *Axioms of Kwame Nkrumah: Freedom fighters' edition*. London: Panaf Books.

O'Regan, T. and Potter, A., 2013. Globalisation from within? The de-nationalising of Australian film and television production. *Media International Australia*, 149, 5–14.

The Overlanders, 1946. Dir: H. Watt.

Pascoe, R., 1979. *The manufacture of Australian history*. Melbourne: Oxford University Press.

Perazzi, J. R. and Merli, G. M., 2017. Análisis de la estructura del mercado laboral en Colombia: Un estudio por género mediante correspondencias multiples. *Cuadernos de Economía*, 40(113), 100–114.

Pusey, M., 1991. *Economic rationalism in Canberra: A nation-building state changes its mind*. Cambridge: Cambridge University Press.

Restrepo, E., Schwartz-Martín, E. and Cárdenas, R., 2014. Nation and difference in the genetic imagination of Colombia. *In*: P. Wade, C. López Beltrán, E. Restrepo and R. Ventura Santos, eds. *Mestizo genomics: Race mixture, nation, and science in Latin America*. Durham: Duke University Press, 55–84.

Rivera, D., 1932. The revolutionary spirit in modern art. *The Modern Quarterly*, 6(3), 51–57.

Rorty, A. O., 1995. Rights: Educational, not cultural. *Social Research*, 62(1), 161–170.

Ross, A., 2009. *Nice work if you can get it: Life and labor in precarious times*. New York: New York University Press.
Scott, W., 1805. *The lay of the last minstrel*. Available from: http://theotherpages.org/poems/minstrel [Accessed 28 December 2017].
Smith, A. D., 2000. *The nation in history: Historiographical debates about ethnicity and nationalism*. Oxford: Polity Press.
Stalin, J., 1946. *Stalin on art and culture*. Available from: Revolutionary democracy. www.northstarcompass.org/nsc0306/stalin.htm [Accessed 28 December 2017].
Strange, S., 1979. The management of surplus capacity: Or how does theory stand up to protectionism 1970s style? *International Organization*, 33(3), 303–334.
Toffler, A., 1983. *Previews and premises*. New York: William Morrow.
Turner, G., 2011. Surrendering the space. *Cultural Studies*, 25(4–5), 685–699.
United Nations, Department of Economic and Social Affairs, Population Division, 2017. *International Migration Report 2017: Highlights* (ST/ESA/SER.A/404). Available from: www.un.org/en/development/desa/population/migration/publications/migrationreport/docs/MigrationReport2017_Highlights.pdf
Vargas Llosa, M., 2017. El nacionalismo en Cataluña. *La Crónica*, 17 December. Available from: http://la-cronica.com.mx/el-nacionalismo-en-cataluna-mario-vargas-llosa.html [Accessed 28 December 2017].
Warhurst, J., 1982. *Jobs or dogma? The Industries Assistance Commission and Australian politics*. St. Lucia: University of Queensland Press.
Wells, H. G., 1902. *Anticipations of the reaction of mechanical and scientific progress upon human life and thought* (2nd ed.). London: Chapman & Hall.
Wittfogel, K. A., 1967. *Oriental despotism: A comparative study of total power*. New Haven: Yale University Press.
Yúdice, G. 2009. Cultural diversity and cultural rights. *Hispanic Issues On Line*, 5(1), 110–137.

Index

Abood, P. 143, 150, 151
Aboriginal art 28–9, 33–4 (*see also* indigenous art practices); and class in Australia 33; ethnographic interpretations 34; and heritage policy 77–8; modes of consumption by white art consumers 34–6; and the tourism industry 35
Aboriginal Memorial, The 36
Acker, T. 31, 39n
Adorno, T.W.157
Ahmed, M. 150–1
Allcock, J.B. 80
Allison, L. 89
Althusser, L. 158
Altman, J. 124
Amazon 21–2
Anderson, B. 2, 137, 155
Anderson, P. 161
Andrejevic, M. 5, 107
Andrejevic, M. and Burdon, M. 107
Ang, I. 151
Ang, I., Hawkins, G. and Dabboussy, L. 146, 147
art fairs 45–9; 'art worlds' 42
art policy agendas 29; and 'critical globalism' 31; institutional developments 30–1; internationalization 30–2 passim; and multiculturalism 141–5; relation to Asian art fields 31
Ashton, P. 80
Ashton, P. and Cornwall, J.L. 76
Athique, A. 4
Attwood, B. 36
Australia Council, the 16, 43, 51, 53, 142, 143–5, 149
Australia's Winning Edge 92–3
Australian Heritage Commission 76–7
Australian Heritage Strategy 75, 81–3

Australian Institute of Sport (AIS) 92
Australian internet 109–110
Australian Rugby Union (ARL) 90, 93
Australian Sports Commission (ASC) 92

Banet-Weiser, S. 69
Banks, J.A. 157
Banks, J. 104
Barrett, J. 20
Barrett, J. and McManus, P. 156
Baudrillard, J. 161
Bauman, Z. 83, 106
Beck, U. 2
Becker, H. 42
Bell, R. 33
Benhabib, S. 158
Bennett, T. 39n
Bennett, T. and Gayo, M. 33
Bennett, T., Frith, S, Grossberg, L. and Turner, G. 56
Benson, R. and Neveu, E. 106, 108
biennales 30–1, 42–7; Venice, 44–5
Billings, A.C., Brown, N., Brown, K., Guo, Q., Leeman, M. Licen, S., Novak, D. and Rowe, D. 90
Book Council of Australia 18
Book Industry Collaborative Council (BICC) 18
Book Industry Strategy Group (BISG) 18
bookselling 21–3
Bourdieu, P. 29, 31, 39n, 41, 42, 87, 89, 93, 94, 95, 105, 106, 108
Brandle, L. 51
Bratich, J. 72
Burns, A. and Eltham, B. 156
Burrawanga, L.L., Maymuru, D., Ganambarr, B, Wright, S., Suchet-Pearson, S. Lloyd, K. and Ganambarr, R. 125

Index

Butterss, P. 17
Byrne, D. 78, 80, 84

Cabral, A. 158
Capon, E. 143
Carey, C. 147
Carey, J.W. 158
Carniel, J. 148
Carriageworks 43
Carroll, L. 96
Carter, D. 19, 20
Carter, D. and Kelly, M. 22
Carter, T. 93
Caruana, W. 36
Castells, M. 106, 108, 111
Castles, S., Cope, B. and Kalantzis, M. 155
Catalunya 160–161
Chadwick, V. 44, 45
Chapple, K. 124
Chenoweth, N. 67
Chopra, R. 106
Clarke, A. 83
Clarke, K. 79
class and rugby union 91–6
Collins, T. 88–9
Colman, M. 90
Colombia 159–60
commercial nationalism 5
commercialization 9–10, 154; and biennales 45; and commodification of culture 107–8; of digital media 110–111; of the heritage field 84–5; of the media 65–6; news media 72; of sport 91–7 passim; and the public good 108; of rugby union, 88–91; and SBS 149–151
Convergence Review 53, 54–5
Cool Britannia 4
Copyright and Digital Economy 55
cosmopolitanism 137–8, 151, 158–160
Couldry, N. 70, 106
Couldry, N. and Hepp, A. 108
Couldry, N. and Turow, J. 110
Couldry, N. and van Dijck, J. 111
Creative Australia 9, 15, 17, 28, 29, 53–4, 59, 119, 140, 144
creative industries and music policy 52, 57
Creative Industries Mapping 53
Creative Nation 1–2, 9, 15, 16–17, 29, 30, 52–3, 59, 103, 108, 112, 116, 140; and digital and media policy 104–6; and heritage policy 79–80; making national culture 109–10; and multiculturalism 140; and tourism 117–18, 123

Crittenden, J. 57
Cultural Engagement Framework 144, 145
cultural nationalism 154, 155
cultural tourism 118–19; Australian investment in 119–21; and cultural consumption 122–3; and cultural production 123–4; and indigenous cultural tourism 124–6; shift from national to local, city and regional 121–3
Cunningham, S. 52, 108
Curran, W. 123
Curtin, M. 7

Daenekindt, S. and Roose, H. 37
Danto, A. 37
Davenport, T.H. and Beck, J. 60
Davidson, D. 66, 67
Davis, M. 20, 22
Davis, T. 131, 132–3
Davison, G. 76
Dayan, D. 66
De Lorenzo, C. Mendelssohn, J., and Speck, C. 30
Decent, T. 97
Deleuze, G. and Guattari, F. 161
Deloitte Access Economics 119, 121
Dermody, S. and Jacka, L. 156
digital, the concept of the field 105–8; copyright and music royalties 55–6; customization 70; and decline in nationing 69; devices for consumption 69–70; and globalization, 22; innovation as culture 104; making national culture 109–110; and publishing 20–1; revolution in, the 15, 112; and shifts in tourism 121–3; social media and heritage 84; and the 'Silicone Valley ethos' 104; and technologies 22; and television 68–9
Dijck, van, J. 65
Dine, P. 88, 95–6
Distinction 87
Dolgopolov, G. 150
Donoughue, P. 21
Driessens, O. 71
Driscoll, B. 20, 22
Durrer, V., Miller, T. and O'Brien, D. 59
Dwyer, T. and Martin, F. 107
Dyer, P. Aberdeen, L, and Schuler, S. 124

Earls, N. 21
ebooks 20–1
Ebrahim-zadeh, C. 155

Economist, The 161
Edwards, J. 54
Elias, N. 106
Eltham, B. 108, 109, 112n
Ensor, J. 22

Fagan, S. 98n
fields of the digital 105–8
Fisher, L. 33, 34
FitzSimons, P. 90
Flew, T. Iosifidis, P. and Steemers, J. 2
Flew, T. and Waisbord. S. 110
Florida, R. 52, 155
Francis, H. 57
Franklin, A. and Paperstegiadis, N. 32, 124
Freestone, R. 78, 84
free-to-air broadcasting in Australia 66–8
Frith, S. and Cloonan, M. 58
Frobel, F., Heinrichs, J. and Kreye, O. 159
Frost, A. 47

Galeano, E. 156
Garcia Canclini, N. 158
Gellner, E. 156
Georgakis, S. 97
Gibson, C., Waite. G., Walmsley, J. and Connell, J. 118
Gibson, C. and Connell, J. 120
Gibson, L. 144
Ginsburg, F. 136
Giorgi, L. 23
Given, J., Goggin, G. Brealey, M. and Gray, C. 67
Gleason, M. 48
Globalization 6–7, 15
Glover, S. 17
Goggin, G. 109–110
Goldblatt, D. 88
Goldlust, J. 89
Grant, I. 75
Grantham, B. and Miller, T. 107
Griffiths, T. 79
Grishin, S. 30, 47, 48
Grodach, C. 56, 123
Groundwater, 119
Gurran, N. and Phibbs, P. 122

Hae, L. 123
Hage, G. 137
Haigh, G. 88
Hall, S. 161
Halliday, F. 157
Hannam, K., Sheller, M. and Urry, J. 116

Hardt, H. and Negri, A. 162
Hargreaves, J. 89
Hartley, J. and McKee, A. 130
Hawkins, G. 141, 142
Head, B. 104
Held, D. 137
Henderson, G. 56
Hepp, A. 71
Herder, von, J.G. 156
Heritage and tourism 82–3; and social media 84
Herman, A. Haidlaw, J. and Swiss, T. 107
history wars 36
Hjarvard, S. 106
Homan, S. 54, 57, 104, 109, 112n
Hope Report, The 75–79
Horkheimer, M. 157
Horowitz, N. 31, 32
hybridity 159–60

Indigenous art practices 33–4, 35; and cosmopolitanism 130; cosmopolitanism and the nation 136–8; cultural tourism 124–6; professional film and television production 132–3; and television 129–136
Indigenous Community Television (ICTV) 130, 131, 132
Inglis, D. 41, 42
Inglis, K. 156
International Rugby Football Board (IRU) 90
Ionnides, D. and Debbage, K. 116
Ireland, T. and Blair, S. 80

Jackson, S.J. 91
James, C.L.R. 158
Jefferies, B. 20
Jones, C. 30, 31
Jordan, D. 19
Junker, U. 124
Jupp, J. 141

Kaneva, N. 4
Kattan 150
Khan, R. Wyatt, D., Yue, A., and Paperstergiadis, N. 142
Khan, R., Wyatt, D. and Yue, A. 140, 142
King, R. 76
Kleist, O. 141
Knell, S. 28, 33, 35, 36
Kristeva, J. 162
Kymlicka, W. 160

170 Index

Lander, E.S and Schmidt, E.E 111
Lee, J. 19
Leiper, N. 116
Lendon, N. 36
Levina, M. and Hasinoff, A. 104
Levy, S. 132–3
Lewis, J. 52
Light, D. 82–3
Literary agents and festivals 23–4
Literature Board of the Australia Council 17
literature, national policy 16–19
Lurie, C. 23
Luxemburg, R. 157
Lyotard, J-F. 158

MacKenzie, D and Wajcman, J. 105
Madaniou, M. 66
Malm, K. and Wallis, R. 51, 58
Mandel, E. 159
marketization 9–10, 66, 112
Marwick, A. 69, 104
Massoud, J. 96
Mastering of a Music City 56
May, T. 159
McCallum, K., Meadows, M., Waller, L., Dunne Breen, M., and Reid, H. 131
McClean, G. 148
McDonald, H. 106
McKay, J. and Miller, T. 91
McKay, J., Hughson, J., Lawrence, G., and Rowe, D. 93
McLean, I. 34, 39n
McQueen, H. 155
McRobbie, A. 58
Meadows, M. 131, 137
Meddows, D. 98n
meta-capital 71–3
Michaels, E. 130
Milhelj, S. 4
Miller, T. 7
Miller, T., Lawrence, G., McKay, J. and Rowe, D. 89
Moran, A. 7
Morphy, H. 30, 124
Morris, H. 119
Multicultural Australia 140–1
multiculturalism 140–1; and community arts 141–2; and cultural diversity 144; and limits to cultural policy 149; and the media 145–8; and multicultural arts 142–3
Mulvaney, J. 80
Music Australia 56
Music Canada 57

'music city' policies 56–8; and the 'music nation' 59
Music Works 57
Myers, F. 39n

Nagel, A. 30
nation formation 3–6 passim
National Contemporary Music Plan 56
National Endowment for Democracy 158
National Gallery of Australia (NGA) 28
National Indigenous Television Network (NITV) 129–138; cosmopolitanism and the nation 136–8; local versus imported content 134–5; nationing remit 136–8; NITV project, the 132–6
National Innovation and Science Agenda 111
National Museum of Australia 36
Nationalism 156–8, 162
nation-branding 4–5, 17–18, 109
'nationing' 2–5; and art museums and public galleries 41; in *Creative Nation* 108–10; decline in digital era 69; and heritage 83–5 passim; international sports competition 90–2 passim; remit of NITV 136–8; television as an instrument of, 64; television's potential for 72
Netflix, and disruption 67–68
Nicholls, S. and Power, J. 123
Nkrumah, K. 158
Noble, G. 141

O'Connor, J. 5, 105
O'Shaughnessy, T. 15
Oakley, K. 52
Oates, G. 120, 121, 122, 125
Overlanders, The 162

Panucci, F. 145, 149, 150
Pascoe, R. 155
Pay-TV 68–9
Peers, A. 44
Perry, J. 97
Picketty, T. 39n
Poland, L. and Indyk, I. 19
Power, Patronage and the Muse 29
Productivity Commission 67
publishing industry, the 15, 17–20,
Pusey, M. 156

Real Wild Child 52
Regulation; copyright and intellectual property 55; local content 56; music broadcasting 54–5

Rennie, E. 130, 131, 132, 134
Rennie, E. and Featherstone, D. 130, 131
Report of the Committee of Inquiry into the National Estate (*see also* the Hope Report) 75–79
Reynolds, H. 36
Richards, H. 89
Rijavec, F. 131
Rivera, D. 155
Rorty, A.O. 160
Rowe, D. 89, 91
Rowe, D., Noble, G., Bennett, T., and Kelly, M. 109
Ruhanen, L., Whitford, M. and McLennan, C. 125
Rules of Art, The 29

Saltz, J. 47
SANZAR 90, 91
Sassatelli, M. 31, 44
Scherer, J. and Rowe, D. 7
Schultz, J. 110–111
Scott, W. 161
Sexton, E. 54
Silver, D. 57
Skeggs, B. and Wood, H., 72
Smith, A. 156
Smith, T. 30
Smith, W. 97
Sparks, C. 7
Special Broadcasting Service (SBS) 129, 130, 131, 145–6; and commercialization 148–150; SBS Independent 130; SBS radio 146; SBS television 146–8
sport, anti-siphoning regime 91–2; participation in 93–4; professionalization of 90–2
Stalin, J. 159
Stallabrass, J. 32, 44
Steen, R. 88
Stegink,V. 19
Stensholt, J. 96
Stevens, I. 17
Stevenson, D. 44
Stewart, C. 23
Stinson, E. 21
Stinson, E. and Manion, A. 21
Strange, S. 156
Strategic Contemporary Music Industry Plan 53
Streeter, T. 103, 104
Sullivan, S. 76, 81, 84

Sunstein, C. 72
Sydney Contemporary 46, 47, 48

Tang, J. 44, 46
Tay, J. and Turner, G. 7, 66
Thompson, D. 46
Thompson, J.B. 19, 23
Thomsen, S. 67
Throsby, D. 17, 18, 23
Tourism Australia 120, 121, 125
transnationalism 7–8, 16, 19; and the art fair 42–3, 48; and the art world 42; and Australian television 64–7; and heritage 82–3; and indigeneity 138
Turner, A. 67
Turner, G. 66, 67, 69, 72, 106, 109, 154
Turner, G. and Tay, J. 109

Upe, R. 125
urban art event 43–4

Van den Bosch, A. 29, 41, 42, 48
Velthius, O. 31
Visions of Australia 28
Volcic, Z. and Andrejevic, M. 109
Volcic, Z. 5
Voltmer, I. 7

Waite, G. and Duffy. M. 122
Waite, G., Figueroa, R. and McGee, L. 124
Waite, G. 124, 126
Wallach, G. 52
Warhurst, J. 156
Watson, S. and Gonzalez-Rodriguez, M. 5, 84
Watson, S. 85
Wells, H.G. 159
Wenner, L.A. 89
White, J. 32, 39n
Whitford, M., and Ruhanen, L.M. 125
Winter, T. 80, 81
Wired 103
Wise, A. and Velayutham, R. 141
World Heritage Convention 79
Wright, F. and Morphy, H. 124
Wu, C. 31
Wynhausen, E. and Perkins, M. 23

Yudice, G. 155

Zarobell, J. 31
Zwar, J. 15, 20, 21, 22